C-4853   CAREER EXAMINATION SERIES

This is your
PASSBOOK for...

Secure Care Treatment Aide II

Test Preparation Study Guide
Questions & Answers

COPYRIGHT NOTICE

This book is SOLELY intended for, is sold ONLY to, and its use is RESTRICTED to individual, bona fide applicants or candidates who qualify by virtue of having seriously filed applications for appropriate license, certificate, professional and/or promotional advancement, higher school matriculation, scholarship, or other legitimate requirements of education and/or governmental authorities.

This book is NOT intended for use, class instruction, tutoring, training, duplication, copying, reprinting, excerption, or adaptation, etc., by:

1) Other publishers
2) Proprietors and/or Instructors of "Coaching" and/or Preparatory Courses
3) Personnel and/or Training Divisions of commercial, industrial, and governmental organizations
4) Schools, colleges, or universities and/or their departments and staffs, including teachers and other personnel
5) Testing Agencies or Bureaus
6) Study groups which seek by the purchase of a single volume to copy and/or duplicate and/or adapt this material for use by the group as a whole without having purchased individual volumes for each of the members of the group
7) Et al.

Such persons would be in violation of appropriate Federal and State statutes.

PROVISION OF LICENSING AGREEMENTS – Recognized educational, commercial, industrial, and governmental institutions and organizations, and others legitimately engaged in educational pursuits, including training, testing, and measurement activities, may address request for a licensing agreement to the copyright owners, who will determine whether, and under what conditions, including fees and charges, the materials in this book may be used them. In other words, a licensing facility exists for the legitimate use of the material in this book on other than an individual basis. However, it is asseverated and affirmed here that the material in this book CANNOT be used without the receipt of the express permission of such a licensing agreement from the Publishers. Inquiries re licensing should be addressed to the company, attention rights and permissions department.

All rights reserved, including the right of reproduction in whole or in part, in any form or by any means, electronic or mechanical, including photocopying, recording, or by any information storage and retrieval system, without permission in writing from the Publisher.

Copyright © 2025 by
National Learning Corporation

212 Michael Drive, Syosset, NY 11791
(516) 921-8888 • www.passbooks.com
E-mail: info@passbooks.com

PASSBOOK® SERIES

THE *PASSBOOK® SERIES* has been created to prepare applicants and candidates for the ultimate academic battlefield – the examination room.

At some time in our lives, each and every one of us may be required to take an examination – for validation, matriculation, admission, qualification, registration, certification, or licensure.

Based on the assumption that every applicant or candidate has met the basic formal educational standards, has taken the required number of courses, and read the necessary texts, the *PASSBOOK® SERIES* furnishes the one special preparation which may assure passing with confidence, instead of failing with insecurity. Examination questions – together with answers – are furnished as the basic vehicle for study so that the mysteries of the examination and its compounding difficulties may be eliminated or diminished by a sure method.

This book is meant to help you pass your examination provided that you qualify and are serious in your objective.

The entire field is reviewed through the huge store of content information which is succinctly presented through a provocative and challenging approach – the question-and-answer method.

A climate of success is established by furnishing the correct answers at the end of each test.

You soon learn to recognize types of questions, forms of questions, and patterns of questioning. You may even begin to anticipate expected outcomes.

You perceive that many questions are repeated or adapted so that you can gain acute insights, which may enable you to score many sure points.

You learn how to confront new questions, or types of questions, and to attack them confidently and work out the correct answers.

You note objectives and emphases, and recognize pitfalls and dangers, so that you may make positive educational adjustments.

Moreover, you are kept fully informed in relation to new concepts, methods, practices, and directions in the field.

You discover that you are actually taking the examination all the time: you are preparing for the examination by "taking" an examination, not by reading extraneous and/or supererogatory textbooks.

In short, this PASSBOOK®, used directedly, should be an important factor in helping you to pass your test.

SECURE CARE TREATMENT AIDE II

DUTIES:

As a Secure Care Treatment Aide II, you would supervise Secure Care Treatment Aides I's and assist with psychiatric treatment, rehabilitation and the care and safety of individuals diagnosed with mental illness or with emotional or social behavior problems. This may include those who are considered to be manipulative, and/or dangerous to themselves and/or others. You would participate in active treatment programming and be responsible for providing a safe, secure, stable environment within which these patients can be given the intensive care and behavioral interactions needed for stabilization and treatment.

SUBJECT OF EXAMINATION:

The written test is designed to test for knowledge, skills, and/or abilities in such areas as:

1. **Characteristics of patient population** - These questions test for basic understanding of abnormal behaviors exhibited by individuals with serious and persistent mental illness. Questions may cover such topics as schizophrenia, mood disorders, personality disorders, developmental disabilities, substance abuse, and sex offenses.
2. **First aid and basic patient care** - These questions test for knowledge of first aid and basic patient care. Questions may cover such topics as blood pressure, body temperatures, respiration, and major seizure disorders; emergency first aid procedures for shock, choking, bleeding, heart attacks, and burns; use of restraints; and commonly used psychotropic medications and their effects.
3. **Preparing written material** - These questions test for the ability to present information clearly and accurately, and to organize paragraphs logically and comprehensibly. For some questions, you will be given information in two or three sentences followed by four restatements of the information. You must then choose the best version. For other questions, you will be given paragraphs with their sentences out of order. You must then choose, from four suggestions, the best order for the sentences.
4. **Supervision** - These questions test for knowledge of the principles and practices employed in planning, organizing, and controlling the activities of a work unit toward predetermined objectives. The concepts covered, usually in a situational question format, include such topics as assigning and reviewing work; evaluating performance; maintaining work standards; motivating and developing subordinates; implementing procedural change; increasing efficiency; and dealing with problems of absenteeism, morale, and discipline.
5. **Treatment for patient population** - These questions test for the ability to function as part of a treatment team. Questions may cover such topics as setting long or short term goals for treatment, contributing to the treatment planning process, implementing treatment plans, assisting with anger management, managing crisis situations, and engaging individuals in activities as prescribed by treatment plans.

HOW TO TAKE A TEST

I. YOU MUST PASS AN EXAMINATION

A. *WHAT EVERY CANDIDATE SHOULD KNOW*

Examination applicants often ask us for help in preparing for the written test. What can I study in advance? What kinds of questions will be asked? How will the test be given? How will the papers be graded?

As an applicant for a civil service examination, you may be wondering about some of these things. Our purpose here is to suggest effective methods of advance study and to describe civil service examinations.

Your chances for success on this examination can be increased if you know how to prepare. Those "pre-examination jitters" can be reduced if you know what to expect. You can even experience an adventure in good citizenship if you know why civil service exams are given.

B. *WHY ARE CIVIL SERVICE EXAMINATIONS GIVEN?*

Civil service examinations are important to you in two ways. As a citizen, you want public jobs filled by employees who know how to do their work. As a job seeker, you want a fair chance to compete for that job on an equal footing with other candidates. The best-known means of accomplishing this two-fold goal is the competitive examination.

Exams are widely publicized throughout the nation. They may be administered for jobs in federal, state, city, municipal, town or village governments or agencies.

Any citizen may apply, with some limitations, such as the age or residence of applicants. Your experience and education may be reviewed to see whether you meet the requirements for the particular examination. When these requirements exist, they are reasonable and applied consistently to all applicants. Thus, a competitive examination may cause you some uneasiness now, but it is your privilege and safeguard.

C. *HOW ARE CIVIL SERVICE EXAMS DEVELOPED?*

Examinations are carefully written by trained technicians who are specialists in the field known as "psychological measurement," in consultation with recognized authorities in the field of work that the test will cover. These experts recommend the subject matter areas or skills to be tested; only those knowledges or skills important to your success on the job are included. The most reliable books and source materials available are used as references. Together, the experts and technicians judge the difficulty level of the questions.

Test technicians know how to phrase questions so that the problem is clearly stated. Their ethics do not permit "trick" or "catch" questions. Questions may have been tried out on sample groups, or subjected to statistical analysis, to determine their usefulness.

Written tests are often used in combination with performance tests, ratings of training and experience, and oral interviews. All of these measures combine to form the best-known means of finding the right person for the right job.

II. HOW TO PASS THE WRITTEN TEST

A. NATURE OF THE EXAMINATION

To prepare intelligently for civil service examinations, you should know how they differ from school examinations you have taken. In school you were assigned certain definite pages to read or subjects to cover. The examination questions were quite detailed and usually emphasized memory. Civil service exams, on the other hand, try to discover your present ability to perform the duties of a position, plus your potentiality to learn these duties. In other words, a civil service exam attempts to predict how successful you will be. Questions cover such a broad area that they cannot be as minute and detailed as school exam questions.

In the public service similar kinds of work, or positions, are grouped together in one "class." This process is known as *position-classification*. All the positions in a class are paid according to the salary range for that class. One class title covers all of these positions, and they are all tested by the same examination.

B. FOUR BASIC STEPS

1) Study the announcement

How, then, can you know what subjects to study? Our best answer is: "Learn as much as possible about the class of positions for which you've applied." The exam will test the knowledge, skills and abilities needed to do the work.

Your most valuable source of information about the position you want is the official exam announcement. This announcement lists the training and experience qualifications. Check these standards and apply only if you come reasonably close to meeting them.

The brief description of the position in the examination announcement offers some clues to the subjects which will be tested. Think about the job itself. Review the duties in your mind. Can you perform them, or are there some in which you are rusty? Fill in the blank spots in your preparation.

Many jurisdictions preview the written test in the exam announcement by including a section called "Knowledge and Abilities Required," "Scope of the Examination," or some similar heading. Here you will find out specifically what fields will be tested.

2) Review your own background

Once you learn in general what the position is all about, and what you need to know to do the work, ask yourself which subjects you already know fairly well and which need improvement. You may wonder whether to concentrate on improving your strong areas or on building some background in your fields of weakness. When the announcement has specified "some knowledge" or "considerable knowledge," or has used adjectives like "beginning principles of..." or "advanced ... methods," you can get a clue as to the number and difficulty of questions to be asked in any given field. More questions, and hence broader coverage, would be included for those subjects which are more important in the work. Now weigh your strengths and weaknesses against the job requirements and prepare accordingly.

3) Determine the level of the position

Another way to tell how intensively you should prepare is to understand the level of the job for which you are applying. Is it the entering level? In other words, is this the position in which beginners in a field of work are hired? Or is it an intermediate or advanced level? Sometimes this is indicated by such words as "Junior" or "Senior" in the class title. Other jurisdictions use Roman numerals to designate the level – Clerk I, Clerk II, for example. The word "Supervisor" sometimes appears in the title. If the level is not indicated by the title, check the description of duties. Will you be working under very close supervision, or will you have responsibility for independent decisions in this work?

4) Choose appropriate study materials

Now that you know the subjects to be examined and the relative amount of each subject to be covered, you can choose suitable study materials. For beginning level jobs, or even advanced ones, if you have a pronounced weakness in some aspect of your training, read a modern, standard textbook in that field. Be sure it is up to date and has general coverage. Such books are normally available at your library, and the librarian will be glad to help you locate one. For entry-level positions, questions of appropriate difficulty are chosen – neither highly advanced questions, nor those too simple. Such questions require careful thought but not advanced training.

If the position for which you are applying is technical or advanced, you will read more advanced, specialized material. If you are already familiar with the basic principles of your field, elementary textbooks would waste your time. Concentrate on advanced textbooks and technical periodicals. Think through the concepts and review difficult problems in your field.

These are all general sources. You can get more ideas on your own initiative, following these leads. For example, training manuals and publications of the government agency which employs workers in your field can be useful, particularly for technical and professional positions. A letter or visit to the government department involved may result in more specific study suggestions, and certainly will provide you with a more definite idea of the exact nature of the position you are seeking.

III. KINDS OF TESTS

Tests are used for purposes other than measuring knowledge and ability to perform specified duties. For some positions, it is equally important to test ability to make adjustments to new situations or to profit from training. In others, basic mental abilities not dependent on information are essential. Questions which test these things may not appear as pertinent to the duties of the position as those which test for knowledge and information. Yet they are often highly important parts of a fair examination. For very general questions, it is almost impossible to help you direct your study efforts. What we can do is to point out some of the more common of these general abilities needed in public service positions and describe some typical questions.

1) General information

Broad, general information has been found useful for predicting job success in some kinds of work. This is tested in a variety of ways, from vocabulary lists to questions about current events. Basic background in some field of work, such as sociology or economics, may be sampled in a group of questions. Often these are principles which have become familiar to most persons through exposure rather than through formal training. It is difficult to advise you how to study for these questions; being alert to the world around you is our best suggestion.

2) Verbal ability

An example of an ability needed in many positions is verbal or language ability. Verbal ability is, in brief, the ability to use and understand words. Vocabulary and grammar tests are typical measures of this ability. Reading comprehension or paragraph interpretation questions are common in many kinds of civil service tests. You are given a paragraph of written material and asked to find its central meaning.

3) Numerical ability

Number skills can be tested by the familiar arithmetic problem, by checking paired lists of numbers to see which are alike and which are different, or by interpreting charts and graphs. In the latter test, a graph may be printed in the test booklet which you are asked to use as the basis for answering questions.

4) Observation

A popular test for law-enforcement positions is the observation test. A picture is shown to you for several minutes, then taken away. Questions about the picture test your ability to observe both details and larger elements.

5) Following directions

In many positions in the public service, the employee must be able to carry out written instructions dependably and accurately. You may be given a chart with several columns, each column listing a variety of information. The questions require you to carry out directions involving the information given in the chart.

6) Skills and aptitudes

Performance tests effectively measure some manual skills and aptitudes. When the skill is one in which you are trained, such as typing or shorthand, you can practice. These tests are often very much like those given in business school or high school courses. For many of the other skills and aptitudes, however, no short-time preparation can be made. Skills and abilities natural to you or that you have developed throughout your lifetime are being tested.

Many of the general questions just described provide all the data needed to answer the questions and ask you to use your reasoning ability to find the answers. Your best preparation for these tests, as well as for tests of facts and ideas, is to be at your physical and mental best. You, no doubt, have your own methods of getting into an exam-taking mood and keeping "in shape." The next section lists some ideas on this subject.

IV. KINDS OF QUESTIONS

Only rarely is the "essay" question, which you answer in narrative form, used in civil service tests. Civil service tests are usually of the short-answer type. Full instructions for answering these questions will be given to you at the examination. But in case this is your first experience with short-answer questions and separate answer sheets, here is what you need to know:

1) Multiple-choice Questions

Most popular of the short-answer questions is the "multiple choice" or "best answer" question. It can be used, for example, to test for factual knowledge, ability to solve problems or judgment in meeting situations found at work.

A multiple-choice question is normally one of three types—
- It can begin with an incomplete statement followed by several possible endings. You are to find the one ending which *best* completes the statement, although some of the others may not be entirely wrong.
- It can also be a complete statement in the form of a question which is answered by choosing one of the statements listed.

- It can be in the form of a problem – again you select the best answer.

Here is an example of a multiple-choice question with a discussion which should give you some clues as to the method for choosing the right answer:

When an employee has a complaint about his assignment, the action which will *best* help him overcome his difficulty is to
   A. discuss his difficulty with his coworkers
   B. take the problem to the head of the organization
   C. take the problem to the person who gave him the assignment
   D. say nothing to anyone about his complaint

In answering this question, you should study each of the choices to find which is best. Consider choice "A" – Certainly an employee may discuss his complaint with fellow employees, but no change or improvement can result, and the complaint remains unresolved. Choice "B" is a poor choice since the head of the organization probably does not know what assignment you have been given, and taking your problem to him is known as "going over the head" of the supervisor. The supervisor, or person who made the assignment, is the person who can clarify it or correct any injustice. Choice "C" is, therefore, correct. To say nothing, as in choice "D," is unwise. Supervisors have and interest in knowing the problems employees are facing, and the employee is seeking a solution to his problem.

2) True/False Questions

The "true/false" or "right/wrong" form of question is sometimes used. Here a complete statement is given. Your job is to decide whether the statement is right or wrong.

SAMPLE: A roaming cell-phone call to a nearby city costs less than a non-roaming call to a distant city.

This statement is wrong, or false, since roaming calls are more expensive.

This is not a complete list of all possible question forms, although most of the others are variations of these common types. You will always get complete directions for answering questions. Be sure you understand *how* to mark your answers – ask questions until you do.

V. RECORDING YOUR ANSWERS

Computer terminals are used more and more today for many different kinds of exams.

For an examination with very few applicants, you may be told to record your answers in the test booklet itself. Separate answer sheets are much more common. If this separate answer sheet is to be scored by machine – and this is often the case – it is highly important that you mark your answers correctly in order to get credit.

An electronic scoring machine is often used in civil service offices because of the speed with which papers can be scored. Machine-scored answer sheets must be marked with a pencil, which will be given to you. This pencil has a high graphite content which responds to the electronic scoring machine. As a matter of fact, stray dots may register as answers, so do not let your pencil rest on the answer sheet while you are pondering the correct answer. Also, if your pencil lead breaks or is otherwise defective, ask for another.

Since the answer sheet will be dropped in a slot in the scoring machine, be careful not to bend the corners or get the paper crumpled.

The answer sheet normally has five vertical columns of numbers, with 30 numbers to a column. These numbers correspond to the question numbers in your test booklet. After each number, going across the page are four or five pairs of dotted lines. These short dotted lines have small letters or numbers above them. The first two pairs may also have a "T" or "F" above the letters. This indicates that the first two pairs only are to be used if the questions are of the true-false type. If the questions are multiple choice, disregard the "T" and "F" and pay attention only to the small letters or numbers.

Answer your questions in the manner of the sample that follows:

32. The largest city in the United States is
    A. Washington, D.C.
    B. New York City
    C. Chicago
    D. Detroit
    E. San Francisco

1) Choose the answer you think is best. (New York City is the largest, so "B" is correct.)
2) Find the row of dotted lines numbered the same as the question you are answering. (Find row number 32)
3) Find the pair of dotted lines corresponding to the answer. (Find the pair of lines under the mark "B.")
4) Make a solid black mark between the dotted lines.

VI. BEFORE THE TEST

Common sense will help you find procedures to follow to get ready for an examination. Too many of us, however, overlook these sensible measures. Indeed, nervousness and fatigue have been found to be the most serious reasons why applicants fail to do their best on civil service tests. Here is a list of reminders:

- Begin your preparation early – Don't wait until the last minute to go scurrying around for books and materials or to find out what the position is all about.
- Prepare continuously – An hour a night for a week is better than an all-night cram session. This has been definitely established. What is more, a night a week for a month will return better dividends than crowding your study into a shorter period of time.
- Locate the place of the exam – You have been sent a notice telling you when and where to report for the examination. If the location is in a different town or otherwise unfamiliar to you, it would be well to inquire the best route and learn something about the building.
- Relax the night before the test – Allow your mind to rest. Do not study at all that night. Plan some mild recreation or diversion; then go to bed early and get a good night's sleep.
- Get up early enough to make a leisurely trip to the place for the test – This way unforeseen events, traffic snarls, unfamiliar buildings, etc. will not upset you.
- Dress comfortably – A written test is not a fashion show. You will be known by number and not by name, so wear something comfortable.

- Leave excess paraphernalia at home – Shopping bags and odd bundles will get in your way. You need bring only the items mentioned in the official notice you received; usually everything you need is provided. Do not bring reference books to the exam. They will only confuse those last minutes and be taken away from you when in the test room.
- Arrive somewhat ahead of time – If because of transportation schedules you must get there very early, bring a newspaper or magazine to take your mind off yourself while waiting.
- Locate the examination room – When you have found the proper room, you will be directed to the seat or part of the room where you will sit. Sometimes you are given a sheet of instructions to read while you are waiting. Do not fill out any forms until you are told to do so; just read them and be prepared.
- Relax and prepare to listen to the instructions
- If you have any physical problem that may keep you from doing your best, be sure to tell the test administrator. If you are sick or in poor health, you really cannot do your best on the exam. You can come back and take the test some other time.

VII. AT THE TEST

The day of the test is here and you have the test booklet in your hand. The temptation to get going is very strong. Caution! There is more to success than knowing the right answers. You must know how to identify your papers and understand variations in the type of short-answer question used in this particular examination. Follow these suggestions for maximum results from your efforts:

1) Cooperate with the monitor

The test administrator has a duty to create a situation in which you can be as much at ease as possible. He will give instructions, tell you when to begin, check to see that you are marking your answer sheet correctly, and so on. He is not there to guard you, although he will see that your competitors do not take unfair advantage. He wants to help you do your best.

2) Listen to all instructions

Don't jump the gun! Wait until you understand all directions. In most civil service tests you get more time than you need to answer the questions. So don't be in a hurry. Read each word of instructions until you clearly understand the meaning. Study the examples, listen to all announcements and follow directions. Ask questions if you do not understand what to do.

3) Identify your papers

Civil service exams are usually identified by number only. You will be assigned a number; you must not put your name on your test papers. Be sure to copy your number correctly. Since more than one exam may be given, copy your exact examination title.

4) Plan your time

Unless you are told that a test is a "speed" or "rate of work" test, speed itself is usually not important. Time enough to answer all the questions will be provided, but this does not mean that you have all day. An overall time limit has been set. Divide the total time (in minutes) by the number of questions to determine the approximate time you have for each question.

5) Do not linger over difficult questions

If you come across a difficult question, mark it with a paper clip (useful to have along) and come back to it when you have been through the booklet. One caution if you do this – be sure to skip a number on your answer sheet as well. Check often to be sure that you have not lost your place and that you are marking in the row numbered the same as the question you are answering.

6) Read the questions

Be sure you know what the question asks! Many capable people are unsuccessful because they failed to *read* the questions correctly.

7) Answer all questions

Unless you have been instructed that a penalty will be deducted for incorrect answers, it is better to guess than to omit a question.

8) Speed tests

It is often better NOT to guess on speed tests. It has been found that on timed tests people are tempted to spend the last few seconds before time is called in marking answers at random – without even reading them – in the hope of picking up a few extra points. To discourage this practice, the instructions may warn you that your score will be "corrected" for guessing. That is, a penalty will be applied. The incorrect answers will be deducted from the correct ones, or some other penalty formula will be used.

9) Review your answers

If you finish before time is called, go back to the questions you guessed or omitted to give them further thought. Review other answers if you have time.

10) Return your test materials

If you are ready to leave before others have finished or time is called, take ALL your materials to the monitor and leave quietly. Never take any test material with you. The monitor can discover whose papers are not complete, and taking a test booklet may be grounds for disqualification.

VIII. EXAMINATION TECHNIQUES

1) Read the general instructions carefully. These are usually printed on the first page of the exam booklet. As a rule, these instructions refer to the timing of the examination; the fact that you should not start work until the signal and must stop work at a signal, etc. If there are any *special* instructions, such as a choice of questions to be answered, make sure that you note this instruction carefully.

2) When you are ready to start work on the examination, that is as soon as the signal has been given, read the instructions to each question booklet, underline any key words or phrases, such as *least, best, outline, describe* and the like. In this way you will tend to answer as requested rather than discover on reviewing your paper that you *listed without describing*, that you selected the *worst* choice rather than the *best* choice, etc.

3) If the examination is of the objective or multiple-choice type – that is, each question will also give a series of possible answers: A, B, C or D, and you are called upon to select the best answer and write the letter next to that answer on your answer paper – it is advisable to start answering each question in turn. There may be anywhere from 50 to 100 such questions in the three or four hours allotted and you can see how much time would be taken if you read through all the questions before beginning to answer any. Furthermore, if you come across a question or group of questions which you know would be difficult to answer, it would undoubtedly affect your handling of all the other questions.

4) If the examination is of the essay type and contains but a few questions, it is a moot point as to whether you should read all the questions before starting to answer any one. Of course, if you are given a choice – say five out of seven and the like – then it is essential to read all the questions so you can eliminate the two that are most difficult. If, however, you are asked to answer all the questions, there may be danger in trying to answer the easiest one first because you may find that you will spend too much time on it. The best technique is to answer the first question, then proceed to the second, etc.

5) Time your answers. Before the exam begins, write down the time it started, then add the time allowed for the examination and write down the time it must be completed, then divide the time available somewhat as follows:
    - If 3-1/2 hours are allowed, that would be 210 minutes. If you have 80 objective-type questions, that would be an average of 2-1/2 minutes per question. Allow yourself no more than 2 minutes per question, or a total of 160 minutes, which will permit about 50 minutes to review.
    - If for the time allotment of 210 minutes there are 7 essay questions to answer, that would average about 30 minutes a question. Give yourself only 25 minutes per question so that you have about 35 minutes to review.

6) The most important instruction is to *read each question* and make sure you know what is wanted. The second most important instruction is to *time yourself properly* so that you answer every question. The third most important instruction is to *answer every question*. Guess if you have to but include something for each question. Remember that you will receive no credit for a blank and will probably receive some credit if you write something in answer to an essay question. If you guess a letter – say "B" for a multiple-choice question – you may have guessed right. If you leave a blank as an answer to a multiple-choice question, the examiners may respect your feelings but it will not add a point to your score. Some exams may penalize you for wrong answers, so in such cases *only*, you may not want to guess unless you have some basis for your answer.

7) Suggestions
    a. Objective-type questions
        1. Examine the question booklet for proper sequence of pages and questions
        2. Read all instructions carefully
        3. Skip any question which seems too difficult; return to it after all other questions have been answered
        4. Apportion your time properly; do not spend too much time on any single question or group of questions

5. Note and underline key words – *all, most, fewest, least, best, worst, same, opposite,* etc.
6. Pay particular attention to negatives
7. Note unusual option, e.g., unduly long, short, complex, different or similar in content to the body of the question
8. Observe the use of "hedging" words – *probably, may, most likely,* etc.
9. Make sure that your answer is put next to the same number as the question
10. Do not second-guess unless you have good reason to believe the second answer is definitely more correct
11. Cross out original answer if you decide another answer is more accurate; do not erase until you are ready to hand your paper in
12. Answer all questions; guess unless instructed otherwise
13. Leave time for review

b. Essay questions
1. Read each question carefully
2. Determine exactly what is wanted. Underline key words or phrases.
3. Decide on outline or paragraph answer
4. Include many different points and elements unless asked to develop any one or two points or elements
5. Show impartiality by giving pros and cons unless directed to select one side only
6. Make and write down any assumptions you find necessary to answer the questions
7. Watch your English, grammar, punctuation and choice of words
8. Time your answers; don't crowd material

8) Answering the essay question

Most essay questions can be answered by framing the specific response around several key words or ideas. Here are a few such key words or ideas:

M's: manpower, materials, methods, money, management
P's: purpose, program, policy, plan, procedure, practice, problems, pitfalls, personnel, public relations

a. Six basic steps in handling problems:
1. Preliminary plan and background development
2. Collect information, data and facts
3. Analyze and interpret information, data and facts
4. Analyze and develop solutions as well as make recommendations
5. Prepare report and sell recommendations
6. Install recommendations and follow up effectiveness

b. Pitfalls to avoid
1. *Taking things for granted* – A statement of the situation does not necessarily imply that each of the elements is necessarily true; for example, a complaint may be invalid and biased so that all that can be taken for granted is that a complaint has been registered

2. *Considering only one side of a situation* – Wherever possible, indicate several alternatives and then point out the reasons you selected the best one
3. *Failing to indicate follow up* – Whenever your answer indicates action on your part, make certain that you will take proper follow-up action to see how successful your recommendations, procedures or actions turn out to be
4. *Taking too long in answering any single question* – Remember to time your answers properly

IX. AFTER THE TEST

Scoring procedures differ in detail among civil service jurisdictions although the general principles are the same. Whether the papers are hand-scored or graded by machine we have described, they are nearly always graded by number. That is, the person who marks the paper knows only the number – never the name – of the applicant. Not until all the papers have been graded will they be matched with names. If other tests, such as training and experience or oral interview ratings have been given, scores will be combined. Different parts of the examination usually have different weights. For example, the written test might count 60 percent of the final grade, and a rating of training and experience 40 percent. In many jurisdictions, veterans will have a certain number of points added to their grades.

After the final grade has been determined, the names are placed in grade order and an eligible list is established. There are various methods for resolving ties between those who get the same final grade – probably the most common is to place first the name of the person whose application was received first. Job offers are made from the eligible list in the order the names appear on it. You will be notified of your grade and your rank as soon as all these computations have been made. This will be done as rapidly as possible.

People who are found to meet the requirements in the announcement are called "eligibles." Their names are put on a list of eligible candidates. An eligible's chances of getting a job depend on how high he stands on this list and how fast agencies are filling jobs from the list.

When a job is to be filled from a list of eligibles, the agency asks for the names of people on the list of eligibles for that job. When the civil service commission receives this request, it sends to the agency the names of the three people highest on this list. Or, if the job to be filled has specialized requirements, the office sends the agency the names of the top three persons who meet these requirements from the general list.

The appointing officer makes a choice from among the three people whose names were sent to him. If the selected person accepts the appointment, the names of the others are put back on the list to be considered for future openings.

That is the rule in hiring from all kinds of eligible lists, whether they are for typist, carpenter, chemist, or something else. For every vacancy, the appointing officer has his choice of any one of the top three eligibles on the list. This explains why the person whose name is on top of the list sometimes does not get an appointment when some of the persons lower on the list do. If the appointing officer chooses the second or third eligible, the No. 1 eligible does not get a job at once, but stays on the list until he is appointed or the list is terminated.

X. HOW TO PASS THE INTERVIEW TEST

The examination for which you applied requires an oral interview test. You have already taken the written test and you are now being called for the interview test – the final part of the formal examination.

You may think that it is not possible to prepare for an interview test and that there are no procedures to follow during an interview. Our purpose is to point out some things you can do in advance that will help you and some good rules to follow and pitfalls to avoid while you are being interviewed.

What is an interview supposed to test?

The written examination is designed to test the technical knowledge and competence of the candidate; the oral is designed to evaluate intangible qualities, not readily measured otherwise, and to establish a list showing the relative fitness of each candidate – as measured against his competitors – for the position sought. Scoring is not on the basis of "right" and "wrong," but on a sliding scale of values ranging from "not passable" to "outstanding." As a matter of fact, it is possible to achieve a relatively low score without a single "incorrect" answer because of evident weakness in the qualities being measured.

Occasionally, an examination may consist entirely of an oral test – either an individual or a group oral. In such cases, information is sought concerning the technical knowledges and abilities of the candidate, since there has been no written examination for this purpose. More commonly, however, an oral test is used to supplement a written examination.

Who conducts interviews?

The composition of oral boards varies among different jurisdictions. In nearly all, a representative of the personnel department serves as chairman. One of the members of the board may be a representative of the department in which the candidate would work. In some cases, "outside experts" are used, and, frequently, a businessman or some other representative of the general public is asked to serve. Labor and management or other special groups may be represented. The aim is to secure the services of experts in the appropriate field.

However the board is composed, it is a good idea (and not at all improper or unethical) to ascertain in advance of the interview who the members are and what groups they represent. When you are introduced to them, you will have some idea of their backgrounds and interests, and at least you will not stutter and stammer over their names.

What should be done before the interview?

While knowledge about the board members is useful and takes some of the surprise element out of the interview, there is other preparation which is more substantive. It *is* possible to prepare for an oral interview – in several ways:

1) Keep a copy of your application and review it carefully before the interview

This may be the only document before the oral board, and the starting point of the interview. Know what education and experience you have listed there, and the sequence and dates of all of it. Sometimes the board will ask you to review the highlights of your experience for them; you should not have to hem and haw doing it.

2) Study the class specification and the examination announcement

Usually, the oral board has one or both of these to guide them. The qualities, characteristics or knowledges required by the position sought are stated in these documents. They offer valuable clues as to the nature of the oral interview. For example, if the job involves supervisory responsibilities, the announcement will usually indicate that knowledge of modern supervisory methods and the qualifications of the candidate as a supervisor will be tested. If so, you can expect such questions, frequently in the form of a hypothetical situation which you are expected to solve. NEVER go into an oral without knowledge of the duties and responsibilities of the job you seek.

3) Think through each qualification required

Try to visualize the kind of questions you would ask if you were a board member. How well could you answer them? Try especially to appraise your own knowledge and background in each area, *measured against the job sought*, and identify any areas in which you are weak. Be critical and realistic – do not flatter yourself.

4) Do some general reading in areas in which you feel you may be weak

For example, if the job involves supervision and your past experience has NOT, some general reading in supervisory methods and practices, particularly in the field of human relations, might be useful. Do NOT study agency procedures or detailed manuals. The oral board will be testing your understanding and capacity, not your memory.

5) Get a good night's sleep and watch your general health and mental attitude

You will want a clear head at the interview. Take care of a cold or any other minor ailment, and of course, no hangovers.

What should be done on the day of the interview?

Now comes the day of the interview itself. Give yourself plenty of time to get there. Plan to arrive somewhat ahead of the scheduled time, particularly if your appointment is in the fore part of the day. If a previous candidate fails to appear, the board might be ready for you a bit early. By early afternoon an oral board is almost invariably behind schedule if there are many candidates, and you may have to wait. Take along a book or magazine to read, or your application to review, but leave any extraneous material in the waiting room when you go in for your interview. In any event, relax and compose yourself.

The matter of dress is important. The board is forming impressions about you – from your experience, your manners, your attitude, and your appearance. Give your personal appearance careful attention. Dress your best, but not your flashiest. Choose conservative, appropriate clothing, and be sure it is immaculate. This is a business interview, and your appearance should indicate that you regard it as such. Besides, being well groomed and properly dressed will help boost your confidence.

Sooner or later, someone will call your name and escort you into the interview room. *This is it.* From here on you are on your own. It is too late for any more preparation. But remember, you asked for this opportunity to prove your fitness, and you are here because your request was granted.

What happens when you go in?

The usual sequence of events will be as follows: The clerk (who is often the board stenographer) will introduce you to the chairman of the oral board, who will introduce you to the other members of the board. Acknowledge the introductions before you sit down. Do not be surprised if you find a microphone facing you or a stenotypist sitting by. Oral interviews are usually recorded in the event of an appeal or other review.

Usually the chairman of the board will open the interview by reviewing the highlights of your education and work experience from your application – primarily for the benefit of the other members of the board, as well as to get the material into the record. Do not interrupt or comment unless there is an error or significant misinterpretation; if that is the case, do not hesitate. But do not quibble about insignificant matters. Also, he will usually ask you some question about your education, experience or your present job – partly to get you to start talking and to establish the interviewing "rapport." He may start the actual questioning, or turn it over to one of the other members. Frequently, each member undertakes the questioning on a particular area, one in which he is perhaps most competent, so you can expect each member to participate in the examination. Because time is limited, you may also expect some rather abrupt switches in the direction the questioning takes, so do not be upset by it. Normally, a board member will not pursue a single line of questioning unless he discovers a particular strength or weakness.

After each member has participated, the chairman will usually ask whether any member has any further questions, then will ask you if you have anything you wish to add. Unless you are expecting this question, it may floor you. Worse, it may start you off on an extended, extemporaneous speech. The board is not usually seeking more information. The question is principally to offer you a last opportunity to present further qualifications or to indicate that you have nothing to add. So, if you feel that a significant qualification or characteristic has been overlooked, it is proper to point it out in a sentence or so. Do not compliment the board on the thoroughness of their examination – they have been sketchy, and you know it. If you wish, merely say, "No thank you, I have nothing further to add." This is a point where you can "talk yourself out" of a good impression or fail to present an important bit of information. Remember, *you close the interview yourself*.

The chairman will then say, "That is all, Mr. _____, thank you." Do not be startled; the interview is over, and quicker than you think. Thank him, gather your belongings and take your leave. Save your sigh of relief for the other side of the door.

How to put your best foot forward

Throughout this entire process, you may feel that the board individually and collectively is trying to pierce your defenses, seek out your hidden weaknesses and embarrass and confuse you. Actually, this is not true. They are obliged to make an appraisal of your qualifications for the job you are seeking, and they want to see you in your best light. Remember, they must interview all candidates and a non-cooperative candidate may become a failure in spite of their best efforts to bring out his qualifications. Here are 15 suggestions that will help you:

1) Be natural – Keep your attitude confident, not cocky

If you are not confident that you can do the job, do not expect the board to be. Do not apologize for your weaknesses, try to bring out your strong points. The board is interested in a positive, not negative, presentation. Cockiness will antagonize any board member and make him wonder if you are covering up a weakness by a false show of strength.

2) Get comfortable, but don't lounge or sprawl

Sit erectly but not stiffly. A careless posture may lead the board to conclude that you are careless in other things, or at least that you are not impressed by the importance of the occasion. Either conclusion is natural, even if incorrect. Do not fuss with your clothing, a pencil or an ashtray. Your hands may occasionally be useful to emphasize a point; do not let them become a point of distraction.

3) Do not wisecrack or make small talk

This is a serious situation, and your attitude should show that you consider it as such. Further, the time of the board is limited – they do not want to waste it, and neither should you.

4) Do not exaggerate your experience or abilities

In the first place, from information in the application or other interviews and sources, the board may know more about you than you think. Secondly, you probably will not get away with it. An experienced board is rather adept at spotting such a situation, so do not take the chance.

5) If you know a board member, do not make a point of it, yet do not hide it

Certainly you are not fooling him, and probably not the other members of the board. Do not try to take advantage of your acquaintanceship – it will probably do you little good.

6) Do not dominate the interview

Let the board do that. They will give you the clues – do not assume that you have to do all the talking. Realize that the board has a number of questions to ask you, and do not try to take up all the interview time by showing off your extensive knowledge of the answer to the first one.

7) Be attentive

You only have 20 minutes or so, and you should keep your attention at its sharpest throughout. When a member is addressing a problem or question to you, give him your undivided attention. Address your reply principally to him, but do not exclude the other board members.

8) Do not interrupt

A board member may be stating a problem for you to analyze. He will ask you a question when the time comes. Let him state the problem, and wait for the question.

9) Make sure you understand the question

Do not try to answer until you are sure what the question is. If it is not clear, restate it in your own words or ask the board member to clarify it for you. However, do not haggle about minor elements.

10) Reply promptly but not hastily

A common entry on oral board rating sheets is "candidate responded readily," or "candidate hesitated in replies." Respond as promptly and quickly as you can, but do not jump to a hasty, ill-considered answer.

11) Do not be peremptory in your answers

A brief answer is proper – but do not fire your answer back. That is a losing game from your point of view. The board member can probably ask questions much faster than you can answer them.

12) Do not try to create the answer you think the board member wants

He is interested in what kind of mind you have and how it works – not in playing games. Furthermore, he can usually spot this practice and will actually grade you down on it.

13) Do not switch sides in your reply merely to agree with a board member

Frequently, a member will take a contrary position merely to draw you out and to see if you are willing and able to defend your point of view. Do not start a debate, yet do not surrender a good position. If a position is worth taking, it is worth defending.

14) Do not be afraid to admit an error in judgment if you are shown to be wrong

The board knows that you are forced to reply without any opportunity for careful consideration. Your answer may be demonstrably wrong. If so, admit it and get on with the interview.

15) Do not dwell at length on your present job

The opening question may relate to your present assignment. Answer the question but do not go into an extended discussion. You are being examined for a *new* job, not your present one. As a matter of fact, try to phrase ALL your answers in terms of the job for which you are being examined.

Basis of Rating

Probably you will forget most of these "do's" and "don'ts" when you walk into the oral interview room. Even remembering them all will not ensure you a passing grade. Perhaps you did not have the qualifications in the first place. But remembering them will help you to put your best foot forward, without treading on the toes of the board members.

Rumor and popular opinion to the contrary notwithstanding, an oral board wants you to make the best appearance possible. They know you are under pressure – but they also want to see how you respond to it as a guide to what your reaction would be under the pressures of the job you seek. They will be influenced by the degree of poise you display, the personal traits you show and the manner in which you respond.

ABOUT THIS BOOK

This book contains tests divided into Examination Sections. Go through each test, answering every question in the margin. We have also attached a sample answer sheet at the back of the book that can be removed and used. At the end of each test look at the answer key and check your answers. On the ones you got wrong, look at the right answer choice and learn. Do not fill in the answers first. Do not memorize the questions and answers, but understand the answer and principles involved. On your test, the questions will likely be different from the samples. Questions are changed and new ones added. If you understand these past questions you should have success with any changes that arise. Tests may consist of several types of questions. We have additional books on each subject should more study be advisable or necessary for you. Finally, the more you study, the better prepared you will be. This book is intended to be the last thing you study before you walk into the examination room. Prior study of relevant texts is also recommended. NLC publishes some of these in our Fundamental Series. Knowledge and good sense are important factors in passing your exam. Good luck also helps. So now study this Passbook, absorb the material contained within and take that knowledge into the examination. Then do your best to pass that exam.

EXAMINATION SECTION

EXAMINATION SECTION
TEST 1

DIRECTIONS: Each question or incomplete statement is followed by several suggested answers or completions. Select the one that BEST answers the question or completes the statement. *PRINT THE LETTER OF THE CORRECT ANSWER IN THE SPACE AT THE RIGHT.*

1. You are assisting with the care of a patient who is suffering from false sensory perceptions and is completely out of touch with reality. These perceptions are referred to as
    A. visions
    B. delusions
    C. hallucinations
    D. flashbacks

   1.____

2. A suicidal patient needs assistance to the bathroom. How should you act when dealing with this situation?
    A. Closely observe the patient
    B. Allow the patient privacy while in the bathroom
    C. Permit the patient to shave
    D. Make sure all sharp items have been removed from the room

   2.____

3. Which of the following is important when caring for a patient with anorexia nervosa?
    A. Allow the patient to have privacy during meal times
    B. Patients should adhere to a strict meal plan
    C. No visitors should be permitted until the patient begins to eat normally
    D. You should be present at all times to make sure the patient eats

   3.____

4. A recently widowed woman is dealing with severe depression and is possibly suicidal. Which of the following questions would be appropriate in order to determine whether or not the patient is suicidal?
    A. "Why do you want to kill yourself?"
    B. "How would you kill yourself?"
    C. "Are you sure you want to kill yourself?"
    D. "Where would you kill yourself?"

   4.____

5. Which of the following characteristics would be evident for a patient who is abusing opiates such as morphine?
    A. Euphoria and dilated pupils
    B. High energy and dilated pupils
    C. Anger and constricted pupils
    D. Slurred speech and dilated pupils

   5.____

6. What is the appropriate action when a patient is having an anxiety attack?
    A. Stay with the patient and speak calmly and slowly
    B. Open windows and turn on lights to avoid claustrophobia
    C. Leave the patient alone in silence
    D. Turn on soothing music

   6.____

7. If a patient has delusions of grandeur, what does this refer to?
   A. The patient feels that he/she is extremely important
   B. The patient is experiencing hallucinations
   C. The patient is suicidal
   D. The patient is severely depressed

8. Enforcing limits on behavior is most important for what type of patient?
   A. Depressed   B. Suicidal
   C. Anxious   D. Manic

9. What are signs and symptoms of post-traumatic stress disorder?
   A. Hostility and violence   B. Behavior changes and anorexia
   C. Hyper alertness and insomnia D. Memory loss and insomnia

10. Which of the following is appropriate for a patient with manic depression?
    A. Encouraging the patient to eat high calorie meals
    B. Insisting on highly exertional activities so patient sleeps at night
    C. Listening closely and avoiding power struggles
    D. Allowing patient to behave with no limits

11. A patient with post-traumatic stress disorder is experiencing nightmares, depression, alcohol abuse, and feelings of hopelessness. Which of the following is important for relieving the symptoms of this patient?
    A. Regular attendance at Alcoholics Anonymous meetings
    B. Family support
    C. Proper anti-anxiety medicine
    D. Encouraging patient to talk about the past experiences

12. If a patient is undergoing detoxification for a heroin overdose and states they can stop using heroin if they want to is an example of which coping mechanism?
    A. Repression   B. Delusion   C. Denial   D. Withdrawal

13. What is a common characteristic among patients who suffer from dependent personality disorder?
    A. Cannot form lasting relationships
    B. Cannot make decisions without seeking advice
    C. Self-destructive behavior
    D. Hopelessness

14. Which of the following is an early sign of alcohol withdrawal?
    A. Slurred speech   B. Perceptual disorders
    C. Agitation   D. Depression

15. Which of the following is a characteristic of a patient with schizotypal personality disorder when faced with a social situation?
    A. Paranoia   B. Depression
    C. Agitation   D. Homicidal impulses

16. When a patient is in a manic state, what is the MOST appropriate action to relieve this situation?
    A. Encourage patient to express feelings
    B. Discourage interaction with other people until manic state passes
    C. Encourage interaction with others to relieve manic state
    D. Reduce any stimulation that may contribute to the manic state

17. Which of the following is imperative in order to care for a patient with bulimia?
    A. Determine which situations cause anxiety
    B. Determine why the patient feels they need to lose weight
    C. Determine what foods the patient likes to eat
    D. Restrict patients to three planned meals per day

18. Which of the following behaviors is indicative of adult cognitive development?
    A. Generating new levels of awareness
    B. Assuming responsibility for actions
    C. Can solve problems and learn new skills
    D. Has reality-based perceptions

19. Which of the following is common when a patient first begins to take lithium for treatment of bipolar disorder?
    A. Excessive thirst
    B. Excessive urination
    C. Constipation
    D. Excessive hunger

20. What characteristics are common for a patient who has overdosed on amphetamines?
    A. Low pulse rate
    B. Low blood pressure
    C. Slurred speech
    D. Irritability

21. Which medications are appropriate for treating patients who commonly suffer from panic attacks?
    A. Opiates
    B. Anti-depressants
    C. Anti-anxiety medications
    D. Barbiturates

22. What is the BEST course of action when a patient is actively having hallucinations that are causing agitation?
    A. Try to bring the patient back to reality
    B. Give the patient a sedative
    C. Try to find out the content of the hallucination
    D. Immediately restrain the patient

23. What is the BEST course of action when a patient with paranoid schizophrenia gets upset and tells you to leave him alone?
    A. Explain that you are in control, not the patient
    B. Continue to do your job regardless of the patient's feelings
    C. Explain that you will leave for now but be back soon
    D. Find out why the patient wants to be left alone

24. What condition is characterized by tonic contractures of the muscles of the neck, mouth, and tongue?   24.____
    A. Dystonia   B. Dyskinesia
    C. Heroin overdose   D. Cocaine overdose

25. Which blood electrolyte level is important to monitor before a patient begins to take lithium?   25.____
    A. Potassium   B. Sodium   C. Calcium   D. Chloride

KEY (CORRECT ANSWERS)

1.	C	11.	D
2.	A	12.	C
3.	B	13.	B
4.	B	14.	B
5.	D	15.	A
6.	A	16.	D
7.	A	17.	A
8.	D	18.	A
9.	C	19.	B
10.	C	20.	D

21.	C
22.	C
23.	C
24.	A
25.	B

TEST 2

DIRECTIONS: Each question or incomplete statement is followed by several suggested answers or completions. Select the one that BEST answers the question or completes the statement. *PRINT THE LETTER OF THE CORRECT ANSWER IN THE SPACE AT THE RIGHT.*

1. Which of the following is defined as the state of well-being where a person can realize his own abilities and cope with normal stresses of life and work?
    A. Mental illness
    B. Mental health
    C. Physical health
    D. Emotional health

    1.____

2. Which duty is appropriately performed by a mental health technician?
    A. Administering medications to a patient
    B. Coordinating the overall care for a patient
    C. Providing information regarding alcohol abuse
    D. Prescribing medications for treatment of a patient

    2.____

3. If a patient states, "Give me a few minutes to remember," this patient is operating on which of the following?
    A. Conscious
    B. Subconscious
    C. Unconscious
    D. Ego

    3.____

4. Which of the following is a characteristic of the superego portion of the psyche?
    A. It is the censoring portion of the mind
    B. It is impulsive and lacks morals
    C. It analyzes prior to making decisions
    D. It uses defensive functions for protection

    4.____

5. Which of the following characteristics is associated with the primary level of prevention?
    A. Rehabilitating a patient to take care of himself
    B. Making sure a suicidal patient cannot harm himself
    C. Performing community-wide disease surveillance
    D. Teaching a patient how to deal with stress

    5.____

6. If you suspect a woman and a child are victims of abuse, which of the following questions is MOST appropriate for you to ask?
    A. "Are you okay?"
    B. "Is something bothering you?"
    C. "What happened to you?"
    D. "Are you being threatened or hurt by your partner?"

    6.____

7. Sexual _____ disorder would be characterized by a female abuse victim who develops a diminished sex drive.
    A. pain
    B. arousal
    C. desire
    D. appetite

    7.____

8. If a patient is still living with an abusive spouse, what is the BEST advice you can offer?
   A. Tell the patient to end the relationship
   B. Tell the patient to summon the family's opinion regarding the relationship
   C. Give the patient information for a crisis center
   D. Tell the patient what you would do if you were in the same situation

9. Which of the following statements could indicate child abuse if made by a parent?
   A. "If I tell my child to do something once, I better not have to tell them again."
   B. "My child tells me no all the time."
   C. "Once my child is potty trained, I can still expect an accident from time to time."
   D. "I encourage my children to try new and different things."

10. What is the PRIMARY concern when dealing with a victim of child abuse?
    A. Understand why the child is being abused
    B. Make sure the patient is safe from further harm
    C. Make sure the patient is now comfortable
    D. Teach the victim how to mentally deal with the abuse

11. Which somatoform disorder is characterized by constant complaints of pain or illness without any medical or clinical explanation?
    A. Hypochondriasis
    B. Conversion disorder
    C. Somatization disorder
    D. Somatoform Pain disorder

12. According to Sigmund Freud, anxiety is defined as
    A. conflict between the id and superego
    B. a hypothalamic-pituitary-adrenal reaction to stress
    C. a conditioned response to stress
    D. functions to satisfy the need for security

13. Which of the following medications would be appropriate for reducing the symptoms of alcohol withdrawal?
    A. Narcan   B. Librium   C. Haldol   D. Phenobarbital

14. Parents of children who develop anorexia nervosa commonly have which of the following characteristics?
    A. History of drug abuse
    B. Generally ignoring their children
    C. Tendency to be strict and overprotective
    D. Tendency to be extremely aggressive and goal oriented

15. What is the FIRST priority when dealing with a spousal abuse victim and the spouse shows up to *finish the job*?
    A. Confront the abusing spouse
    B. Remain with the victim and stay calm
    C. Call security and another staff member for assistance
    D. Ask the abusing spouse why this happened

16. Which aspect is very important when dealing with a patient with bulimia in which strict management of dietary intake is necessary?
    A. Allowing the patient to eat meals in private
    B. Allowing the patient to choose their own food and staying with them for an hour after the meal is finished
    C. Choosing the food for the patient and making sure they eat at least half of the meal
    D. Keeping patient engaged in activities for two hours after each meal time

17. Patients being treated with Antabuse need to carefully read the labels on which products to avoid potential reactions?
    A. Sodas
    B. Cologne and aftershaves
    C. Toothpaste
    D. Juices

18. If you are caring for an injured child, what specific action would lead you to believe the child is being abused?
    The child
    A. does not cry when being examined
    B. does not make eye contact with the caregiver
    C. cries uncontrollably throughout the examination
    D. resists contact from the caregiver

19. The patient's _____ needs is the highest priority when encountering a patient who has taken PCP.
    A. medical
    B. psychological
    C. physical
    D. safety

20. How would you proceed if you entered a room and found a patient sitting on the floor with cuts on both wrists and surrounded by broken glass?
    A. Approach the patient slowly, speak in a calm voice, call the patient by name and tell them you are here to help
    B. Move the glass away and sit down next to the patient
    C. Call for additional staff before entering the room and restraining the patient
    D. Enter the room quietly and get beside the patient to assess him

21. Clonidine is useful for treating which condition other than hypertension?
    A. Alcohol withdrawal
    B. Opiate withdrawal
    C. Cocaine withdrawal
    D. Heroin withdrawal

22. Which of the following are early signs of alcohol withdrawal? 22.____
    A. Sweating, tremors, nervousness
    B. Hypertension, sweating, seizures
    C. Dehydration, fever, itching
    D. Vomiting, diarrhea, slow heart rate

23. What are some behavioral characteristics for a person with antisocial personality disorder? 23.____
    A. Continuously talks of violence
    B. Silence and disobedient
    C. Rigid posture, restlessness, glaring
    D. Depression and physical withdrawal

24. How long after the last alcoholic drink will early withdrawal symptoms begin to become evident? 24.____
    A. 6 hours
    B. 12 hours
    C. 24-48 hours
    D. 60-72 hours

25. What is the proper treatment for a patient experiencing hallucinations secondary to alcohol abuse? 25.____
    A. Keep patient restrained until hallucinations stop
    B. Check blood pressure every 15 minutes and force fluids
    C. Keep environment calm and quiet and give medications as needed
    D. Continuously monitor the patient and check blood pressure every 30 minutes

KEY (CORRECT ANSWERS)

1.	B		11.	D
2.	A		12.	A
3.	B		13.	B
4.	A		14.	C
5.	D		15.	C
6.	D		16.	B
7.	C		17.	B
8.	C		18.	A
9.	A		19.	D
10.	B		20.	A

21.	B
22.	D
23.	C
24.	C
25.	C

EXAMINATION SECTION

TEST 1

DIRECTIONS: Each question or incomplete statement is followed by several suggested answers or completions. Select the one that BEST answers the question or completes the statement. *PRINT THE LETTER OF THE CORRECT ANSWER IN THE SPACE AT THE RIGHT.*

1. Which of the following findings is MOST consistent with early alcohol withdrawal?
    A. Heart rate of 50-60 beats per minute
    B. Heart rate of 120-140 beats per minute
    C. Blood pressure of 90/60 mmHg
    D. Blood pressure of 140/80 mmHg

2. Which of the following patients would have the HIGHEST risk for suicide?
    A. Patient who talks about wanting to die
    B. Patient who plans a violent death and has the means to do so
    C. Patient who appears depressed, frequently thinks about dying, and gives away all personal possessions
    D. Patient who says they may do something if life does not improve soon

3. Which medical condition is commonly associated with patients with bulimia nervosa?
    A. Diabetes   B. HIV   C. Cancer   D. Hepatitis C

4. What action would be considered as a primary nursing intervention for a victim of child abuse?
    A. Teach the victim coping skills
    B. Ensure the safety of the victim
    C. Analyze the family dynamics
    D. Assess the scope of the problem

5. Somatoform disorder is defined as
    A. management consisting of a specific medical treatment
    B. expression of conflicts through bodily symptoms
    C. a voluntary expression of psychological conflicts
    D. physical symptoms explained by organic causes

6. What is a proper plan for treating a school-age child with attention deficit hyperactivity disorder?
    A. Ignore the child's hyperactivity
    B. Child should be removed from the classroom when disruptive
    C. Child should have as much structure as possible
    D. Encourage the child to play to release excess energy

7. Which characteristic is common for a child with conduct disorder?
   A. Ritualistic behaviors
   B. Preference for inanimate objects
   C. Severe violations of age-related normal behavior
   D. Easily distracted

8. School phobia is commonly relieved by
   A. allowing the parent to be with the child in the classroom
   B. immediately returning the child to school with a family member
   C. telling the student why attendance at school is important
   D. allowing the child to enter the school before the other children

9. If a child has an I.Q. of 45, what classification of mental retardation does this value represent?
   A. Mild   B. Moderate   C. Severe   D. Profound

10. Which characteristics are common for a child with autistic disorder?
    A. Aggression, stealing, lying
    B. Easily distracted, impulsive, and hyperactive
    C. Intolerant to change, disturbed relatedness, stereotypes
    D. Angry, argumentative, and disobedient

11. Which of the following would NOT be an acceptable therapeutic approach for caring for an autistic child?
    A. Providing safety measures
    B. Rearranging the environment to motivate the child
    C. Engaging a diversion when acting out
    D. Providing an atmosphere of acceptance

12. According to Piaget's Cognitive Stages of Development, a 5-year-old child is in what stage of development?
    A. Sensorimotor stage   B. Concrete operations
    C. Pre-operational   D. Formal operation

13. What is indicated if a patient states they have to increase their level of alcohol intake to achieve the desired effect?
    A. Tolerance   B. Withdrawal
    C. Intoxication   D. Weight gain

14. If an alcoholic patient is experiencing tremors, irritability, hypertension, and fever, what condition will soon follow?
    A. Esophageal varices   B. Korsakoff's syndrome
    C. Wernicke's syndrome   D. Delirium tremens

15. What would be the proper treatment for a patient in delirium tremens?
    A. Adequate fluids and high nutrient foods
    B. Placed in a quiet, dimly lit room
    C. Administration of Librium
    D. Monitoring vital signs every hour

16. If a patient presents with hallucinations, agitation, and an irritated nasal septum, which illicit drug did the patient MOST likely ingest?
    A. Marijuana
    B. Cocaine
    C. Heroin
    D. Methamphetamine

17. What would be the appropriate medication for a patient who presents with needle tracks in the arm, in a stupor, and with a pinpoint pupil?
    A. Narcan
    B. Methadone
    C. Naltrexone
    D. Disulfiram

18. If an elderly patient presents with increasing forgetfulness, decreasing daily function, and using a toothbrush to comb his hair, which of the following conditions is being exhibited by this patient?
    A. Aphasia
    B. Amnesia
    C. Apraxia
    D. Agnosia

19. What would be a PRIMARY treatment intervention for a patient with moderate stage dementia?
    A. Providing a safe and secure environment
    B. Providing adequate nutrition and hydration
    C. Encouraging memories to decrease isolation
    D. Encouraging to independently care for themselves

20. Through which characteristic is dementia different from delirium?
    A. Dementia promotes slurred speech
    B. Dementia has a gradual onset
    C. Dementia includes clouding of the consciousness
    D. Dementia includes a sensory perceptual change

21. What would be the BEST advice you could give to a patient who feels the need to starve themselves?
    A. Exercise until the need to starve passes
    B. Allow the patient to starve to relieve anxiety
    C. Tell the patient's family immediately
    D. Tell the patient to approach a nurse and talk out their feelings

22. Which characteristic is a sign of improvement for patients with anorexia nervosa?
    A. Weight loss
    B. Weight gain
    C. Eating meals in the dining room
    D. Participation in group activities

23. What is the MAJOR difference between anorexia nervosa and bulimia nervosa?
    Bulimic patients
    A. will have periods of binge eating and purging
    B. will have lesser anxiety
    C. will have peculiar food handling patterns
    D. have poor self-esteem

24. A caregiver can build a therapeutic relationship with a bulimic patient by performing all of the following actions EXCEPT
    A. discussing their eating behavior
    B. establishing an atmosphere of trust
    C. helping patients identify feelings associated with binging and purging
    D. educating the patient about the condition of bulimia nervosa

25. Which condition would be characterized by an intense fear of riding in an elevator?
    A. Arachnophobia   B. Agoraphobia
    C. Xenophobia   D. Claustrophobia

KEY (CORRECT ANSWERS)

1.	B	11.	B
2.	B	12.	C
3.	A	13.	A
4.	C	14.	D
5.	B	15.	D
6.	C	16.	B
7.	C	17.	A
8.	B	18.	D
9.	B	19.	A
10.	C	20.	B

21. D
22. B
23. A
24. A
25. D

TEST 2

DIRECTIONS: Each question or incomplete statement is followed by several suggested answers or completions. Select the one that BEST answers the question or completes the statement. *PRINT THE LETTER OF THE CORRECT ANSWER IN THE SPACE AT THE RIGHT.*

1. What should be the INITIAL treatment action for a patient with claustrophobia?
   A. Accept the patient's fear without opinion or criticism
   B. Assist the patient to find the cause of the fear
   C. Allow the patient to talk about their fear as much as possible
   D. Establish a trusting relationship

   1._____

2. Which is evidence of a caregiver developing a countertransference reaction?
   A. Confronting the patient about discrepancies in their behavior
   B. Revealing personal information to the patient
   C. Focusing on the feelings of the patient
   D. Ignoring the patient's wants and needs

   2._____

3. In attempting to be accomplished when conducting desensitization, the patient
   A. stops using illicit drugs
   B. stops abusing alcohol
   C. overcomes disabling fear
   D. admits to all wrongdoings

   3._____

4. Which of the following should you advise patients who are prescribed to take valium?
   A. Increase fluid intake
   B. Decrease fluid intake
   C. Avoid caffeinated beverages
   D. Avoid alcoholic beverages

   4._____

5. How does malingering differ from somatoform disorder?
   A. Malingering is stress that is expressed through physical symptoms
   B. Malingering is gratification from the environment
   C. Malingering has evidence from an organic basis
   D. Malingering is a deliberate effort to handle upsetting events

   5._____

6. What is the MOST successful form of therapy for a somatoform disorder?
   A. Prescription medications
   B. Stress management
   C. Psychotherapy
   D. Milieu therapy

   6._____

7. What method would you use to treat a psychiatric patient who speaks a foreign language?
   A. Use pictures to communicate
   B. Speak in universal phrases
   C. Simply use nonverbal communication
   D. Employ the services of an interpreter

   7._____

13

8. The _____ theory attempts to explain obsessive compulsive behaviors related to unconscious conflicts between id impulses and the superego.
   A. cognitive
   B. psychoanalytic
   C. behavioral
   D. interpersonal

9. _____ the patient's obsessive compulsive disorder is the MOST successful behavior when caring for a patient with obsessive-compulsive disorder?
   A. Rejecting
   B. Preventing
   C. Accepting
   D. Challenging

10. Which of the following characteristics would NOT be a factor for a patient having diminished sexual arousal?
    A. Medications
    B. Health status
    C. Education and work history
    D. Relationship with spouse

11. Getting the patient to _____ is the ultimate goal of treating a patient with somatoform disorder.
    A. take the prescribed medications
    B. recognize the signs and symptoms of physical illness
    C. cope with physical illness
    D. express anxiety verbally rather than through physical symptoms

12. What is MOST important when counseling a family whose teenage son has just been diagnosed with schizophrenia?
    A. The distressing symptoms of schizophrenia can respond to medications.
    B. Symptoms of this disease imbalance the brain.
    C. Genetic history is a factor for developing schizophrenia.
    D. Schizophrenia can affect every aspect of a patient's functioning.

13. A patient who states they only abuse alcohol and cocaine to deal with a stressful marriage and stressful job is exhibiting which defense mechanism?
    A. Displacement
    B. Rationalization
    C. Sublimation
    D. Projection

14. A pregnant female continues to use heroin throughout her pregnancy. Which of the following conditions would this child be at risk for developing?
    A. Heroin dependence
    B. Mental retardation
    C. Schizophrenia
    D. Anorexia nervosa

15. What is the MOST important medical intervention when caring for a victim of sexual assault?
    A. Preserving an unbroken chain of evidence
    B. Preserving the patient's privacy
    C. Determining the identity of the attacker
    D. Assessing for sexually transmitted diseases

16. Which of the following is NOT a factor for a victim of family violence to safely remain in the home?
    A. Ability of patient to relocate
    B. Socioeconomic status of the family
    C. Availability of community shelters
    D. A non-abusive family member to intervene on behalf of the victim

17. Inability to _____ would be a sign of early onset of Alzheimer's disease.
    A. balance a checkbook
    B. take care of self
    C. relate to family members
    D. remember own name

18. Which neurotransmitter is responsible for the development of Alzheimer's disease?
    A. Serotonin
    B. Dopamine
    C. Epinephrine
    D. Acetylcholine

19. What products should be avoided by patients who are taking lithium carbonate to stabilize moods?
    A. Caffeine   B. Diuretics   C. Antacids   D. Antibiotics

20. Which of the following situations would NOT increase stress on a healthy family system?
    A. Birth of a child
    B. Parental arguments
    C. Child going away to college
    D. Death of a grandparent

21. Patients who take monoamine oxidase inhibitors as antidepressants should avoid
    A. dairy and green vegetables
    B. red meat and poultry
    C. aged cheese and red wine
    D. flour, grains, and rice

22. What should a caregiver assess prior to administering thorazine to an agitated patient?
    A. Pulse rate
    B. Blood pressure
    C. Blood urea nitrogen level
    D. Liver enzymes

23. A patient who is prescribed benzodiazepine oxazepam should avoid excessive consumption of
    A. shellfish   B. coffee   C. sugar   D. salt

24. What is the PRIMARY purpose of Alcoholics Anonymous?
    A. Teach positive coping mechanisms
    B. Alleviate stress
    C. Help members maintain sobriety
    D. Provide fellowship among members

25. What would be the initial treatment intervention if a patient experiences a panic attack in your presence?
    A. Remain with patient and promote a safe environment
    B. Reduce external stimuli
    C. Encourage physical activity
    D. Teach coping mechanisms

25._____

KEY (CORRECT ANSWERS)

1. A
2. B
3. C
4. D
5. D

6. B
7. D
8. B
9. C
10. C

11. D
12. A
13. B
14. A
15. A

16. B
17. A
18. D
19. B
20. B

21. C
22. B
23. B
24. C
25. A

EXAMINATION SECTION
TEST 1

DIRECTIONS: Each question or incomplete statement is followed by several suggested answers or completions. Select the one that BEST answers the question or completes the Statement. *PRINT THE LETTER OF THE CORRECT ANSWER IN THE SPACE AT THE RIGHT.*

Questions 1-5.

DIRECTIONS: Answer questions 1 through 5 on the basis of the following passage.

Mental disorders are found in a fairly large number of the inmates in correctional institutions. There are no exact figures as to the inmates who are mentally disturbed -- partly because it is hard to draw a precise line between "mental disturbance" and "normality" -- but experts find that somewhere between 15% and 25% of inmates are suffering from disorders that are obvious enough to show up in routine psychiatric examinations. Society has not yet really come to grips with the problem of what to do with mentally disturbed offenders. There is not enough money available to set up treatment programs for all the people identified as mentally disturbed; and there would probably not be enough qualified psychiatric personnel available to run such programs even if they could be set up. Most mentally disturbed offenders are therefore left to serve out their time in correctional institutions, and the burden of dealing with them falls on correction officers. This means that a correction offcer must be sensitive enough to human behavior to know when he is dealing with a person who is not mentally normal, and that the officer must be imaginative enough to be able to sense how an abnormal individual might react under certain circumstances.

1. According to the above passage, mentally disturbed inmakes in correctional institutions

    A. are usually transferred to mental hospitals when their condition is noticed
    B. cannot be told from other inmates, because tests cannot distinguish between insane people and normal people
    C. may constitute as mich as 25% of the total inmate population
    D. should be regarded as no different from all the other inmates

    1._____

2. The passage says that today the job of handling mentally disturbed inmates is MAINLY up to

    A. psychiatric personnel   B. other inmates
    C. correction officers   D. administrative officials

    2._____

3. Of the following, which is a reason given in the passage for society's failure to provide adequate treatment programs for mentally disturbed inmates?

    A. Law-abiding citizens should not have to pay for fancy treatment programs for criminals.
    B. A person who breaks the law should not expect society to give him special help.
    C. It is impossible to tell whether an inmate is mentally disturbed.
    D. There are not enough trained people to provide the kind of treatment needed.

    3._____

17

4. The expression *abnormal individual,* as used in the last sentence of the passage, refers to an individual who is

   A. of average intelligence
   B. of superior intelligence
   C. completely normal
   D. mentally disturbed

5. The reader of the passage would MOST likely agree that

   A. correction officers should not expect mentally disturbed persons to behave the same way a normal person would behave
   B. correction officers should not report infractions of the rules committed by mentally disturbed persons
   C. mentally disturbed persons who break the law should be treated exactly the same way as anyone else
   D. mentally disturbed persons who have broken the law should not be imprisoned

Questions 6-12.

DIRECTIONS: Questions 6 through 12 are based on the roster of patients, the instructions, the table, and the sample question given below.

Twelve patients of a mental institution are divided into three permanent groups in their workshop. They must be present and accounted for in these groups at the beginning of each workday. During the day, the patients check out of their groups for various activities. They check back in again when those activities have been completed. Assume that the day is divided into three activity periods.

ROSTER OF PATIENTS

GROUP X	Ted	Frank	George	Harry
GROUP Y	Jack	Ken	Larry	Mel
GROUP Z	Phil	Bob	Sam	Vic

The following table shows the movements of these patients from their groups during the day. Assume that all were present and accounted for at the beginning of Period I.

		GROUP X	GROUP Y	GROUP Z
Period I	Check-outs	Ted, Frank	Ken, Larry	Phil
Period II	Check-ins	Frank	Ken, Larry	Phil
	Check-outs	George	Jack, Mel	Bob, Sam, Vic
Period III	Check-ins	George	Mel, Jack	Sam, Bob, Vic
	Check-outs	Frank, Harry	Ken	Vic

SAMPLE QUESTION: At the end of Period II, the patients remaining in Group X were

   A. Ted, Frank, Harry
   B. Frank, Harry
   C. Ted, George
   D. Frank, Harry, George

During Period I, Ted and Frank were checked out from Group X. During Period II, Frank was checked back in and George was checked out. Therefore, the members of the group remaining out are Ted and George. The two other members of the group, Frank and Harry, should be present. The CORRECT answer is B.

6. At the end of Period I, the TOTAL number of patients remaining in their own permanent groups was

    A. 8 B. 7 C. 6 D. 5

7. At the end of Period I, the patients remaining in Group Z were

    A. George and Harry B. Jack and Mel
    C. Bob, Sam, and Vic D. Phil

8. At the end of Period II, the patients remaining in Group Y were

    A. Ken and Larry B. Jack, Ken, and Mel
    C. Jack and Ken D. Ken, Mel, and Larry

9. At the end of Period II, the TOTAL number of patients remaining in their own permanent groups was

    A. 8 B. 7 C. 6 D. 5

10. At the end of Period II, the patients who were NOT present in Group Z were

    A. Phil, Bob, and Sam B. Sam, Bob, and Vic
    C. Sam, Vic, and Phil D. Vic, Phil, and Bob

11. At the end of Period II, the patients remaining in Group Y were

    A. Ted, Frank, and George B. Jack, Mel, and Ken
    C. Jack, Larry, and Mel D. Frank and Harry

12. At the end of Period III, the TOTAL number of patients NOT present in their own permanent groups was

    A. 4 B. 5 C. 6 D. 7

13. The one of the following conditions which bears no causative relationship to feeblemindedness is

    A. heredity B. cerebral defect
    C. early postnatal trauma D. dementia

14. Physical conditions which are caused by emotional conflicts are generally referred to as being

    A. psycho-social B. hypochondriacal
    C. psychosomatic D. psychotic

15. Of the following conditions, the one in which anxiety is NOT generally found is

    A. psychopathic personality
    B. mild hysteria
    C. psychoneurosis
    D. compulsive-obsessive personality

16. Kleptomania may BEST be described as a   16.___

    A. neurotic drive to accumulate personal property through compulsive acts in order to dispose of it to others with whom one wishes friendship
    B. type of neurosis which manifests itself in an uncontrollable impulse to steal without economic motivation
    C. psychopathic trait which is probably hereditary in nature
    D. manifestation of punishment-inviting behavior based upon guilt feelings for some other crime or wrong-doing, fantasied or real, committed as a child

17. The one of the following tests which is NOT ordinarily used as a protective technique is the   17.___

    A. Wechsler Bellevue Scale
    B. Rorschach Test
    C. Thematic Apperception Test
    D. Jung Free Association Test

18. The outstanding personality test in use at the present time is the Rorschach Test. Of the following considerations, the GREATEST value of this test to the psychiatrist and social worker is that it   18.___

    A. provides practical recommendations with reference to further educational and vocational training possibilities for the person tested
    B. reveals in quick, concise form the hereditary factors affecting the individual personality
    C. helps in substantiating a diagnosis of juvenile delinquency
    D. helps in a diagnostic formulation and in determining differential treatment

19. Of the following, the one through which ethical values are MOST generally acquired is   19.___

    A. heredity
    B. early training in school
    C. admonition and strict corrective measures by parents and other supervising adults
    D. integration into the self of parental values and attitudes

20. Delinquent behavior is MOST generally a result of   20.___

    A. living and growing up in an environment that is both socially and financially deprived
    B. a lack of educational opportunity for development of individual skills
    C. multiple factors -- psychological, bio-social, emotional and environmental
    D. low frustration tolerance of many parents toward problems of married life

21. Alcoholism in the United States is USUALLY caused by   21.___

    A. the sense of frustration in one's work
    B. inadequacy of recreational facilities
    C. neurotic conflicts expressed in drinking excessively
    D. shyness and timidity

22. The MOST distinctive characteristic of the chronic alcoholic is that he drinks alcohol 22.____

    A. socially   B. compulsively
    C. periodically   D. secretly

23. The chronic alcoholic is the person who cannot face reality without alcohol, and yet 23.____
    whose adequate adjustment to reality is impossible so long as he uses alcohol.
    On the basis of this statement, it is MOST reasonable to conclude that individuals
    overindulge in alcohol because alcohol

    A. deadens the sense of conflict, giving the individual an illusion of social competence
       and a feeling of well-being and success
    B. provides the individual with an outlet to display his feelings of good-fellowship and
       cheerfulness which are characteristic of his extroverted personality
    C. affords an escape technique from habitual irrational fears, but does not affect rational fears
    D. offers an escape from imagery and feelings of superiority which cause tension and
       anxiety

24. The one of the following drugs to which a person is LEAST likely to become addicted is 24.____

    A. opium   B. morphine   C. marijuana   D. heroin

25. Teenagers who become addicted to the use of drugs are MOST generally 25.____

    A. mentally defective   B. paranoid
    C. normally adventurous   D. emotionally disturbed

26. In the light of the current high rate of addiction to drugs among youths throughout the 26.____
    country, the one of the following statements which is generally considered to be LEAST
    correct is that

    A. a relatively large number of children and youths who experiment with drugs
       become addicts
    B. youths who use narcotics do so because of some emotional and personality disturbance
    C. youthful addicts are found largely among those who suffer to an abnormal extent
       deprivations in their personal development and growth
    D. the great majority of youthful addicts have had unfortunate home experiences and
       practically no contact with established community agencies

27. The one of the following terms which BEST describes the psychological desire to repeat 27.____
    the use of a drug intermittently or continously because of emotional needs is

    A. habituation   B. euphoria   C. tolerance   D. addiction

28. The desire for special clothing in a mental institution usually is concerned with 28.____

    A. shoes   B. sox   C. trousers   D. underwear

29. A study entitled "*A preliminary evaluation of the relationship between group psychotherapy and the adjustment of adolescent inmates (16-21 years) in a short-term penal institution*" was conducted by the Diagnostic Staff at Rikers Island in New York. A conclusion 29.____
    which was drawn as a result of the study was that

A. a repetition of the study was necessary with smaller therapy and non-therapy groups
B. group psychotherapy subjects displayed a better institutional adjustment than those not receiving group therapy
C. no follow-up study was necessary because of the negative results from the original study
D. a smaller proportion of experimental group subjects improved after receiving group psychotherapy when compared to those who did not receive group therapy

30. The one of the following statements which is MOST accurate concerning group psychotherapy is that group psychotherapy

   A. is in a way an outgrowth of the concept of patient self-government
   B. is of little value with deviant personality types
   C. should make the group members resent help from their fellow patients
   D. reflects a punitive rather than a rehabilitative aim

31. In group counseling and psychotherapy it is USUALLY true that persons are more defensive and argumentative than in individualized counseling and therapy sessions. The reason for this tendency is that

   A. individuals in a group setting feel it more necessary to protect their personality
   B. people in group settings are motivated by the characteristically free atmosphere
   C. people would rather argue in a group setting than in an individualized setting
   D. the group session is more poorly organized and therefore uncontrolled

32. There is a group of mentally ill patients who have a functional psychosis. The word "functional" in this case indicates that

   A. it is an organic psychosis
   B. the psychosis is caused by alcoholism or drug addiction
   C. there are no demonstrable changes in the brain
   D. there are clinical findings of senile arteriosclerosis

33. "Sociopaths" is a fairly new word used to describe

   A. confirmed narcotics addicts
   B. latent male homosexuals
   C. neurotic adolescents
   D. psychopathic personalities

34. The incarceration of the geriatric presents many problems in mental administration. The word "geriatric" means MOST NEARLY

   A. dipsomanic (alcoholic)
   B. moronic (mentally deficient)
   C. pertaining to split personality types
   D. pertaining to individuals of advanced years

35. Jobs for ex-patients can MOST often be found in

   A. big corporations
   B. domestic service
   C. government agencies
   D. small private enterprises

KEY (CORRECT ANSWERS)

1.	C	16.	B
2.	C	17.	A
3.	D	18.	D
4.	D	19.	D
5.	A	20.	C
6.	B	21.	C
7.	C	22.	B
8.	A	23.	A
9.	D	24.	C
10.	B	25.	D
11.	C	26.	A
12.	B	27.	A
13.	D	28.	A
14.	C	29.	B
15.	A	30.	A

31.	A
32.	C
33.	D
34.	D
35.	D

EXAMINATION SECTION
TEST 1

DIRECTIONS: Each question or incomplete statement is followed by several suggested answers or completions. Select the one that BEST answers the question or completes the statement. *PRINT THE LETTER OF THE CORRECT ANSWER IN THE SPACE AT THE RIGHT.*

1. A patient tells you that the other patients are plotting to kill him. This is MOST likely an example of

    A. a manic-depressive reaction
    B. a paranoid reaction
    C. excellent perceptual skills on the part of the patient
    D. a compulsive reaction

    1._____

2. Which of the following statements is TRUE?

    A. Diagnoses are, by their very nature, always accurate.
    B. Phobic reactions are the most common reasons people are admitted to mental hospitals.
    C. People with neuroses are far less likely to be hospitalized than people with psychoses.
    D. Severely depressed patients are less of a suicide risk than any other patient group, except paranoid schizophrenics.

    2._____

3. The LARGEST single diagnostic group of psychotic patients are

    A. neurotic depressive   B. schizophrenic
    C. obsessive-compulsive   D. paranoid reactive

    3._____

4. The personality type that would BEST be characterized by the description that *he or she has no conscience* would be the

    A. drug addict   B. exhibitionist
    C. sociopath   D. manic-depressive

    4._____

5. Of the following, the marked inability to organize one's thoughts is found MOST commonly and severely in

    A. schizophrenics
    B. amnesiacs
    C. those suffering from anxiety neuroses
    D. sociopaths

    5._____

6. Someone who constantly feels tense, anxious, and worried but is unable to identify exactly why is MOST likely to be suffering from

    A. anxiety neurosis   B. schizophrenia
    C. dissociative reaction   D. a conversion reaction

    6._____

7. A patient always insists upon twirling around six times before entering a new room, or she fears she will die. This is an example of

    A. paranoid reaction   B. obsessive-compulsive reaction
    C. dissociative reaction   D. anxiety neurosis

    7._____

25

8. Of the following, those who suffer from neuroses would USUALLY complain of

   A. rejections, dissociation, and frequent inability to remember what day it is
   B. delusions, rejections, and feeling tired
   C. tiredness, fears, and hallucinations
   D. fears, physical complaints, and anxieties

9. The category that is caused by a disorder of the brain for which physical pathology can be demonstrated is

   A. neurotic depressive reaction   B. schizophrenia
   C. functional psychoses   D. organic psychoses

10. Of the following, which is NOT true?

    A. Someone who is suddenly unable to hear for psychological reasons would be considered to be suffering from a conversion reaction.
    B. If someone is in fugue, they have combined amnesia with flight.
    C. *Multiple personalities* is a dissociative reaction that affects primarily the elderly.
    D. General symptoms of schizophrenia include an ability to deal with reality, the presence of delusions or hallucinations, and inappropriate affect.

11. Which one of the following is TRUE?

    A. Calling an elderly person *gramps* or *granny* makes them feel more secure.
    B. It is important for an elderly person to maintain his or her independence whenever possible.
    C. When elderly patients start acting like children, they should be treated like children.
    D. It is important to encourage the elderly to hurry because they tend to move so slowly.

12. It has been found that older patients learn BEST when one does all but which one of the following?

    A. Allowing plenty of time for them to practice and learn
    B. Creating a relaxing environment for them
    C. Dealing with one thing at a time
    D. Assuming little knowledge on their part

13. Which of the following contains the main factors that should be considered before administering medications to elderly patients?

    A. How popular the medication is with the patient and the team leader's recommendations
    B. Any organic brain damage, liver dysfunction, and body weight
    C. Liver dysfunction, the patient's medical history, and decreased body weight
    D. Decreased body weight, impaired circulation, liver dysfunction, and increased sensitivity to medications

14. When communicating with the hearing impaired, it is BEST to do all of the following EXCEPT

    A. make sure the person can see your lips
    B. speak slowly and clearly
    C. use gestures
    D. shout

15. The three most common visual disorders in the elderly are cataracts, diabetic retinopathy, and glaucoma.
    Of the following statements about these, the one that is NOT true is that

    A. the symptoms for cataracts are a need for brighter light and a need to hold things very near the eyes
    B. diabetic retinopathy, if untreated, can cause blindness, so any vision or eye problems in diabetics should be promptly reported
    C. glaucoma develops slowly, so it is much easier to detect than cataracts or diabetic retinopathy
    D. some of the symptoms of glaucoma are loss of vision out of the corner of the eye, headaches, nausea, eye pain, tearing, blurred vision, and halos around objects of light

16. Which of the following is NOT true?

    A. Most of the elderly hospitalized for psychiatric problems suffer from senile brain atrophy or brain changes that occur due to arteriosclerosis.
    B. It is important to allow the elderly who wish to, the right to always live in the past.
    C. The majority of the elderly are competent, alert, and functioning well in their communities.
    D. Many elderly patients feel that they are no longer valued members of our society.

17. Of the following, which is NOT a good reason for helping the elderly patient stay active?
    Activity

    A. promotes good health by stimulating appetite and regulating bowel function
    B. prevents the complications of inactivity such as pneumonia, bed sores, and joint immobility
    C. can create an interest in taking more medication
    D. can increase blood circulation

18. Staff members must come to an understanding of their own feelings about the elderly because

    A. the staff may then be more helpful
    B. any negative feelings one has may be difficult to hide
    C. feelings of fear or aversion can be easily transmitted
    D. all of the above

19. An elderly patient will probably eat better if

    A. food servings are large
    B. the foods are chewy
    C. he or she is allowed to finish his/her meals at a leisurely pace
    D. cooked food is served cold

20. The MOST common accident to the elderly involves

    A. falls   B. burns   C. bruises   D. cuts

21. Which of the following is TRUE?

    A. Children should be considered and treated as miniature adults.
    B. Children are growing, developing human beings who will react to situations according to their level of development and the experiences to which they have been subjected.
    C. Children who are brought to a mental health center are usually calm and non-apprehensive on their first visit.
    D. The problems of adolescents are usually overestimated.

22. In working with adolescents, it would be BEST to

    A. neither bend over backwards to give in to demands, nor control them by rigid and punitive means
    B. dress the way most adolescents do
    C. staff those units with young people
    D. watch television with them regularly

23. Of the following, when working with children, it is MOST important to be

    A. consistent
    B. strict
    C. more concerned for their welfare than for the welfare of the other patients
    D. well-liked

24. Of the following, the element that is MOST lacking in relationships between adolescents and adults is

    A. respect   B. fear   C. trust   D. sensitivity

25. Of the following, the BEST reason for grouping children together would be

    A. they should be protected from the influences of all adult patients
    B. children tend to feel more comfortable with other children
    C. children are less likely to *act out* when they are with other children
    D. they would be unable to bother adult patients

26. All of the following statements are true EXCEPT:

    A. Accidents, reactions to drugs, fevers, and disease may each contribute to mental or emotional problems
    B. How effectively an individual reacts to and manages stress contributes to his or her mental health
    C. There is significant research that indicates that mental illness is caused primarily by genetic transmittal
    D. A person's upbringing, his or her relationships with family or friends, past experiences, and present living conditions may all contribute to the status of his or her mental health

27. All of the following are basic psychological needs which must be met for a person to have self-esteem EXCEPT

    A. acceptance and understanding
    B. trust, respect, and security
    C. a rewarding romantic relationship
    D. pleasant interactions with other people

28. All of the following statements are true EXCEPT:

    A. Most people become mentally ill because they are unable to cope with or adapt to the stresses and problems of life
    B. People with emotional problems can rarely be helped enough to live independently
    C. Most of the diseases and symptoms of the body which plague people have a large emotional component as their cause
    D. Environmental and familial factors are more important than genetic factors in mental illness

29. The following are all optimal aspects of family functioning EXCEPT

    A. communication is open and direct
    B. expression of emotion is more often positive than negative
    C. minor problems are ignored, knowing they will go away on their own
    D. there is a high degree of congruence or harmony between the family's values and the actual realities of the society

30. All of the following statements are true EXCEPT:

    A. People who are wealthy rarely become mentally ill
    B. Physical disease may influence emotional balance
    C. People who are mentally ill are often very sensitive to what is happening in their environment
    D. Most people doubt their own sanity at one time or another

31. All of the following statements are true EXCEPT:

    A. Hereditary factors are not the primary cause of mental illness
    B. A person may react to an extremely traumatic experience by becoming mentally ill
    C. Early recognition and treatment does not affect the course of mental illness
    D. Mental illness can develop suddenly

32. All of the following statements are true EXCEPT:

    A. Emotionally disturbed people are usually very sensitive to how other people feel towards them
    B. People do not inherit mental disorders, but may inherit a predisposition to certain types of mental problems
    C. There are many factors which can cause mental illness
    D. Mood swings are signs of mental illness

33. Which of the following statements is LEAST accurate?

    A. The difference between being mentally healthy and mentally ill often lies in the intensity and frequency of inappropriate behavior.
    B. The way a person views a situation determines his or her response to the situation.
    C. The mentally ill are permanently disabled.
    D. Different personal experiences cause a difference in what a person perceives as stressful, and how much stress a person can tolerate.

34. All of the following statements are true EXCEPT:

    A. Most experts in the field of mental health believe that the experiences which occur during the first twenty, or the first six, years of life are the most significant
    B. An unfortunate characteristic of children is that they tend to blame themselves for failures of their parents, and thus may develop feelings of inadequacy which may affect them all of their lives
    C. If neglect is severe enough, an infant or young child may withdraw from reality into a fantasy world which feels less threatening
    D. Human beings develop in the exact same pattern and almost at the same rate

35. Schizophrenia is

    A. genetically caused
    B. most often caused by the habitual use of drugs
    C. the result of a complex relationship between biological, psychological, and sociological factors
    D. most commonly caused by the inhalation of toxic gases

KEY (CORRECT ANSWERS)

1.	B	16.	B
2.	C	17.	C
3.	B	18.	D
4.	C	19.	C
5.	A	20.	A
6.	A	21.	B
7.	B	22.	A
8.	D	23.	A
9.	D	24.	C
10.	C	25.	B
11.	B	26.	C
12.	D	27.	C
13.	D	28.	B
14.	D	29.	C
15.	C	30.	A

31. C
32. D
33. C
34. D
35. C

TEST 2

DIRECTIONS: Each question or incomplete statement is followed by several suggested answers or completions. Select the one that BEST answers the question or completes the statement. *PRINT THE LETTER OF THE CORRECT ANSWER IN THE SPACE AT THE RIGHT.*

1. Tardive dyskenesia is a(n)   1.____

    A. antidepressant
    B. birth-related serious injury
    C. serious side effect of phenothiazine derivatives
    D. antiparkinsons drug

2. People taking psychotropic drugs are MOST likely to be sensitive to   2.____

    A. long exposures to sunlight
    B. darkness
    C. noise
    D. other patients

3. An antipsychotic drug that is a phenothiazine derivative would MOST likely be used for   3.____

    A. helping a patient lose weight
    B. calming a patient
    C. helping a patient sleep
    D. reducing the frequency of delusions in a patient

4. Of the following, an antidepressant such as Elavil would MOST likely be used for   4.____

    A. the immediate prevention of suicidal action in a newly admitted patient
    B. helping a patient lose weight
    C. elevating a patient's mood
    D. diuretic purposes

5. Which of the following statements is NOT true?   5.____

    A. Antianxiety tranquilizers such as sparine, librium, and vistaril are useful primarily with psychoneurotic and psychosomatic disorders.
    B. Minor or antianxiety tranquilizers tend to be less habit-forming than major or antipsychotic tranquilizers.
    C. Akinesia, pseudoparkinsonism, and tardive dyskenesia are serious side effects of antipsychotic drugs, or phenothiazine derivatives.
    D. Generally, those using tranquilizers like sparine or librium are in less danger of deadly drug overdoses than those using barbituates.

6. All of the following statements are false EXCEPT: 6.____

    A. Antipsychotic drugs promote increased sexual interest
    B. Patients no longer need to take their medication when they feel better
    C. Phenothiazines are psychotropic drugs
    D. One of the main difficulties with antipsychotic drugs is that they tend to be habit-forming

7. Yellowing of the skin or eyes, sensitivity to light and pseudoparkinsonism may occur in patients receiving

    A. mellaril or thorazine
    B. librium or tranxene
    C. valium or vistaril
    D. antiparkinson drugs

8. Which of the following is NOT true of extrapyramidal symptoms (EPS)? They

    A. may appear after many weeks of use of phenothiazines
    B. can safely be controlled without medical assistance
    C. may appear after the patient has been taking the drug for only a few days
    D. may include pseudoparkinsonism

9. The time required to reach an effective blood level for an antidepressant medication would MOST likely be three

    A. days   B. hours   C. weeks   D. months

10. An example of a psychotropic drug would be

    A. seconal   B. aspirin   C. librium   D. perichloz

11. In evaluating a patient you are meeting for the first time, it would be best NOT to

    A. be as objective as possible
    B. question one's own motives and reactions when processing data during and after the meeting
    C. be extremely goal-oriented
    D. not allow any praise or criticism directed at you by the patient to influence your assessment

12. All of the following statements are true EXCEPT:

    A. People communicate non-verbally via their behavior and their body posture
    B. Non-verbal clues may be a better indication of a patient's true feelings than what the patient actually says
    C. A patient who is highly anxious is easier to evaluate than a patient who is relatively calm
    D. People should be judged objectively

13. When asking a patient a question, one should do all of the following EXCEPT

    A. phrase questions in order to receive a yes or no response
    B. ask only relevant questions
    C. listen carefully to the response before asking the next question
    D. phrase questions clearly

14. The MAIN purpose for extensive record keeping is to

    A. provide an accurate description of the patient's diagnosis
    B. provide a subjective report of the patient's behavior
    C. provide an objective report of the patient's behavior
    D. give mental health personnel something to do

15. When talking to a patient for the first time, one must realize that

    A. hostile behavior indicates an extremely severe disorder in the patient
    B. a patient's physical appearance will indicate how successful you will be in communicating with the patient
    C. the patient is extremely nervous
    D. you are both strangers to each other

16. Of the following, which statement is NOT true?

    A. The rapid assessment of a patient is not necessarily accomplished by asking a series of routine questions.
    B. There is value, in assessing a patient, in creating a conversational bridge which has *here and now* relevance.
    C. One can assess a patient's state by his or her reaction to a warm greeting given to him or her.
    D. There is some value in routinely asking certain questions, when needed, in order to check a patient's orientation and memory.

17. All of the following could be signs that someone is moving towards mental illness EXCEPT

    A. exhibiting a degree of prolonged, constant anxiety, apprehension, or fear which is out of proportion with reality
    B. severe appetite disturbances
    C. occasional depression
    D. abrupt changes in a person's behavior

18. The first few minutes of interaction with a patient can reveal all but

    A. a patient's contact with reality
    B. whether you are comfortable with a patient
    C. a patient's mood
    D. a patient's chances for recovery

19. Which of the following statements is TRUE?

    A. The tentative diagnosis made when a patient is first admitted is the most accurate diagnosis.
    B. One should always try and keep in mind the state the patient was in when first admitted.
    C. A diagnosis is actually an ongoing process.
    D. When assessing patients' behavior, it is best to be suspicious of what may look like progress.

20. All of the following are examples of defense mechanisms EXCEPT

    A. projection
    B. complimenting someone
    C. displacement
    D. regression

21. A treatment plan is likely to be MOST effective if the

    A. patient's suggestions are always incorporated
    B. patient is voluntarily and wholeheartedly participating in the treatment plan designed for him or her

C. patient has daily contact with his or her family
D. patient respects the team leader

22. All of the following are true EXCEPT:

    A. Patients do not become well simply by people doing something for them
    B. A patient's well-being is enhanced when one or more team members can forge a *therapeutic alliance* with that patient
    C. The most important purpose of the treatment team is to administer the proper medications to patients
    D. It is important that a patient be seen as an individual, and not just as a *case* or a *number*

23. Of the following, a member of the treatment team can BEST assist a patient by

    A. commanding respect from other team members
    B. carefully observing the behavior of patients
    C. avoiding spending too much time with patients
    D. becoming friends with a patient

24. Of the following, which is LEAST important when considering a treatment plan?

    A. Involving the patient
    B. Setting reasonable goals
    C. Being as specific as possible in setting completion dates for goals, and sticking to them
    D. Detailing the methods to be followed, and the work assignments

25. All of the following are true EXCEPT:

    A. A treatment team should help patients understand that they can improve their condition if they will cooperate with the treatment plan
    B. Patients should be encouraged to participate in the programs designed for them
    C. Patients should be encouraged to revise their treatment plans
    D. One's approach should be tailored for each individual, whenever possible

26. All of the following could be considered appropriate goals for patients to work towards, EXCEPT to

    A. expand one's capacity to find or create acceptable options
    B. learn to be less dependent
    C. give up feeling persecuted
    D. learn how to get what one needs, at any cost

27. In working in treatment teams, it is MOST important for team members to

    A. communicate effectively with each other
    B. enjoy working with each other
    C. keep morale high
    D. attend meetings on time

28. One of the purposes of the treatment team is to

    A. decrease the amount of work
    B. coordinate and integrate services to patients
    C. provide training
    D. provide patients with basic counseling skills they can use

29. When working with someone exhibiting a manic-depressive psychosis, depressed type, it is BEST to

    A. concern yourself primarily with his or her eating habits
    B. focus primarily on their sleeping habits
    C. take every statement he or she may make about suicide seriously
    D. allow them to watch a great deal of television

30. In working with a paranoid patient, all of the following are true EXCEPT:
    It

    A. is important to listen with respect
    B. is helpful to establish a trusting relationship
    C. is good to try and talk the patient out of his or her fears
    D. would not be a good practice to agree with their statements, if they are not true

31. It is important, when dealing with verbally abusive patients, to keep in mind all of the following EXCEPT:

    A. Patients usually become abusive because of frustrating circumstances beyond their control
    B. In most cases, the patients do not mean anything personal by their abusive remarks; they are displacing anger
    C. It is important for staff members to remain calm and controlled when patients have emotional outbursts
    D. It is a good idea to allow an angry patient to draw you into an argument, as this will eventually help calm him or her down

32. When dealing with a patient who insists upon doing a number of rituals before brushing his teeth, it would be BEST to

    A. attempt to tease him out of his behavior
    B. not be critical of the ritualistic behavior
    C. perform the same rituals so that he feels more secure
    D. insist that he eliminate one step of the ritual each week

33. A patient tells you that he is balancing an automobile on the top of his head, and asks you what you think of that.
    An APPROPRIATE response for you to make would be:

    A. to ask him to take you for a ride
    B. *Stop saying ridiculous things*
    C. *I know you believe you are balancing a car on your head but I don't see it, therefore I have to assume that you're not*
    D. *Is it an invisible car*

34. A new patient, who is very paranoid, refuses to take off his clothes before getting into bed.
    Which would be MOST helpful?

    A. Getting another staff member to assist in removing his clothes
    B. Leaving the room until he comes to his senses
    C. Trying to find out why the patient does not want to undress
    D. Allowing the patient to stay up all night

35. In handling depressed patients, it is BEST to

    A. encourage them to participate in activities
    B. remind them often that things will be better tomorrow
    C. remember that depressed patients have few feelings of guilt
    D. let them know that you know just how they are feeling

36. A patient tells you that she is very depressed over the recent death of her brother.
    Which of the following would be the MOST appropriate response?

    A. *Everybody gets depressed when they lose someone they love.*
    B. *It could have been worse; at least he was ill only a short time.*
    C. *I know just how you feel.*
    D. *This must be very difficult for you.*

37. A patient who recently suffered a stroke refuses to let you help her bathe.
    This is probably because

    A. it is hard for her to accept that she can no longer do things for herself that she could do before the stroke
    B. she does not like you
    C. she is extremely independent and should be encouraged to be less so
    D. you need to review your methods for bathing patients

38. All of the following would be appropriate in working with a patient who is hallucinating EXCEPT

    A. carefully watch what you are non-verbally communicating
    B. ask concrete, reality-oriented questions
    C. provide a calm, structured environment
    D. agree with the patient, if asked, that you are experiencing the same state he or she is

39. In dealing with overactive patients, it is BEST to

    A. not give most of your attention to these patients, leaving the quieter patients to look after themselves
    B. keep in mind that overactive patients are always more interesting than other patients
    C. remember that overactive patients need more care than other patients
    D. forcibly restrain them whenever possible

40. A patient with mild organic brain damage is very withdrawn and negativistic. 40.____
    The BEST approach, of the following, would be
    A. *I need a partner to play cards with me*
    B. *Your family is very disappointed in you when you act like this*
    C. *Your doctor said you should participate in all activities here, so you'd better do that*
    D. *Would you like to go to your room so you can be alone?*

KEY (CORRECT ANSWERS)

1.	C	11.	C	21.	B	31.	D
2.	A	12.	C	22.	C	32.	B
3.	D	13.	A	23.	B	33.	C
4.	C	14.	C	24.	C	34.	C
5.	B	15.	D	25.	C	35.	A
6.	C	16.	C	26.	D	36.	D
7.	A	17.	C	27.	A	37.	A
8.	B	18.	D	28.	B	38.	D
9.	C	19.	C	29.	C	39.	A
10.	C	20.	B	30.	C	40.	A

EXAMINATION SECTION
TEST 1

DIRECTIONS: Each question or incomplete statement is followed by several suggested answers or completions. Select the one that BEST answers the question or completes the statement. *PRINT THE LETTER OF THE CORRECT ANSWER IN THE SPACE AT THE RIGHT.*

1. According to Freudian theory, the _____ functions to encourage a person's tolerance of frustration. 1.____

    A. subconscious B. id
    C. ego D. superego

2. Which of the following hormones controls the use of glucose by the body's cells? 2.____

    A. Cortisone B. Insulin
    C. Adrenal steroids D. Thyroxine

3. A client who is receiving lithium carbonate should undergo regular monitoring of 3.____

    A. blood pressure B. blood level
    C. weight D. urine

4. According to intrapsychic theory, the problem of separation anxiety is MOST likely to occur during the _____ stage. 4.____

    A. latency B. oral C. anal D. phallic

5. A client with adrenal insufficiency is weak and dizzy upon arising in the morning. The MOST likely cause of this is 5.____

    A. lack of sodium
    B. increased intracavity fluid volume
    C. hypertension
    D. hypoglycemic reaction

6. The administration of Anectine prior to electroconvulsive therapy involves the major complication of 6.____

    A. loss of bowel control
    B. inhibition of breathing muscles
    C. memory loss
    D. the bite reflex

7. An infant with congenital hyperthyroidism is at risk for _____ if care is not given immediately. 7.____

    A. thyrotoxicosis B. acromegaly
    C. myxedema D. mental retardation

8. For which of the following is lithium carbonate used as a control or modifier? 8.____

    A. Manic episode of bipolar disorder
    B. Acute agitation of schizophrenia

39

C. Agitated phase of paranoia
D. Depressive phase of major depression

9. Which of the following is the cause of acromegaly?

   A. Oversecretion of adrenal steroids
   B. Undersecretion of thyroid hormone
   C. Oversecretion of growth hormone
   D. Undersecretion of testosterone

10. At what approximate age does a person demonstrate the primary emergence of his or her personality?

    A. 6 months
    B. 18 months
    C. 2 years
    D. 8 years

11. Diabetic acidosis is caused by elevated _____ levels in the blood.

    A. lactic acid
    B. ketone
    C. albumin
    D. glucose

12. Which of the following behaviors is MOST likely to be demonstrated by an autistic child?

    A. Lack of response to external stimuli
    B. Sad facial expression
    C. Irrelevant smiling
    D. Rocking and flapping of hands

13. To evaluate the effectiveness of DDAVP in treating diabetes insipidus, which of the following should be monitored?

    A. Blood pressure
    B. Intake and output
    C. Pulse rate
    D. Serum glucose

14. Glucagon

    A. retards glycogenesis
    B. causes the release of insulin
    C. elevates blood sugar levels
    D. improves the storage of glucose

15. Of the following, the clearest evidence of mental illness is when a client

    A. does not seem to be able to complete tasks
    B. has difficulty relating to others
    C. has little interest in social activities or work
    D. encounters frequent periods of high anxiety

16. For a client with insulin-dependent diabetes mellitus, insulin needs will *decrease* when the client

    A. exercises
    B. is infected
    C. reaches middle age
    D. is emotionally stressed

17. The treatment for a client suffering from depression should focus on getting the client to

    A. express anger toward others
    B. admit an emotional problem
    C. articulate feelings of low self-esteem
    D. accept care and comfort willingly

18. A child who is about to undergo surgery to correct a congenital megacolon should be given a preoperative enema of

    A. barium
    B. isotonic saline
    C. tap water
    D. hypertonic phosphate

19. Which of the following is a common side effect associated with the use of Thorazine?

    A. Jaundice
    B. Melanocytosis
    C. Photosensitivity
    D. Excessive thirst

20. Piaget's theory of cognitive development states that at the age of six months, an infant should demonstrate

    A. a sense of time
    B. the ability to remember
    C. the onset of object permanence
    D. coordinated motor responses

21. Which of the following would MOST clearly reveal congenital hip dysplasia in a newborn infant?

    A. Different leg lengths
    B. Asymmetrical gluteal folds
    C. Limited adduction
    D. Skewed leg alignment

22. A client is diagnosed with an organic mental disorder. Which of the following nursing strategies would be MOST helpful to this client?

    A. Providing a diet high in carbohydrates
    B. Providing a variety of stimuli to keep the client's interest high
    C. Eliminating the need for choices
    D. Asking the client for input concerning the nursing care plan

23. Which of the following would be included in the early treatment of diabetic acidosis?

    A. IV fluids
    B. Kayexalate
    C. Potassium
    D. NPH insulin

24. Which level of consciousness BEST represents a person's feelings and attitudes?

    A. Conscious
    B. Unconscious
    C. Preconscious
    D. Foreconscious

25. What is the MOST common cause of diabetic ketoacidosis?

    A. Inadequate fluid intake
    B. Psychological stress
    C. Elevated insulin level
    D. Infection

25.____

KEY (CORRECT ANSWERS)

1.	C	11.	B
2.	C	12.	D
3.	B	13.	B
4.	B	14.	C
5.	D	15.	B
6.	B	16.	A
7.	D	17.	A
8.	A	18.	B
9.	C	19.	C
10.	C	20.	C

21.	B
22.	C
23.	A
24.	B
25.	D

TEST 2

DIRECTIONS: Each question or incomplete statement is followed by several suggested answers or completions. Select the one that BEST answers the question or completes the statement. *PRINT THE LETTER OF THE CORRECT ANSWER IN THE SPACE AT THE RIGHT.*

1. A client with an anxiety disorder is likely to handle the anxiety in each of the following ways EXCEPT

    A. projecting it onto nonthreatening objects
    B. converting it into a physical symptom
    C. demonstrating regressive behavior
    D. acting out with antisocial behavior

1.____

2. What type of diet is recommended for a client with Graves' disease?

    A. High roughage
    B. Low sodium
    C. Liquid
    D. High-calorie

2.____

3. Which of the following is the cause of primary degenerative dementia?

    A. Anatomic brain changes
    B. Atrophy of the frontal lobes
    C. An extended history of malnutrition
    D. Excessive use of narcotics

3.____

4. Which of the following blood gas results would indicate diabetic acidosis?

    A. Reduced HCO_3
    B. Elevated pH
    C. Reduced PO_2
    D. Elevated PCO_2

4.____

5. The primary difference between a psychophysiologic disorder and a somatoform disorder is that a

    A. psychophysiologic disorder involves an actual change in tissues
    B. somatoform disorder is caused by emotions
    C. psychophysiologic disorder restricts the client's activities
    D. somatoform disorder is accompanied by a feeling of illness

5.____

6. Which of the following is MOST likely to be a complication following the insertion of a ventriculoperitoneal shunt in a child with communicating hydrocephalus?

    A. Violent tremors
    B. Distended abdomen
    C. Yellowish discharge from shunt
    D. Fever

6.____

7. Each of the following is a common physiological response to anxiety EXCEPT

    A. respiratory constriction
    B. dilated pupils
    C. hyperglycemia
    D. increased pulse rate

7.____

8. It is MOST important for a nurse to monitor a client suffering from alcohol and cirrhosis for

   A. gastric pain
   B. blood in the stool
   C. dizziness
   D. constipation

9. To encourage a withdrawn and noncommunicative client to talk, the BEST nursing plan would include the attempt to

   A. ask the client to describe feelings
   B. ask simply-phrased questions that require yes or no answers
   C. join the client in an activity that the client enjoys
   D. concentrate on subjects that are nonthreatening

10. What is the function of glucose in a cell?

    A. Energy extraction
    B. Protein synthesis
    C. Cellular respiration
    D. Genetic coding

11. Which of the following treatments would be included in a plan for a client with severe and intractable depression and suicidal tendency?

    A. High doses of tranquilizers
    B. Electroconvulsive therapy
    C. Nondirective psychotherapy
    D. Thorazine

12. A *decrease* in the anterior pituitary secretion of ACTH would be caused by

    A. ketosis
    B. a *decrease* in the blood concentration of adrenal steroids
    C. an *increase* in the blood concentration of cortisol
    D. acidosis

13. A client is experiencing a phase of extreme elation and hyperactivity. Which of the following nursing interventions would BEST meet the client's nutritional needs?

    A. Assuming that the client will eat when hungry
    B. Firmly suggesting that the client sit and eat the meal that has been prepared
    C. Inducing an IV feeding to insure that the client is properly nourished
    D. Giving the client frequent high-calorie feedings that the client can feed to herself

14. Which of the following would be experienced by a client with acute cholecystitis accompanied by biliary colic?

    A. Melena
    B. Lipid intolerance
    C. Diarrhea
    D. Pain in lower left quadrant

15. Which of the following must be monitored especially closely following a hypophysectomy?

    A. Motor reflexes
    B. Urinary output
    C. Intracranial pressure
    D. Respiration

16. Which of the following would MOST accurately characterize the personality of a client with obsessive-compulsive personality disorder?

    A. Deep depression
    B. Indecisiveness and doubt
    C. Rapid mood swings
    D. Detailed delusions

17. Which of the following symptoms would MOST likely be revealed during an assessment of a client with Cushing's syndrome?

    A. Dehydration
    B. Migraine headaches
    C. Menorrhagia
    D. Hypertension

18. Most commonly, the behavior of a client with schizophrenia can be described as

    A. euphoric
    B. angry and hostile
    C. flat and apathetic
    D. depressed

19. Which of the following medications would be used to treat a child with cystic fibrosis?

    A. Antimetabolite
    B. Pancreatic enzymes
    C. Fat-soluble vitamins
    D. Aerosol mists

20. Which of the following would NOT be a helpful component of a nursing care plan for a severely depressed client?

    A. Short-term projects
    B. Client participation in activity planning
    C. Repetitive activities
    D. Simple instructions to be followed

21. A client with Addison's disease is experiencing hypotension. Most likely, this involves a disturbance in the production of

    A. mineralocorticoids
    B. proteins
    C. glucocorticoids
    D. insulin

22. Which of the following medications would be used to counter an overdose of narcotics?

    A. Methadone
    B. Thorazine
    C. Benzedrine
    D. Narcan

23. Prior to a serum glucose test, a client with Type II diabetes mellitus should

    A. have a clear liquid breakfast
    B. take prescribed medications
    C. void the bladder
    D. avoid food and fluids

24. Which of the following is the BEST description of a somatoform disorder? A(n)

    A. conscious defense against stress
    B. sublimation of stress
    C. psychological defense against anxiety
    D. unconscious means of controlling conflict

25. Which of the following tests is conducted to detect PKU in infant children?   25._____

    A. OCT
    B. Phenistix test
    C. BUN
    D. Guthrie blood test

KEY (CORRECT ANSWERS)

1. D	11. B
2. D	12. C
3. B	13. D
4. A	14. B
5. A	15. C
6. D	16. B
7. A	17. B
8. B	18. C
9. D	19. B
10. A	20. B

21. A
22. D
23. D
24. D
25. D

TEST 3

DIRECTIONS: Each question or incomplete statement is followed by several suggested answers or completions. Select the one that BEST answers the question or completes the statement. *PRINT THE LETTER OF THE CORRECT ANSWER IN THE SPACE AT THE RIGHT.*

1. A client recently admitted to an alcohol detoxification unit would probably exhibit each of the following EXCEPT

    A. hypertension
    B. nausea
    C. hyperactivity
    D. loss of appetite

2. Prior to an adrenalectomy, the client should

    A. increase fluid intake
    B. receive steroids
    C. have all medication withheld for 48 hours
    D. be placed on a high-protein diet

3. A client with an antisocial personality disorder

    A. learns quickly through experience and punishment
    B. is generally unable to defer gratification
    C. often masks his disorder by articulate communication
    D. suffers from a high level of anxiety

4. Which of the following is a defense mechanism that helps an individual channel unacceptable desires into socially approved behavior?

    A. Regression
    B. Denial
    C. Conversion
    D. Sublimation

5. Which of the following would NOT be a likely result of a laboratory test performed on a client suffering from diabetic ketoacidosis?

    A. Low CO_2
    B. Increased acidity
    C. High bicarbonate
    D. Increased blood sugar

6. Following an adrenalectomy, a client is MOST likely to exhibit the symptoms of

    A. sodium retention
    B. dehydration
    C. hypotension
    D. increased urinary output

7. It is MOST important for a nurse to _____ when attempting to resolve a crisis situation with a client.

    A. encourage socialization
    B. meet all of the client's dependency needs
    C. nurture the client's ego strengths
    D. introduce the client to a therapy group

8. Which of the following is NOT a typical indication of a hypoglycemic reaction to insulin?

    A. Paleness
    B. Excessive thirst
    C. Tremors
    D. Perspiration

9. A client is admitted to the hospital with a diagnosis of conversion disorder. The nurse should expect the client's attitude toward his physical symptoms to be one of

   A. hysteria
   B. indifference
   C. anger
   D. great sadness

10. Along with vitamin D, the regulatory agent that controls the overall calcium balance in the body is

    A. parathyroid hormone
    B. growth hormone
    C. thyroid hormone
    D. ACTH

11. A client is admitted to the hospital with Wernicke's encephalopathy caused by chronic alcoholism. The client's initial treatment would include

    A. an increase in fluid intake
    B. IM injection of thiamine
    C. administration of an anti-opiate
    D. administration of paraldehyde

12. Each of the following is a defect commonly associated with tetralogy of Fallot EXCEPT

    A. pulmonary artery stenosis
    B. mitral valve stenosis
    C. right ventricular hypertrophy
    D. overriding aorta

13. Which of the following statements, spoken to a nurse by a patient diagnosed with Alzheimer's disease, would indicate a need to accomplish Erikson's developmental task of ego integrity versus despair?

    A. I don't understand why I have to go through this.
    B. Please leave me alone.
    C. I can take care of myself.
    D. I am useless to everyone now.

14. The purpose of administering Mycifradin to a client with liver disease is to

    A. increase the urea digestive activity of enteric bacteria
    B. protect the liver from bacteria
    C. reduce ammonia-forming bacteria in the intestinal tract
    D. aid the digestion of complex proteins

15. Emotionally disturbed children

    A. seem unresponsive to their environment
    B. respond equally to all stimuli
    C. respond violently to most stimuli
    D. are immersed in their environment to the point of distraction

16. A client exhibiting cold intolerance may have

    A. increased levels of CO_2
    B. decreased blood pH

C. insufficient bile salts
D. decreased levels of T_3 and T_4

17. The part of the psyche that develops from internalizing the concepts of parents and other significant relations is the

    A. foreconscious
    B. id
    C. ego
    D. superego

18. Which of the following is NOT a typical sign of hypo-kalemia?

    A. Weakness
    B. Abdominal distention
    C. Edema
    D. Apathy

19. Which of the following might be experienced by a person who makes an abrupt withdrawal from habitual use of barbiturates?

    A. Gastric bleeding
    B. Cardiac arrhythmia
    C. Convulsions
    D. Ataxia

20. Which of the following would be observed in a toddler with cyanotic congenital heart disease?

    A. Orthopnea
    B. Blotchy skin
    C. Increased hematocrit
    D. Pitting edema

21. A delusional client is admitted for psychiatric treatment after harming a close relative. In talking about the incident, the client refers to herself in the third person. This is an example of the defense mechanism of

    A. conversion
    B. transference
    C. dissociation
    D. displacement

22. Which of the following is the clearest indication of diabetes insipidus?

    A. Elevated blood glucose
    B. Increased blood pressure
    C. Decreased urinary specific gravity
    D. Increased BUN

23. Which of the following is the MOST common cause of functional mental illness?

    A. Infection
    B. Chemical imbalance
    C. Social environment
    D. Genes

24. Which gland regulates the rate of oxygenation in the body's cells?

    A. Thyroid
    B. Adrenal
    C. Thalamus
    D. Pituitary

25. Which of the following is NOT thought to be a significant formative component of personality?

    A. Cultural setting
    B. Genetic background
    C. Psychologic development
    D. Biologic constitution

KEY (CORRECT ANSWERS)

1. C
2. B
3. B
4. D
5. C

6. C
7. C
8. B
9. B
10. A

11. B
12. B
13. D
14. C
15. A

16. D
17. D
18. C
19. C
20. C

21. C
22. B
23. C
24. A
25. B

TEST 4

DIRECTIONS: Each question or incomplete statement is followed by several suggested answers or completions. Select the one that BEST answers the question or completes the statement. *PRINT THE LETTER OF THE CORRECT ANSWER IN THE SPACE AT THE RIGHT.*

1. The preservation of sodium in the body's cells is accomplished by the hormone

    A. parathyroid hormone
    B. thyrocalcitonin
    C. aldosterone
    D. insulin

2. Which of the following behaviors would be LEAST likely to be demonstrated by a client with an organic mental disorder?

    A. An inclination to ignore the present circumstances while dwelling in the past
    B. A steadfast resistance to change
    C. The inability to focus on new interests
    D. A fixation on personal appearance and hygiene

3. Which of the following is a complication associated with hyperparathyroidism?

    A. Bone destruction
    B. Graves' disease
    C. Hypotension
    D. Tetany

4. Which of the following interventions should be undertaken to prevent thrombus formation in a client with sickle-cell anemia?

    A. Administer heparin or other anticoagulants
    B. Encourage exercise
    C. Maintain a high-roughage diet
    D. Increase oral fluid intake

5. A client with an obsessive-compulsive personality disorder will MOST likely react with _____ if he is interrupted in the performance of a ritual.

    A. hostility
    B. indifference
    C. confusion
    D. withdrawal

6. Which of the following would be experienced by a patient in a diabetic coma, but not by a patient in an HHNK coma?

    A. Kussmaul respirations
    B. Glycosuria
    C. Fluid loss
    D. Elevated blood glucose

7. Which of the following daily patterns tends to work best with clients who are depressed?

    A. Numerous sensory stimuli
    B. A simple daily schedule
    C. Removing the need for complicated decisions
    D. Multiple and varied activities

8. Glucocorticoids are secreted by the

    A. hypophysis cerebri
    B. adrenal glands
    C. thyroid
    D. pancreas

9. Prior to beginning lithium carbonate therapy, a client should undergo

   A. fluid and electrolyte evaluation
   B. renal evaluation
   C. psychomotor
   D. BUN evaluation

10. Which of the following is the result of an underproduction of thyroxin?

    A. Acromegaly
    B. Cushing's disease
    C. Myxedema
    D. Addison's disease

11. Which of the following is a common side effect of the major tranquilizers?

    A. Tremors
    B. Diaphoresis
    C. Jaundice
    D. Photosensitivity

12. Each of the following is likely to be revealed during the assessment of a client with hyperthyroidism EXCEPT

    A. weight loss
    B. increased appetite
    C. constipation
    D. nervousness

13. Severe emotional disturbances are often treated with tranquilizers to

    A. prevent complications
    B. make the client less dangerous to himself and others
    C. improve the client's mood
    D. make the client more receptive to psychotherapy

14. Which of the following symptoms would cause a nurse to stop giving Thorazine to a client?

    A. Uncoordinated movements
    B. Jaundice
    C. Withdrawal
    D. Tremors

15. What is the MOST likely cause of ascites in a patient with cirrhosis?

    A. Inhibited portal venous return
    B. Undersecretion of bile salts
    C. Gastric bleeding
    D. Overproduction of serum albumin

16. The defense mechanism used by clients who express anxiety through physical symptoms can BEST be described as

    A. psychosomatic
    B. regressive
    C. psychoneurotic
    D. dissociative

17. A 42-year-old client is admitted to the hospital with a diagnosis of Addison's disease. She is weak, hypotensive, and has low sodium and high potassium levels.
    The focus of the client's therapy should be

    A. lowering the level of eosiniphils
    B. restoring electrolyte balance
    C. increasing carbohydrate intake
    D. increasing lymph

18. A client who has been hospitalized for major depression has recently begun to receive 18.____
    Parnate. It is important that the nurse explain to the client that the use of this drug

    A. typically causes extreme photosensitivity
    B. may cause drowsiness
    C. increases the heart rate
    D. involves dietary restrictions

19. The MOST frequent cause of Cushing's syndrome is 19.____

    A. hyperplasia of pituitary
    B. hyperplasia of adrenal cortex
    C. decreased adrenocortical hormones
    D. insufficient production of ACTH

20. A group setting is particularly conducive to therapy because it 20.____

    A. takes the focus off the individual client
    B. forces clients to notice similarities with others
    C. establishes a learning environment
    D. encourages individual relationships

21. What is the purpose of installing a T-tube after a cholecystectomy? 21.____

    A. Draining bile from the cystic duct
    B. Protecting the common bile duct
    C. Preventing infection
    D. Providing a port for cholangiogram dye

22. A nurse notices that a socially agressive elderly client, who has been receiving Thora- 22.____
    zine for several months, is sitting rigidly in a chair. What other adverse effects of the drug
    should the nurse watch for?

    A. Tremors   B. Slurred speech
    C. Excessive salivation   D. Withdrawal

23. For what reason is an infant born with a cleft palate prone to infection? 23.____

    A. Mouth breathing
    B. Leakage of nasal mucus
    C. Poor nutrition from feeding disturbances
    D. Poor circulation in defective locus

24. Which of the following is a defense mechanism in which emotional conflicts are 24.____
    expressed through sensorimotor or somatic disability?

    A. Dissociation   B. Conversion
    C. Displacement   D. Regression

25. For the emergency treatment of ketoacidosis, what type of insulin should be administered? 25.____

    A. Zinc suspension
    B. NPH insulin
    C. Protamine zinc suspension
    D. Regular insulin injection

KEY (CORRECT ANSWERS)

1. C	11. A
2. D	12. C
3. A	13. D
4. D	14. B
5. A	15. A
6. A	16. C
7. B	17. B
8. D	18. D
9. B	19. B
10. C	20. C

21. B
22. A
23. A
24. B
25. D

EXAMINATION SECTION
TEST 1

DIRECTIONS: Each question or incomplete statement is followed by several suggested answers or completions. Select the one that BEST answers the question or completes the statement. *PRINT THE LETTER OF THE CORRECT ANSWER IN THE SPACE AT THE RIGHT.*

1. In regard to first aid procedures, priority in treatment should be given FIRST to cases of

    A. internal poisoning
    B. severe eye injuries
    C. stoppage of breathing
    D. severe bleeding at the neck

    1._____

2. The American Red Cross advocates that for an insect sting on the neck, the first aider apply to the injured part

    A. a cut in the skin at the spot to encourage bleeding in order to remove impurities
    B. suction in order to remove the injected toxin
    C. ice applications
    D. hot, wet applications

    2._____

3. The group of symptoms BEST describing a case of shock is

    A. extreme thirst, skin dry, breathing deep, pulse irregular
    B. face flushed, pulse full, pupils constricted, nauseous-ness
    C. pulse absent, skin hot, breathing heavy, face ashen
    D. body weakness, skin moist, pupils dilated, breathing shallow

    3._____

4. According to the American Red Cross, the four types of wounds are

    A. scrapes, cuts, burns, stabs
    B. punctures, lacerations, incisions, abrasions
    C. friction burns, open blisters, gashes, punctures
    D. scratches, infections, sores, bleeding cuts

    4._____

5. When administering first aid to a pupil experiencing an epileptic attack, the teacher should FIRST

    A. loosen clothing about the neck and chest
    B. remove the victim to a room other than a classroom filled with pupils
    C. place an object between the victim's upper and lower teeth on one side of the mouth
    D. apply an ammonia ampule to the victim's nostrils

    5._____

6. In the execution of the back pressure-arm lift method of artificial respiration, all of the following are correct procedures EXCEPT the one in which the operator

    A. places the victims in the prone position with the face turned to one side
    B. rocks foward with bent elbows as he exerts pressure at a 70° angle
    C. draws the arms of the victim upward and toward him during the final step of the cycle
    D. repeats the cycle at a steady rate of 12 times per minute

    6._____

7. In second or third degree burns, all of the following are correct first aid procedures EXCEPT 7.___

   A. applying mineral oil to the area
   B. giving fluids by mouth
   C. providing immediate first aid for shock
   D. covering the burned area with sterile dressing

8. Of the following symptoms a person might display after receiving a blow to the head, the one MOST indicative of serious injury is 8.___

   A. pallor
   B. swelling
   C. dizziness
   D. inequality in size of pupils of the eye

9. When reassuring a victim of an accident, of the following, it is MOST advisable to 9.___

   A. explain his condition to him as you find it and state you will stay with him
   B. tell him what first aid steps you are going to take and how they will help him
   C. state to the victim that, since there is no doctor around, you will take his place
   D. keep the victim talking about the accident to relieve tension

10. The rate at which artificial respiration should be given to adults is 10.___

    A. about 12 times a minute
    B. about 20 times a minute
    C. as fast as you can work
    D. slightly faster than normal breathing

KEY (CORRECT ANSWERS)

1.	D	6.	B
2.	C	7.	A
3.	D	8.	D
4.	B	9.	B
5.	C	10.	A

TEST 2

DIRECTIONS: Each question or incomplete statement is followed by several suggested answers or completions. Select the one that BEST answers the question or completes the statement. *PRINT THE LETTER OF THE CORRECT ANSWER IN THE SPACE AT THE RIGHT.*

1. In rendering the mouth-to-mouth method of artificial respiration, the one hand of the operator should

    A. cover the victim's nose and the other hand should be placed on the chest
    B. be on the ground near the victim's shoulder and in such position as to assist the other hand in maintaining equal support of his body weight
    C. hold the victim's jaw up and back and the other hand should pinch the victim's nostrils together
    D. be placed around the victim's mouth and the other hand should hold the nape of the victim's neck rigid

1.____

2. In the case of a severely burned victim who needs fluids, of the following, it is MOST advisable to give him at fifteen-minute intervals

    A. a full cup of hot tea or hot coffee
    B. a teaspoonful of spirits of ammonia in a glass of water
    C. half-glass doses of one-half teaspoon of table salt and of baking soda in a quart of water
    D. a mild stimulant

2.____

3. In caring for burns, the first aider should

    A. break the blisters caused by the burn
    B. apply wet dressings to the burned area
    C. apply large amounts of lukewarm water to a chemical burn before treating the burn
    D. remove scorched clothing on or near the burn

3.____

4. A person, in rendering first aid, should

    A. administer medication internally
    B. apply antiseptics to broken skin
    C. attempt to remove foreign bodies from eyes
    D. use the method of artificial respiration best known to him

4.____

5. In cases of shock, the first aider should elevate the lower part of the victim's body is

    A. the blood loss is great
    B. he complains of pain at a fracture site in the lower extremity
    C. there is a head injury
    D. breathing is difficult

5.____

6. When rendering first aid to a diabetic who suddenly becomes confused, incoherent, and faint, the FIRST thing to be done is to

    A. keep him warm and comfortable until a doctor arrives
    B. give him some form of sugar if he can swallow
    C. use a mild stimulant to keep him from losing consciousness
    D. take steps to summon an ambulance

6.____

7. During the winter months, in cases of first aid care for victims of shock, the first aider should

   A. wrap the victim in excess covering while waiting for the arrival of the doctor
   B. cover the victim sparingly in spite of a possible low temperature
   C. always apply hot water bottles to the victim's body
   D. protect the victim's body so that a flushed condition of the skin appears and is then maintained

8. In order to minimize the possibility of infection, the first aider, when caring for a wound, should

   A. wash the body surface toward the wound before applying a gauze dressing
   B. use soap and clean running tap water on both the wound and its surrounding area
   C. apply a two percent iodine solution as his first step in treating the wound
   D. cover the wound with adhesive tape in order to prevent contact with germs

9. If a particle is on the eyeball, one should NOT

   A. close his eyes for a few minutes in order to allow the tears to wash out the foreign matter
   B. grasp the lashes of the upper lid and draw it out and down over the lower lid in order to dislodge the particle
   C. use an eye dropper in order to flush the eye so that the particle will float out of the eye
   D. examine the eye in order to determine the location of the foreign particle and, when found, remove it from the eyeball by touching lightly with the moistened corner of a clean handkerchief

10. Of the following concerning mouth-to-mouth resuscitation, the operator can BEST be sure that no obstruction exists in the victim's air passage by following his first blowing efforts with a

    A. sharp tilt backward of the victim's head so that the chin points almost directly upward
    B. forceful opening of the victim's mouth as the victim's nostrils are held in a closed position
    C. removal of his mouth by turning his head to the side in order to listen for the return rush of air from the victim's body
    D. removal of mucous and foreign matter in the victim's mouth

KEY (CORRECT ANSWERS)

1. C
2. C
3. B
4. D
5. A
6. B
7. B
8. B
9. D
10. C

TEST 3

DIRECTIONS: Each question or incomplete statement is followed by several suggested answers or completions. Select the one that BEST answers the question or completes the statement. *PRINT THE LETTER OF THE CORRECT ANSWER IN THE SPACE AT THE RIGHT.*

1. The universal antidote to be administered in poisoning cases if no specific antidote is known consists of

    A. several teaspoonfuls of baking soda in half a glass of water
    B. a large glass of milk diluted with an equal amount of water
    C. one part tea, two parts crumbled burnt toast, one part milk of magnesia
    D. one part milk, one part egg white, one part water

2. In the case of severe bleeding from a hand, the first aider should IMMEDIATELY

    A. locate the pressure point above the wound and apply digital pressure at that point
    B. apply pressure directly on the wound with clean gauze or a towel
    C. apply a tourniquet in order to limit the flow of blood from the artery to the wound
    D. locate the pressure point and apply a tourniquet at that point

3. The INCORRECT association of first aid bandage and body area of use is

    A. four-tailed bandage - nose
    B. cravat bandage - knee
    C. triangular bandage - head
    D. figure-eight bandage - chest

4. With victims of shock, when medical help is not immediate, water should NOT be given to those who have

    A. suffered marked bleeding
    B. burns involving more than ten percent of the body surface
    C. a penetrating abdominal wound
    D. a fracture of the femur

5. The MAIN objective in first aid care for a victim of poison by mouth is to

    A. first induce vomiting
    B. dilute the poison
    C. give an antidote
    D. look around for tell-tale evidence of the poison

6. The LATEST accepted method (American Red Cross) of administering artificial respiration is known as the _____ method.

    A. back-pressure arm-lift
    B. chest-pressure arm-lift
    C. mouth-to-mouth
    D. prone pressure

2 (#3)

7. All of the following statements regarding first aid care are correct EXCEPT: 7.____

   A. Soap and clean water may be used to wash the wounded area in case of minor wounds
   B. A modified back-pressure arm-lift method of artificial respiration is recommended for infants and children under 4 years of age
   C. Direct pressure is recommended for most cases of severe bleeding
   D. Shock victims should be kept slightly cool rather than *toasting* warm with little or no surface covering used on warm days

8. In poisoning, the first aider should induce vomiting for all of the following taken through the mouth EXCEPT   8.____

   A. lye
   B. barbiturates
   C. mushrooms
   D. iodine

9. A recommended first aid procedure in the treatment of heat stroke is to   9.____

   A. give a stimulant
   B. keep the head lower than the chest
   C. apply external heat to the body
   D. sponge the body with lukewarm water

10. Of the following, the distinctive symptom in cases of heat stroke is   10.____

    A. a desire to sleep
    B. nausea
    C. absence of perspiration
    D. dizziness

KEY (CORRECT ANSWERS)

1. C
2. B
3. D
4. C
5. B

6. C
7. B
8. A
9. D
10. C

TEST 4

DIRECTIONS: Each question or incomplete statement is followed by several suggested answers or completions. Select the one that BEST answers the question or completes the statement. *PRINT THE LETTER OF THE CORRECT ANSWER IN THE SPACE AT THE RIGHT.*

1. All of the following are recommended first aid measures for insect bites and stings EXCEPT the application of   1.____

    A. a compress moistened with ammonia water
    B. calamine lotion
    C. ice
    D. light massage in order to remove the sting

2. According to the American Red Cross, the INCORRECT association of type of bandage and injury is   2.____

    A. four-tail bandage - fracture of the jaw
    B. spiral-reverse bandage - wound on the forearm
    C. figure-of-eight bandage - sprained ankle
    D. cravat bandage - eye injury

3. A compound fracture is one in which the bone is   3.____

    A. broken in many pieces
    B. broken with a connecting wound on the surface of the body
    C. twisted apart
    D. broken longitudinally

4. One of the shop workers strikes heavily against the wall. You recognize that he is in a state of shock because of his   4.____

    A. strong pulse
    B. regular but deep breathing
    C. moist, pale skin
    D. high body temperature

5. According to the American Red Cross, first aid care for an individual who gives evidence of possible insulin reaction when there is no other reason to account for the trouble includes the   5.____

    A. usual treatment for shock
    B. giving of candy or sugar to the victim
    C. application of artificial respiration
    D. swallowing of a stimulant

6. In caring for frostbite cases, one should   6.____

    A. apply woolen material to the injured area
    B. rub the injured part with snow
    C. massage the affected part
    D. have the victim soak the injured part in water as hot as possible

61

7. When applying wet applications to infected wounds, one should AVOID 7.____
   A. boiling the water prior to its use
   B. adding salt to the liquid
   C. half-hour periods of application followed by alternate free periods of the same length
   D. having the solution hot

8. According to the American Red Cross, tourniquets may be applied in all of the following situations EXCEPT 8.____
   A. when severe bleeding involves an extremity in which large arteries are severed
   B. to individuals who are known to be allergic to a bee or wasp sting, if the sting is on an extremity
   C. in cases where there is partial severance of a body part accompanied by severe bleeding
   D. to a limb in which there is an infected wound and there is indication of a spread of the infection

9. According to the American Red Cross, it is MOST NEARLY accurate to state that the danger of tetanus is present in _____ wounds. 9.____

   A. puncture   B. lacerated
   C. incised   D. all

10. All of the following men have developed a method of artificial respiration EXCEPT 10.____

    A. Schafer   B. Neilsen
    C. Cureton   D. Silvester

KEY (CORRECT ANSWERS)

1.	D	6.	A
2.	A	7.	D
3.	B	8.	D
4.	C	9.	D
5.	B	10.	C

TEST 5

DIRECTIONS: Each question or incomplete statement is followed by several suggested answers or completions. Select the one that BEST answers the question or completes the statement. *PRINT THE LETTER OF THE CORRECT ANSWER IN THE SPACE AT THE RIGHT.*

1. The recommended American Red Cross first aid care for sunburns in which the skin is blistered is the application of

    A. a burn ointment or medicated cream
    B. butter or oleomargarine
    C. a sterile, dry dressing
    D. a dressing saturated with a warm salt solution

    1.____

2. The MOST serious harm from tiny foreign objects on the eye surface is

    A. their irritating effect
    B. the danger of their becoming embedded in the outer layer of the eyeball
    C. their creating an increased secretion of tears
    D. their interference with the individual's normal vision

    2.____

3. All of the following are complete fractures EXCEPT a(n) _____ fracture.

    A. impacted   B. Greenstick
    C. Colles'   D. Pott's

    3.____

4. The CORRECT statement in regard to the first aid care for burns is:

    A. Burns must be treated only with moist materials
    B. Greasy substances are the best medicines for all types of burns
    C. Burns must be treated only with dry materials
    D. The depth to which the body tissues are injured determines the first aid care

    4.____

5. In applying a strapping to a sprained ankle, the person applying the strapping should

    A. pull the tape tight over the bony prominence of the ankle
    B. bind the toes as well as the rest of the foot
    C. have the injured foot in a position of 90 dorsi-flexion
    D. have the injured person keep the knee of the injured leg straight

    5.____

6. To clean a thermometer after use, the American Red Cross advises the use of

    A. formaldehyde   B. cool water and soap
    C. peroxide   D. liquid soap in hot water

    6.____

7. Hot applications should be applied

    A. in case of a sting from an insect
    B. in case of nosebleed
    C. to an ankle immediately after it is sprained
    D. none of the above cases

    7.____

2 (#5)

8. If a victim complains of increased pain after traction has been applied to a fractured leg, the first aider would MOST likely conclude that 8.___
   A. the traction bands are too loose
   B. the traction bands are too tight
   C. a tourniquet must be applied
   D. the simple fracture has turned into a compound fracture

9. Care of an unconscious victim, when the cause of unconsciousness is unknown, is based upon the 9.___
   A. pulse rate   B. odor of the breath
   C. color of the face   D. location of the accident

10. A victim of heat exhaustion will MOST likely have 10.___
    A. a moist skin   B. a strong pulse
    C. a red face   D. high temperature

KEY (CORRECT ANSWERS)

1.	C	6.	B
2.	B	7.	D
3.	B	8.	A
4.	D	9.	C
5.	C	10.	A

EXAMINATION SECTION
TEST 1

DIRECTIONS: Each question or incomplete statement is followed by several suggested answers or completions. Select the one that BEST answers the question or completes the statement. *PRINT THE LETTER OF THE CORRECT ANSWER IN THE SPACE AT THE RIGHT.*

1. The word *supervision* is subject to many interpretations, depending on the area in which it functions.
   Of the following, the statement which represents the BEST definition of supervision as it functions in nursing is that it is a(n)

   A. educational process for the training of personnel
   B. administrative process aimed at economy of performance
   C. leadership process for the development of new leaders
   D. cooperative process for the improvement of service

   1.____

2. Of the following, the one which BEST defines a *philosophy of supervision* in nursing is that it is a(n)

   A. practical application of the principles of public health nursing
   B. general statement of the overall purposes of the supervisory process
   C. unchanging guide based on the functions of the supervisor
   D. adaptation of the principles of public health nursing to the service of a particular agency

   2.____

3. Principles of supervision are generally accepted rules governing the supervisory process.
   They are PRIMARILY important because they

   A. are guides to methods and activities
   B. are standards for evaluating supervision
   C. eliminate the need for *techniques* for nursing performance
   D. reflect administrative policies

   3.____

4. Of the following, the one on which the objectives of a supervisory program in nursing should PRIMARILY be based is

   A. the health problems of the community
   B. a job analysis of supervisory functions
   C. administrative policies of the agency
   D. the needs of the staff nurses

   4.____

5. Certain restrictions on the functions of the supervisor are inherent in the nature of the process of supervision. Of the following statements, the one which will BEST serve as a guide in determining supervisory functions is that

   A. since supervision is educational, the supervisor should require each staff nurse to further her own education through advanced study
   B. the supervisor has some responsibility for social reforms since public health nursing is interested in improving living standards

   5.____

C. supervision should not extend beyond the point where its influence affects the service program of the agency
D. the supervisor has some responsibility for the health of the staff nurses and should guide their recreational and social activities

6. Of the following, the BEST method for a supervisor to use in order to develop the staff nurse's understanding of nursing is to

   A. encourage all nurses to further their professional growth through advanced study
   B. help the nurses to solve family problems by the use of all community agencies
   C. develop concepts of family and community health through individual supervision of each nurse's work
   D. plan group education programs which will bring in speakers from all kinds of health agencies in the community

6.____

7. Democratic supervision recognizes individual differences and values.
Of the following statements, the one which represents the BEST interpretation of a democratic approach to the staff nurse is that

   A. each nurse should receive an equal amount of guidance from the supervisor
   B. each nurse has something of value to contribute to the service
   C. staff nurses and supervisors should accept equal responsibility for the work of the agency
   D. the work of each nurse is of equal value to the agency

7.____

8. Changes in public health and nursing practice affect the function of the supervisor in public health nursing.
Of the following, the one which represents a trend in public health or nursing practice which will affect supervisory functions is that the

   A. intangible nature of present day health guidance increases the need for staff nurses prepared as *specialists* in many areas
   B. public health nurse is expected to function as a partner in the health team
   C. modern public health nurse is expected to function independently
   D. multiplicity of community agencies and health workers has decreased the demands made on public health nurses for participation in community activities

8.____

9. Of the following methods, the one which represents the BEST supervisory practice with regard to scheduling work for nurses is to

   A. schedule each nurse's work on a daily basis to insure even distribution of work
   B. schedule routine assignments on a monthly basis and special assignments on a daily basis
   C. make scheduling of work a staff responsibility except for relief assignments
   D. make it a cooperative activity for supervisor and staff

9.____

10. Assignment of work is one means which may be utilized by the supervisor as a method of staff development.
Of the following, the principle which it would be BEST to follow in making work assignments, considering the total functions of the supervisor, is to

10.____

A. plan varying work assignments for the districts so that the needs of each individual nurse can be met
B. give primary consideration to the needs of the nurse, since service demands can be distributed among the entire staff
C. consider the nurse's ability and potential growth since both the nurse and the service will profit
D. discontinue the services of a nurse who cannot carry a routine work assignment in any area

11. The maintenance of *morale* within the staff group is one of the important responsibilities of the supervisor.
Of the following, the BEST way to strengthen morale in a staff group where dissatisfaction exists because of heavy case loads is to

    A. recommend to administration that nurses receive extra compensation for overtime hours on duty
    B. reduce large case loads by discharging families where only minor problems exist
    C. present the problem for discussion at a staff meeting and ask for suggested solutions
    D. rotate work assignments, alternating the heavy and light districts among all the staff

12. Of the following statements, the one which BEST represents the philosophy of the recommended ratio of supervisors to staff nurses is that

    A. the ratio can be reduced when more qualified public health workers are available
    B. the trend toward employment of non-nurses for some tasks will make it possible to reduce the ratio
    C. the ratio can be reduced when qualified specialist consultants are available
    D. since the work of the public health nurse is becoming increasingly more complex, the ratio may need to be increased

13. Older staff nurses are frequently resistant to new ideas and present a problem to the supervisor.
The BEST approach in handling this situation is to

    A. encourage the nurses to take courses which will bring them *up to date*
    B. avoid situations which tend to generate resistance
    C. have the nurses assist in conducting activities which include new ideas
    D. use supervisory authority to request their cooperation

14. Field observation as a supervisory technique is of *particular* value PRIMARILY because it

    A. keeps the supervisor in touch with the realities of the work
    B. best reveals the strengths and weaknesses of the staff
    C. is an economical procedure
    D. gives the supervisor an opportunity to check on the nurse's techniques

15. An individual conference between supervisor and staff nurse can be considered *successful* if

A. all of the nurse's problems have been discussed
B. the nurse accepts all the supervisor's suggestions
C. free discussion takes place between supervisor and nurse
D. the nurse assumes responsibility for self-evaluation

16. The development of citizens advisory committees for official health agencies is a definite trend in community health organizations.
The PARTICULAR value of such a committee is that it

    A. develops general citizen interest in community health and community health projects
    B. encourages the hiring of better prepared personnel
    C. develops new health programs in accordance with community needs
    D. provides volunteer service for community health work

17. Evaluation of the overall performance of the staff nurses as a group is an administrative as well as an educational function.
From the *administrative* point of view, it serves as a(n)

    A. aid to the director in securing the necessary budget
    B. means of justifying the service
    C. basis for planning staff education
    D. basis for setting up job qualifications

18. Of the following, the one which is the BEST criterion of the success of the supervisor is her ability to

    A. mold the staff nurses into a desirable pattern established by her
    B. develop the resources of the staff nurses with the maximum degree of efficiency
    C. secure the consent of the staff nurses to follow established nursing policies
    D. develop and maintain cooperation between staff and administrative groups

19. Of the following, the one which would be *irrelevant* in a self-analysis of supervisory efficiency is:

    A. Is there evidence of job satisfaction among members of the staff?
    B. Do vital statistics show a reduction in morbidity and mortality rates in the community?
    C. Do nurses' case records show an improvement in the type of nursing service rendered?
    D. Is there evidence of cooperative working relationships with other agencies in the community?

20. Of the following statements, the one which BEST represents the responsibility of the nurse in the community health program is

    A. planning and putting into action a community-wide health program
    B. interpreting the public health program to the community
    C. giving health guidance to families and individuals
    D. participating in the public relations program of community health agencies

21. When selecting a case load for a new staff nurse during her period of introduction to a public health nursing agency, it is MOST advisable to assign her to 21.____

    A. a variety of cases to give her a complete picture of the agency program
    B. cases involving contact with many community agencies to give her a picture of the community
    C. cases with difficult and varied health and social problems to determine her ability to adjust to the work
    D. cases which will give her an opportunity to see the function of a public health nurse in family health service

22. In evaluating personal qualities which are desirable in nurses, it is important to base judgments on objective behavior. 22.____
    Of the following statements, the one that describes *objective* behavior is:

    A. Does not show loyalty to the organization
    B. Has made several excellent suggestions for staff conferences
    C. Is well liked by patients and secures their cooperation
    D. Seems incapable of any sustained effort towards improvement

23. A staff nurse who needs help in planning and organizing her work can BEST be assisted by 23.____

    A. encouraging her to analyze her work as a basis for planning
    B. having her keep a careful record of all her activities
    C. having her work scheduled carefully by the supervisor
    D. suggesting that she not plan for more than one day's work at a time

24. Many facets of the work of the nurse cannot be developed in a short period of introduction to the service. 24.____
    Of the following, the one which needs *particularly* long time guidance and supervision is for the nurse to

    A. acquire the ability to adjust to the general field of public health nursing
    B. appreciate the dynamic nature of public health nursing
    C. acquire knowledge of the routine techniques required
    D. develop skill in family health teaching

25. The level of achievement which should be reached by an average staff nurse at the end of a two-month introductory period in a public health nursing agency is 25.____

    A. knowledge of the total health program in the community
    B. ability to plan a program of health instruction
    C. ability to accept responsibility for nursing service to a selected number of families
    D. awareness of the chief health problems of the community

KEY (CORRECT ANSWERS)

1. D
2. B
3. A
4. A
5. C

6. C
7. B
8. B
9. D
10. C

11. C
12. D
13. C
14. A
15. C

16. A
17. B
18. B
19. B
20. C

21. D
22. B
23. A
24. D
25. C

TEST 2

DIRECTIONS: Each question or incomplete statement is followed by several suggested answers or completions. Select the one that BEST answers the question or completes the statement. *PRINT THE LETTER OF THE CORRECT ANSWER IN THE SPACE AT THE RIGHT.*

1. The successful staff education program is one which is carefully planned by the supervisor and the staff nurses. Of the following statements, the one which represents the BEST basis for planning a staff education program is the   1.____

    A. needs of the staff nurses as expressed by the supervisory group
    B. chief health problems of the community
    C. needs of the staff nurses as they are related to the needs of the service
    D. problems in nursing service as seen by the administrator

2. A procedure manual is a supervisory tool which can be of assistance to the nursing supervisor in that it   2.____

    A. frees her of the necessity of routine checking of technique
    B. gives her assurance that the staff nurses will give safe nursing care
    C. provides a basis for the necessary standardization of nursing techniques
    D. insures that administrative policies are understood by the staff

3. The staff education program is a major responsibility of the supervisor in a nursing program. To do an effective job, the supervisor needs a knowledge of the principles that govern teaching-learning situations.
   These principles are based PRIMARILY on   3.____

    A. psychological factors that operate in the teaching-learning situation
    B. standardized tests
    C. practical experience of teachers
    D. studies made by experts in the field

4. Dramatization of incidents by means of role playing as a technique of staff education is of particular value PRIMARILY because it   4.____

    A. helps the nurse to understand patient attitudes
    B. gives the nurse confidence in meeting difficult situations
    C. develops leadership and teaching potentialities
    D. gives the nurse the feeling of true life situations

5. The *particular* value of the case study method of teaching in staff education is to   5.____

    A. give nurses help in solving the problems of the family under discussion
    B. provide training in problem solving by making problem situations more concrete
    C. familiarize the nurse with community agencies which may assist in solving family problems
    D. help nurses understand why families do not always cooperate with plans made for them

6. Assume that a staff nurse under your supervision is familiar with teaching principles and methods and that her knowledge is adequate, yet she fails to put her teaching across to the families.
Of the following methods, the one which would be BEST for the supervisor to use to help this nurse is to

   A. suggest additional reading references
   B. encourage her to make written teaching plans
   C. give her practice in teaching large groups
   D. assist her in making practical applications in specific cases

7. The use of special lecturers in staff education has definite value in certain instances. A *specific* value of this method is that it

   A. provides information not readily available in printed form
   B. stimulates group participation in discussion
   C. presents material of a controversial nature
   D. promotes cooperation between agencies

8. Proper preparation is an important factor for a group discussion and is the responsibility of the discussion leader.
Of the following, the one which does NOT constitute part of the leader's preparation is

   A. preparing an outline for the discussion
   B. assembling the necessary visual aids
   C. providing factual material for the discussants
   D. determining the conclusion he desires

9. Of the following, the MOST important requirement for a discussion leader is that he

   A. be an *expert* on the subject to be discussed
   B. have the ability to stimulate others to think and to express themselves
   C. have an aggressive personality
   D. have the ability to lead others toward an acceptance of his opinions

10. Of the following suggested criteria, the one which is MOST valid in judging the success of a group discussion is whether

    A. there were no more than 40 nor fewer than 30 participants
    B. the discussion resulted in complete agreement among the members
    C. all issues were resolved at the close of the discussion
    D. effective and constructive group action resulted from the discussion

11. Supervision of recording includes various activities, one of which is the routine checking of records.
Of the following, the CHIEF purpose of this type of record review is to

    A. build staff interest in records
    B. promote accuracy and completeness
    C. assure that visits are made on schedule
    D. secure information for use in record revision

12. Assume that a staff nurse does good work but keeps poor records.
Of the following, the method which would contribute MOST toward the improvement of her record keeping is to

    A. give her close individual supervision and guidance
    B. assign her to check the records of other staff nurses for inaccuracies
    C. check all her records daily for omissions and errors
    D. make her responsible for a staff education meeting on *Records*

13. A staff nurse constantly meets resistance from families in attempting to secure information for records.
Of the following, it would be MOST advisable for the supervisor to suggest to the staff nurse that she

    A. defer asking for information for records until she knows the families and is accepted by them
    B. try getting the required information without letting the families know that it is going to be recorded
    C. let the families see the record and assist the nurse in filling it out
    D. explain to the families the need of the information and that it is kept confidential

14. Leadership is an important technique in the supervisory process.
Of the following characteristics, the one which would provide for the BEST kind of leadership in nursing is

    A. aggressiveness in attacking problems
    B. confidence in one's ability to lead others
    C. a dynamic, extrovert type of personality
    D. ability to inspire confidence in others

15. Field experience for university students in public health nursing programs provides an opportunity for the integration of theory with practic The agency is not expected to duplicate material covered in the classroom, but to develop it.
Of the following, the one for which the university has the *right* to expect the field agency to accept PRIMARY responsibility is

    A. developing the nurse's ability to plan teaching
    B. having the nurse understand the purposes and functions of records
    C. helping the nurse to recognize and appreciate teaching opportunities
    D. teaching the nurse to understand the psychological basis of teaching and learning

16. If the shortage of public health nurses continues, agencies giving services will be required to make adjustments in their programs. Decisions will have to be made as to which services are essential and which can be cut to a minimum or discontinued.
Of the following services, the one which under these circumstances could be *curtailed* is home visits to

    A. give bedside care in acute illness
    B. tuberculosis patients and their families
    C. mothers and newborn babies delivered in the hospitals
    D. patients under adequate treatment for syphilis

17. The use of time studies is a method which the nursing supervisor may use to advantage in self-evaluation. Of the following information secured as a result of a time study made by a supervisor, the one which would be an *indication* of the need for better work planning and organization is that there has been a(n)

    A. *increase* in the time spent on *patient not home* visits
    B. *decrease* in the doctor's time in the clinics
    C. *increase* in the time spent by volunteers in the clinics
    D. *decrease* in the time spent by nurses in the office

18. Assume that you were newly assigned to replace a supervisor who had created resentment among the staff by her authoritarian methods.
    In order to secure acceptance by the staff, it would be BEST for you to

    A. concentrate on the managerial aspects of supervision until the staff has learned to accept you
    B. continue authoritarian supervision for a while, tapering it off gradually as the staff becomes accustomed to democratic methods
    C. explain democratic supervision at an early staff meeting and let the staff know that they will now have more freedom
    D. maintain authoritarian methods but appeal to the staff for their loyal cooperation

19. A council of social agencies is a community agency which

    A. acts as a social planning agency for those organizations in the community that belong to the council
    B. registers identifying information about families known to social agencies
    C. supplies confidential information about families known to social agencies
    D. acts as a money raising group for social agencies

20. Of the following statements, the one which BEST represents one of the values of vital statistics in public health is: A(n)

    A. study of birth registration data shows the causes of infant deaths
    B. study of national mortality statistics will point out ways to save the lives of mothers and newborn babies
    C. analysis of morbidity statistics will indicate the prevalence of certain diseases that constitute health problems
    D. analysis of mortality statistics will help to estimate the possibility of epidemics

21. Administration of school health services is a difficult problem because of the official responsibilities of both public health agencies and departments of education for the welfare of the school age child. There are arguments in favor of administration for each group. However, of the following, the MOST valid argument in favor of administration by official public health agencies is that

    A. educators are not qualified by either experience or education to understand the health problems of children
    B. the supervision of school nurses and physicians can best be done by a public health agency
    C. departments of health are by law responsible for the protection of health and the prevention of disease

D. educators are primarily interested in their own specific educational problems and exhibit only secondary interest in the health program

22. In order to make the best use of available public health nursing personnel in school health services, it is essential that nurses in the schools carry out only those functions which require their skills and judgment.
Of the following functions, the one which could BEST be delegated to *non-nursing* personnel is

    A. caring for acute injuries and illnesses
    B. instructing teachers and assisting them with the health observation of children
    C. assisting physicians with medical examinations
    D. reviewing physicians' recommendations and planning for follow-up

23. In making field observations, it is usually MOST advisable for the supervisor

    A. not to let the nurse know when she will be observed
    B. to select with the staff nurse the cases to be observed
    C. to observe the nurse on the day when the nurse invites her to do so
    D. to allow the nurse to select the cases she wishes the supervisor to observe

24. The recommended ratio of supervisors to staff nurses in public health nursing is one supervisor to _____ students.

    A. twelve staff workers, including
    B. ten staff nurses, including
    C. six graduate staff nurses and two
    D. eight workers, including

25. The National Institute of Mental Health of the Public Health Service has as its MAJOR purpose

    A. financial aid to states to provide better care for the indigent mentally ill
    B. stimulation of research in medical schools into the causes of mental illness
    C. training of mental health personnel, and assistance in developing community mental health programs
    D. case finding and treatment of people with mild mental disorders, to prevent the development of more severe psychoses

KEY (CORRECT ANSWERS)

1.	C	11.	B
2.	C	12.	A
3.	A	13.	D
4.	D	14.	D
5.	B	15.	C
6.	D	16.	D
7.	A	17.	A
8.	D	18.	A
9.	B	19.	A
10.	D	20.	C

21. C
22. C
23. B
24. B
25. C

PREPARING WRITTEN MATERIAL
EXAMINATION SECTION
TEST 1

DIRECTIONS: Each short paragraph below is followed by four restatements or summaries of the information contained within it. Select the one that most completely and accurately restates the information given in the paragraph. *PRINT THE LETTER OF THE CORRECT ANSWER IN THE SPACE AT THE RIGHT.*

1. India's night jasmine, or hurshinghar, is different from most flowering plants, in that its flowers are closed during the day, and open after dark. The scientific reason for this is probably that the plant has avoided competing with other flowers for pollinating insects and birds, and relies instead on the service of nocturnal bats that are drawn to the flower's nectar. According to an old Indian legend, however, the flowers sprouted from the funeral ashes of a beautiful young girl who had fallen hopelessly in love with the sun.
    A. Despite the Indian legend that explains why the hurshinghar's flowers open at dusk, scientists believe it has to do with competition for available pollinators.
    B. The Indian hurshinghar's closure of its flowers during the day is due to a lack of available pollinators.
    C. The hurshinghar of India has evolved an unhealthy dependency on nocturnal bats.
    D. Like most myths, the Indian legend of the hurshinghar's night-flowering has been disproved by science.

1.____

2. Charles Lindbergh's trans-Atlantic flight from New York to Paris made him an international hero in 1927, but he lived nearly another fifty years, and by most accounts they weren't terribly happy ones. The two greatest tragedies of his life—the 1932 kidnapping and murder of his oldest son, and an unshakeable reputation as a Nazi sympathizer during World War II—he blamed squarely on the rabid media hounds who stalked his every move.
    A. Despite the fact that Charles Lindbergh had a hand in the two greatest tragedies of his life, he insisted on blaming the media for his problems.
    B. Charles Lindbergh lived a largely unhappy life after the glory of his 1927 trans-Atlantic flight, and he blamed his unhappiness on media attention
    C. Charles Lindbergh's later life was marked by despair and disillusionment.
    D. Because of the rabid media attention sparked by Charles Lindbergh's 1927 trans-Atlantic flight, he would later consider it the last happy event of his life

2.____

3. The United States, one of the world's youngest nations in the early twentieth century, had yet to spread its wings in terms of foreign affairs, preferring to remain isolated and opposed to meddling in the affairs of others. But the fact remained that as a young nation situated on the opposite side of the globe from Europe, Africa, and Asia, the United States had much work to do in

3.____

establishing relations with the rest of the world. So, too, as the European colonial powers continued to battle for influence in North and South America, did the United States come to believe that it was proper for them to keep these nations from encroaching into their sphere of influence.
- A. The roots of the Monroe Doctrine can be traced to the foreign policy shift of the United States during the early nineteenth century.
- B. In the early nineteenth century, the United States shifted its foreign policy to reflect a growing desire to actively protect its interests in the Western Hemisphere.
- C. In the early nineteenth century, the United States was too young and undeveloped to have devised much in the way of foreign policy.
- D. The United States adopted a more aggressive foreign policy in the early nineteenth century in order to become a diplomatic player on the world stage.

4. Hertha Ayrton, a nineteenth-century Englishwoman, pursued a career in science during a time when most women were not given the opportunity to go to college. Her series of successes led to her induction into the Institution of Electrical Engineers in 1899, when she was the first woman to receive this professional honor. Her most noted accomplishment was the research and invention of an anti-gas fan that the British War Office used in the trench warfare of World War I.   4.____
- A. The British Army's success in World War I can be partly attributed to Hertha Ayrton, a groundbreaking British scientist.
- B. Hertha Ayrton was the first woman to be inducted into the Institution of Electrical Engineers.
- C. The injustices of nineteenth-century England were no match for the brilliant mind of Hertha Ayrton.
- D. Hertha Ayrton defied the restrictions of her society by building a successful scientific career.

5. Scientists studying hyenas in Tanzania's Ngorongoro Crater have observed that hyena clans have evolved a system of territoriality that allows each clan a certain space to hunt within the 100-square-mile area. These territories are not marked by natural boundaries, but by droppings and excretions from the hyenas' scent glands. Usually, the hyenas take these boundary lines very seriously; some hyena clans have been observed abandoning their pursuit of certain prey after the prey has crossed into another territory, even though no members of the neighboring clan are anywhere in sight.   5.____
- A. The hyenas of Ngorongoro Crater illustrate that the best way to peacefully co-exist within a limited territory is to strictly delineate and defend territorial borders.
- B. While most territorial boundaries are marked using geographical features, the hyenas of Ngorongoro Crater have devised another method.
- C. The hyena clans of Ngorongoro Crater, in order to co-exist within a limited hunting territory, have developed a method of marking strict territorial boundaries.
- D. As with most species, the hyenas of Ngorongoro Crater have proven the age-old motto: "To the victor go the spoils."

3 (#1)

6. The flood control policy of the U.S. Army Corps of Engineers has long been an obvious feature of the American landscape—the Corps seeks to contain the nation's rivers with an enormous network of dams and levees, "channelizing" rivers into small, confined routes that will stay clear of settled flood—plains when rivers rise. As a command of the U.S. Army, the Corps seems to have long seen the nation's rivers as an enemy to be fought; one of the agency's early training films speaks of the Corps' "battle" with its adversary, Mother Nature.

    A. The dams and levees built by the U.S. Army Corps of Engineers have at least defeated their adversary, Mother Nature.
    B. The flood control policy of the U.S. Army Corps of Engineers has often reflected a military point of view, making the nation's rivers into enemies that must be defeated.
    C. When one realizes that the flood policy of the U.S. Army Corps of Engineers has always relied on a kind of military strategy, it is only possible to view the Corps' efforts as a failure.
    D. By damming and channelizing the nation's rivers, the U.S. Army Corps of Engineers have made America's flood plains safe for farming and development.

6.____

7. Frogs with extra legs or missing legs have been showing up with greater frequency over the past decade, and scientists have been baffled by the cause. Some researchers have concluded that pesticide runoff from farms is to blame; others say a common parasite, the trematode, is the culprit. Now, a new study suggests that both these factors in combination have disturbed normal development in many frogs, leading to the abnormalities.

    A. Despite several studies, scientists still have no idea what is causing the widespread incidence of deformities among aquatic frogs.
    B. In the debate over what is causing the increase in frog deformities, environmentalists tend to blame pesticide runoff, while others blame a common parasite, the trematode.
    C. A recent study suggests that both pesticide runoff and natural parasites have contributed to the increasing rate of deformities in frogs.
    D. Because of their aquatic habitat, frogs are among the most susceptible organisms to chemical ad environmental change, and this is illustrated by the increasing rate of physical deformities among frog populations.

7.____

8. The builders of the Egyptian pyramids, to insure that each massive structure was built on a completely flat surface, began by cutting a network of criss-crossing channels into the pyramid's mapped-out ground space and partly filling the channels with water. Because the channels were all interconnected, the water was distributed evenly throughout the channel system, and all the workers had to do to level their building surface was cut away any rock above the waterline.

    A. The modern carpenter's level uses a principle that was actually invented several centuries ago by the builders of the Egyptian pyramids.
    B. The discovery of the ancient Egyptians' sophisticated construction techniques is a quiet argument against the idea that they were built by slaves.

8.____

C. The use of water to insure that the pyramids were level mark the Egyptians as one of the most scientifically advanced of the ancient civilizations.
D. The builders of the Egyptian pyramids used a simple but ingenious method for ensuring a level building surface with interconnected channels of water

9. Thunderhead Mountain, a six-hundred-foot-high formation of granite in the Black Hills of South Dakota, is slowly undergoing a transformation that will not be finished for more than a century, when what remains of the mountain will have become the largest sculpture in the world. The statue, begun in 1947 by a Boston Sculptor named Henry Ziolkowski, is still being carved and blasted by his wife and children into the likeness of Crazy Horse, the legendary chief of the Sioux tribe of American natives. The enormity of the sculpture—the planned length of one of the figure's arms is 263 feet—is understandable, given the historical greatness of Crazy Horse.   9.____
   A. Only a hero as great as Crazy Horse could warrant a sculpture so large that it will take morae than a century to complete.
   B. In 1947, sculptor Henry Ziolkowski began work on what he imagined would be the largest sculpture in the world—even though he knew he would not live to see it completed.
   C. The huge Black Hills sculpture of the great Sioux chief Crazy Horse, still being carried out by the family of Henry Ziolkowski, will some day be the largest sculpture in the world.
   D. South Dakota's Thunderhead Mountain will soon be the site of the world's largest sculpture, a statue of the Sioux chief Crazy Horse.

10. Because they were some of the first explorers to venture into the western frontier of North America, the French were responsible for the naming of several native tribes. Some of these names were poorly conceived—the worst of which was perhaps Eskimo, the name for the natives of the far North, which translates roughly as "eaters of raw flesh." The name is incorrect; these people have always cooked their fish and game, and they now call themselves the Inuit, a native term that means "the people."   10.____
   A. The first to explore much of North America's western frontier were the French, and they usually gave improper or poorly-informed names to the native tribes.
   B. The Eskimos of North America have never eaten raw flesh, so it is curious that the French would give them a name that means "eaters of raw flesh."
   C. The Inuit have fought for many years to overcome the impression that they eat raw flesh.
   D. Like many native tribes, the Inuit were once incorrectly named by French explorers, but they have since corrected the mistake themselves.

11. Of the 30,000 species of spiders worldwide, only a handful are dangerous to human beings, but this doesn't prevent many people from having a powerful fear of all spiders, whether they are venomous or not. The leading scientific theory about arachnophobia, as this fear is known, is that far in our evolutionary past, some species of spider must have presented a serious enough threat to people that the sight of a star-shaped body or an eight-legged walk was coded into our genes as a danger signal.
    A. Scientists theorize that peoples' widespread fear of spiders can be traced to an ancient spider species that was dangerous enough to trigger this fearful reaction.
    B. The fear known as arachnophobia is triggered by the sight of a star-shaped body or an eight-legged walk.
    C. Because most spiders have a uniquely shaped body that triggers a human fear response, many humans are afflicted with the fear of spiders known as arachnophobia.
    D. Though only a few of the planet's 30,000 spider species are dangerous to people, many people have an unreasonable fear of them.

11.____

12. From the 1970s to the 1990s, the percentage of Americans living in the suburbs climbed from 37% to 47%. In the latter part of the 1990s, a movement emerged that questioned the good of such a population shift—or at least, the good of the speed and manner in which this suburban land was being developed. Often, people began to argue, the planning of such growth was flawed, resulting in a phenomenon that has become known as suburban "sprawl," or the growth of suburban orbits around cities at rates faster than infrastructures could support, and in ways that are damaging to the environment
    A. The term "urban sprawl" was coined in the 1990s, when the movement against unchecked suburban development began to gather momentum.
    B. In the 1980s and 1990s, home builders benefited from a boom in their most favored demographic segment, suburban new home buyers.
    C. Suburban development tends to suffer from poor planning, which can lead to a lower quality of life for residents
    D. The surge in suburban residences in the late twentieth century was criticized by many as "sprawl" that could not be supported by existing resources

12.____

13. Medicare, a $200 billion-a-year program, processes 1 billion claims annually, and in the year 2000, the computer system that handles these claims came under criticism. The General Accounting Office branded Medicare's financial management system as outdated and inadequate—one in a series of studies and reports warning that the program is plagued with duplication, overcharges, double billings, and confusion among users.
    A. The General Accounting Office's 2000 report proves that Medicare is bloated bureaucracy in need of substantial reform.
    B. Medicare's confusing computer network is an example of how the federal government often neglects the programs that mean the most to average American citizens.

13.____

C. In the year 2000, the General Accounting Office criticized Medicare's financial accounting network as inefficient and outdated.
D. Because it has to handle so many claims each year, Medicare's financial accounting system often produces redundancies and errors.

14. The earliest known writing materials were thin clay tablets, used in Mesopotamia more than 5,000 years ago. Although the tablets were cheap and easy to produce, they had two major disadvantages: they were difficult to store, and once the clay had dried and hardened, a person could not write on them. The ancient Egyptians later discovered a better writing material—the thin bark of the papyrus reed, a plant that grew near the mouth of the Nile River, which could be peeled into long strips, woven into a mat-like layer, pounded flat with heavy mallets, and then dried in the sun. 14.____
    A. The Egyptians, after centuries of frustration with clay writing tablets, were finally forced to invent a better writing surface.
    B. With the bark of the papyrus reed, ancient Egyptians made a writing material that overcame the disadvantages of clay tablets.
    C. The Egyptian invention of the papyrus scroll was necessitated in part by a relative lack of available clay.
    D. The word "paper" can be traced to the innovations of the Egyptians, who made the first paper-like writing material from the bark of papyrus plant.

15. In 1850, the German pianomaker Heinrich Steinweg and his family stepped off an immigrant ship in New York City, threw themselves into competition with dozens of other established craftsmen, and defeated them all by reinventing the instrument. The company they created commanded the market for nearly the next century and a half, while their competitors—some of the most acclaimed pianomakers in the business—faded into obscurity. And all the while, Steinway & Sons, through their sponsorship and encouragement of the world's most distinguished pianists, helped define the cultural life of the young United States. 15.____
    A. The Steinways capitalized on weak competition during the mid-nineteenth century to capture the American piano market.
    B. Because of their technical and cultural innovations, the Steinways had an advantage over other American pianomakers.
    C. Heinrich Steinweg founded the Steinway piano empire in 1850.
    D. From humble immigrant origins, the Steinway family rose to dominate both the pianomaking industry and American musical culture.

16. Feng Shui, the ancient Chinese science of studying the natural environment's effect on a person's well-being, has gained new popularity in the design and decoration of buildings. Although a complex area of study, a basic premise of Feng Shui is that each building creates a unique field of energy which affects the inhabitants of that building or home. In recent years, decorators and realtors have begun to offer services which include a diagnosis of a building's Feng Shui, or energy. 16.____
    A. Feng Shui, the Chinese science of balancing environmental energies, has been given more aesthetic quality by recent practitioners.

B. Generally, practitioners of Feng Shui work to create balance within a room, carefully arranging sharp and soft surfaces to create a positive environment that suits the room's primary purpose.
C. The idea behind the Chinese "science" of Feng Sui objects give off certain energies that affect a building's inhabitants has been a difficult one for most Westerners to accept, but it is gaining in popularity.
D. The ancient Chinese science of Feng Shui, which studies the balance of energies in a person's environment, has become popular among those who design and decorate buildings.

17. Because the harsh seasonal variations of the Kansas plains make survival difficult for most plant life, the area is dominated by tall, sturdy grasses. The only tree that has been able to survive and prosper throughout the wide expanse of prairie is the cottonwood, which can take root and grow in the most extreme climatic conditions. Sometimes a storm will shear off a living branch and carry it downstream, where it may snag along a sandbar and take root.   17.____
    A. Among the plant life of the Kansas plains, the only tree is the cottonwood.
    B. The only prosperous tree on the Kansas plains is the cottonwood, which can take root and grow in a wide range of conditions.
    C. Only the cottonwood, whose branches can grow after being broken off and washed down a river, is capable of surviving the climatic extremes of the Kansas plains.
    D. Because it is the most widespread and hardiest tree on the Kansas plains, the cottonwood had become a symbol of pioneer grit and fortitude.

18. In the twenty-first century, it's easy to see the automobile as the keystone of American popular culture. Subtract linen dusters, driving goggles, and women's *crepe de chine* veils from our history, and you've taken the Roaring out of the Twenties. Take away the ducktail haircuts, pegged pants, and upturned collars from the teen Car Cult of the Fifties, and the decade isn't nearly as Fabulous. Were the chromed and tailfinned muscle cars of the automobile' Golden Age modeled after us, or were we mimicking them?   18.____
    A. Ever since its invention, the automobile has shaped American culture.
    B. Many of the familiar names we give historical era, such as "Roaring Twenties" and "Fabulous Fifties," were given because of the predominance of the automobile.
    C. Americans' tastes in clothing have been determined primarily by the cars they drive.
    D. Teenagers have had a fascination for automobiles ever since the motorcar was first invented.

19. Since the 1960s, an important issue for Canada has been the status of minority French-speaking Canadians, especially in the province of Quebec, whose inhabitants make up 30% of the Canadian population and trace their ancestry back to a Canada that preceded British influence. In response to pressure from Quebec nationalists, the government in 1982 added a Charter of Rights to the constitution, restoring important rights that dated back to the time of aboriginal treaties. Separatism is still a prominent issue, though successive   19.____

referendums and constitutional inquiries have not resulted in any realistic progress toward Quebec's independence.
- A. Despite the fact that Quebec's inhabitants have their roots in Canada's original settlers, they have been constantly oppressed by the descendants of those who came later, the British.
- B. It seems unavoidable that Quebec's linguistic and cultural differences with the rest of Canada will some day lead to its secession.
- C. French-speaking Quebec's activism over the last several decades has led to concessions by the Canadian government, but it seems that Quebec will remain a part of the country for some time.
- D. The inhabitants of Quebec are an aboriginal culture that has been exploited by the Canadian government for years, but they are gradually winning back their rights.

20. For years, musicians and scientists have tried to discover what it is about an eighteenth-century Stradivarius violin—which may sell for more than $1 million on today's market—that gives it its unique sound. In 1977, American scientist Joseph Nagyvary discovered that the Stradivarius is made of a spruce wood that came from Venice, where timber was stored beneath the sea, and unlike the dry-seasoned wood from which other violins were made, this spruce contains microscopic holes which add resonance to the violin's sound. Nagyvary also found the varnish used on the Stradivarius to be equally unique, containing tiny mineral crystals that appear to have come from ground-up gemstones, which would filter out high-pitched tones and give the violin a smoother sound.
    - A. After carefully studying Stradivarius violins to discover the source of their unique sound, an American scientist discovered two qualities in the construction of them that set them apart from other instruments: the wood from which they were made, and the varnish used to coat the wood.
    - B. The two qualities that give the Stradivarius violin such a unique sound are the wood, which adds resonance, and the finish, which filters out high-pitched tones.
    - C. The Stradivarius violin, because of the unique wood and finish used in its construction, is widely regarded as the finest string instrument ever manufactured in the world.
    - D. A close study of the Stradivarius violin has revealed that the best wood for making violins is Venetian spruce, stored underwater.

20.____

21. People who watch the display of fireflies on a clear summer evening are actually witnessing a complex chemical reaction called "bioluminescence," which turns certain organisms into living light bulbs. Organisms that produce this light undergo a reaction in which oxygen combines with a chemical called lucerfin and an enzyme called luciferase. Depending on the organism, the light produced from this reaction can range from the light green of the firefly to the bright red spots of a railroad worm.
    - A. Although the function of most displays of bioluminescence is to attract mates, as is the case with fireflies, other species rely on bioluminescence for different purposes.

21.____

B. Bioluminescence, a phenomenon produced by several organisms, is the result of a chemical reaction that takes place within the body of the organism.
C. Of all the organisms in the world, only insects are capable of displaying bioluminescence.
D. Despite the fact that some organisms display bioluminescence, these reactions produce almost no heat, which is why the light they create is sometimes referred to as cold light.

22. The first of America's "log cabin" presidents, Andrew Jackson rose from humble backcountry origins to become a U.S. congressman and senator, a renowned military hero, and the seventh president of the United States. Among many Americans, especially those of the western frontier, he was acclaimed as a symbol of the "new" American: self-made, strong through closeness to nature, and endowed with a powerful moral courage.   22.____
    A. Andrew Jackson was the first American president to rise from modest origins.
    B. Because he was born poor, President Andrew Jackson was more popular among Americans of the western frontier.
    C. Andrew Jackson's humble background, along with his outstanding achievements, made him into a symbol of American strength and self-sufficiency.
    D. Andrew Jackson achieved success as a legislator, soldier, and president because he was born humbly and had to work for every honor he ever received.

23. In the past few decades, while much of the world's imagination has focused on the possibilities of outer space, some scientists have been exploring a different frontier—the ocean floor. Although ships have been sailing the oceans for centuries, only recently have scientists developed vehicles strong enough to sustain the pressure of deep-sea exploration and observation. These fiberglass vehicles, called submersibles, are usually just big enough to take two or three people to the deepest parts of the oceans' floors.   23.____
    A. Modern submersible vehicles, thanks to recent technological innovations, are now exploring underwater cliffs, crevices, and mountain ranges that were once unreachable.
    B. While most people tend to fantasize about exploring outer space, they should be turning toward a more accessible realm—the depths of the earth's oceans.
    C. Because of the necessarily small size of submersible vehicles, exploration of the deep ocean is not a widespread activity.
    D. Recent technological developments have helped scientists to turn their attention from deep space to the deep ocean.

24. The panda—a native of the remote mountainous regions of China—subsists almost entirely on the tender shoots of the bamboo plant. This restrictive diet has allowed the panda to evolve an anatomical structure that is completely different from that of other bears, whose paws are aligned for running, stabbing, and scratching. The panda's paw has an over-developed wrist bone that juts out below the other claws like a thumb, and the panda uses this "thumb" to grip bamboo shoots while it strips them of their leaves.
    A. The panda is the only bear-like animal that feeds on vegetation, and it has a kind of thumb to help it grip bamboo shoots.
    B. The panda's limited diet of bamboo has led it to evolve a thumb-like appendage for grasping bamboo shoots.
    C. The panda's thumb-like appendage is a factor that limits its diet to the shoots of the bamboo plant.
    D. Because bamboo shoots must be held tightly while eaten, the panda's thumb-like appendage ensure that it is the only bear-like animal that eats bamboo.

24.____

25. The stability and security of the Balkan region remains a primary concern for Greece in post-Cold War Europe, and Greece's active participation in peacekeeping and humanitarian operations in Georgia, Albania, and Bosnia are substantial examples of this commitment. Due to its geopolitical position, Greece believes it necessary to maintain, at least for now, a more nationalized defense force than other European nations. It is Greece's hope that the new spirit of integration and cooperation will help establish a common European foreign affairs and defense policy that might ease some of these regional tensions, and allow a greater level of Greek participation in NATO's integrated military structure.
    A. Greece's proximity to the unstable Balkan region has led it to keep a more nationalized military, though it hopes to become more involved in a common European defense force.
    B. The Balkan states present a greater threat to Greece than any other European nation, and Greece has adopted a highly nationalist military force as a result.
    C. Greece, the only Balkan state to belong to NATO, has an isolationist approach to defense, but hopes to achieve greater integration in the organization's combined forces.
    D. Greece's failure to become more militarily integrated with the rest of Europe can be attributed to the failure to establish a common European defense policy.

25.____

KEY (CORRECT ANSWERS)

1.	A		11.	A
2.	B		12.	D
3.	B		13.	C
4.	D		14.	B
5.	C		15.	D
6.	B		16.	D
7.	C		17.	B
8.	D		18.	A
9.	C		19.	C
10.	D		20.	A

21. B
22. C
23. D
24. B
25. A

PREPARING WRITTEN MATERIAL

PARAGRAPH REARRANGEMENT
COMMENTARY

The sentences that follow are in scrambled order. You are to rearrange them in proper order and indicate the letter choice containing the correct answer at the space at the right.

Each group of sentences in this section is actually a paragraph presented in scrambled order. Each sentence in the group has a place in that paragraph; no sentence is to be left out. You are to read each group of sentences and decide upon the best order in which to put the sentences so as to form a well-organized paragraph.

The questions in this section measure the ability to solve a problem when all the facts relevant to its solution are not given.

More specifically, certain positions of responsibility and authority require the employee to discover connection between events sometimes, apparently, unrelated. In order to do this, the employee will find it necessary to correctly infer that unspecified events have probably occurred or are likely to occur. This ability becomes especially important when action must be taken on incomplete information.

Accordingly, these questions require competitors to choose among several suggested alternatives, each of which presents a different sequential arrangement of the events. Competitors must choose the MOST logical of the suggested sequences.

In order to do so, they may be required to draw on general knowledge to infer missing concepts or events that are essential to sequencing the given events. Competitors should be careful to infer only what is essential to the sequence. The plausibility of the wrong alternatives will always require the inclusion of unlikely events or of additional chains of events which are NOT essential to sequencing the given events.

It's very important to remember that you are looking for the best of the four possible choices, and that the best choice of all may not even be one of the answers you're given to choose from.

There is no one right way to solve these problems. Many people have found it helpful to first write out the order of the sentences, as they would have arranged them, on their scrap paper before looking at the possible answers. If their optimum answer is there, this can save them some time. If it isn't, this method can still give insight into solving the problem. Others find it most helpful to just go through each of the possible choices, contrasting each as they go along. You should use whatever method feels comfortable and works for you.

While most of these types of questions are not that difficult, we've added a higher percentage of the difficult type, just to give you more practice. Usually there are only one or two questions on this section that contain such subtle distinctions that you're unable to answer confidently. And you then may find yourself stuck deciding between two possible choices, neither of which you're sure about.

PREPARING WRITTEN MATERIAL
PARAGRAPH REARRANGEMENT
EXAMINATION SECTION
TEST 1

DIRECTIONS: The sentences listed below are part of a meaningful paragraph, but they are not given in their proper order. You are to decide what would be the BEST order to put sentences to form a well-organized paragraph. Each sentence has a place in the paragraph; there are no extra sentences. *PRINT THE LETTER OF THE CORRECT ANSWER IN THE SPACE AT THE RIGHT.*

1. I. At first, I had very low enrollment, but then I started passing out flyers describing my services.
    II. Last summer I started a carwashing venture.
    III. I hope to save enough to buy my own carwash business one day.
    IV. I've been in business almost a year.
    V. After the advertising, I was booked every weekend during the summer.
    The CORRECT answer is:
    A. II, I, V, IV, III   B. I, II, IV, III, V   C. II, I, IV, V, III   D. V, III, IV, I, II

    1.____

2. I. Yesterday, John had to call work and tell them he wouldn't be able to come in.
    II. She wanted to eat at the new seafood restaurant in town.
    III. Two days ago, John and Sally went to dinner for Sally's birthday.
    IV. However, later John realized the sushi made him sick.
    V. They both tried the sushi and thought it tasted good.
    The CORRECT answer is:
    A. I, V, IV, III, II   B. III, II, V, IV, I   C. III, V, IV, I, II   D. V, IV, III, I, II

    2.____

3. I. Music programs should not be cut when school funds are tight.
    II. Some will argue that music programs are too costly.
    III. According to many experts, music programs have even shown the ability to re-engage student populations who have lost interest in scholastic endeavors.
    IV. There is a direct connection between school improvement and a student's connection to music.
    V. However, there are many different programs to choose from that are not as expensive.
    The CORRECT answer is:
    A. IV, II, V, I, III   B. I, III, IV, II, V   C. II, I, III, IV, V   D. I, IV, III, II, V

    3.____

4. I. The hockey team went undefeated in their tournament.
    II. Because the coach and their parents believed in them, the players played with great confidence.
    III. No one wanted to go home after they won the championship.
    IV. Their coach made them believe they could beat anyone they played.
    V. They were not expected to beat all of the teams in their bracket.
    The CORRECT answer is:
    A. III, II, V, IV, I   B. I, II, III, IV, V   C. I, V, IV, II, III   D. I, IV, V, II, III

    4.____

5. I.   The problem started when my alarm clock was set for 6:00 P.M. not 6:00 A.M., so I woke up late.
    II. I guess a neighbor's dog got loose before practice started, so it was delayed and no one notices I was a little tardy.
    III. I rode my bike as fast as I could and thought I was going to be in trouble for sure.
    IV. This morning was crazy because if I was late, I would get cut from the team.
    V.   When I got to the field, everyone was standing on the outside of the fence and there were policemen all on the field.
    The CORRECT answer is:
    A. I, IV, III, V, II   B. IV, III, I, II, V   C. I, V, II, III, IV   D. IV, I, III, V, II

6. I.   Lastly, do not eat food off of your date's plate unless they have offered it to you first.
    II. Do not tell jokes that aren't funny and especially do not laugh at them yourself.
    III. Remember, there are many ways to screw up a date, but these are the worst ways.
    IV. When on a first date, there are many ways to screw it up, but here are the three worst.
    V.   Do not forget to shower and groom yourself before showing up.
    The CORRECT answer is:
    A. IV, V, II, I, III   B. I, V, IV, II, III   C. IV, III, II, I, V   D. V, IV, II, I, III

7. I.   We could prevent drunk drivers from harming themselves or others by by providing this service.
    II. Thousands each year die because of accidents caused by drugs or alcohol.
    III. Many are not willing to pay for a taxi and decide to drive themselves home instead.
    IV. While the cost may be a burden to the wallet, it would be small compared to the loss of a loved one because of drunk driving.
    V.   Lives could be saved if the town started a free taxi service.
    The CORRECT answer is:
    A. I, III, V, IV, II   B. II, V, III, I, IV   C. II, III, I, V, IV   D. V, III, II, IV, I

8. I.   These amazing animals are disappearing at a startling rate.
    II. Do people really want to explain to our grandchildren why they can only see these majestic animals in a book?
    III. Zoos all across the country do not want the Siberian tiger to vanish.
    IV. We can also make donations to charities and sanctuaries that protect the Siberian tiger.
    V.   If we write to local governments, we could let them know we demand the preservation of this species.
    The CORRECT answer is:
    A. I, III, V, II, IV   B. V, II, I, III, IV   C. III, I, V, IV, II   D. II, IV, V, I, III

9.
I. Often, they have been described as eating machines, and their design certainly matches perfectly for that activity.
II. Of all the creatures that live in water, Orcas are the greediest eaters and killers.
III. As soon as they finish a meal, Orcas are on the prowl for more food.
IV. Orcas, better known as killer whales, are powerful swimmers, with sleek, muscled, stream-lined bodies.
V. They suffer from continual hunger.
The CORRECT answer is:
A. II, V, III, I, IV   B. II, III, I, IV, V   C. V, II, III, IV, I   D. I, IV, II, III, V

10.
I. Sleep researchers have recently concluded that high school students need more sleep than they currently get.
II. In an attempt to aid high school students get more sleep, some schools have delayed start times so students can perform better.
III. In addition to having difficulty with thinking, students who are sleep deprived often see more stress in their lives because of an increase in stress hormones like cortisol.
IV. Consistent data has determined that sleep is necessary to help with creating memories and solving complex issues.
V. At school, teens have difficulty with complex thought because many of them do not get enough sleep each night.
The CORRECT answer is:
A. I, V, III, II, IV   B. IV, III, I, V, II   C. I, IV, V, III, II   D. II, III, V, IV, I

11.
I. It took me twice as long to pack because I was so excited.
II. That all changed on the last day of school.
III. Until last year, I had never been out of the state, let alone out of the country.
IV. My sister decided to take me on a trip to London.
V. Now I think I want to be a travel agent, so I can see the world.
The CORRECT answer is:
A. II, IV, I, V, III   B. III, II, IV, I, V   C. IV, V, I, III, II   D. III, IV, II, I, V

12.
I. The owner felt that tattoos gave a negative image for the coffee shop.
II. Furthermore, a clean cut appearance would attract better customers.
III. Since then, the policy has seen few complaints from residents or employees.
IV. In 2008, a coffee shop in Billings, Montana instituted a policy that banned employees from having tattoos that can be seen by customers.
V. When one of the employees refused to wear a long sleeve shirt to cover up, he was told he could no longer work at the coffee shop.
The CORRECT answer is:
A. IV, II, III, I, V   B. V, I, II, IV, III   C. I, II, V, III, IV   D. IV, I, II, V, III

13. I.   Our household might have been described as uncooperative.
    II. When the tide was high, she would be standing on the inlet bridge with her waders on.
    III. Everything was subservient to the disposal of the tides.
    IV. I grew up with buckets, shovels, and nets waiting by the back door.
    V.   When the tide was low, Mom could be found down on the mudflats.
    The CORRECT answer is:
    A. I, V, IV, V, III   B. IV, I, III, V, II   C. V, IV, II, I, III   D. II, IV, I, III, V

13._____

14. I.   A 2012 survey found that over 50% of those polled thought educators were prohibited from teaching about religion.
    II. The result is that many schools and teachers are hesitant to educate students about world religions.
    III. However, for many it is impossible to deny the role that religion plays in history and literature.
    IV. As many people know, the First Amendment guarantees the separation of church and state.
    V.   Ultimately, this is a dilemma that will continue to plague Social Studies and World History educators.
    The CORRECT answer is:
    A. IV, I, III, V, II   B. I, III, V, II, IV   C. IV, III, II, I, V   D. II, III, V, IV, I

14._____

15. I.   The Wampanoag religion was similar to that of the other Algonquin tribes.
    II. They also had spiritual beliefs about animals, and the forest.
    III. Then, they told their stories of the cycle of life and the Great Spirit.
    IV. They expressed their religious beliefs during festivals and at night when they sat at huge campfires.
    V.   In those times, people believed in a Great Spirit and many other things that Nature had a part of the Great Spirit in them.
    The CORRECT answer is:
    A. I, V, II, IV, III   B. V, II, III, I, IV   C. I, II, III, IV, V   D. III, IV, II, V, I

15._____

16. I.   Consumers spend an endless amount of money each year on cutting, lengthening, highlighting and curling hair.
    II. Brunettes want to be blonde, redheads long to be brunettes, and all cringe at the thought of gray hair.
    III. Why is everyone so obsessed with the hair on their heads?
    IV. These thoughts all crossed my mind as I examine the result of my most recent hair adventure.
    V.   The result was not quite what I expected, but I resolved to live with it, as it's my hair and no one else's!
    The CORRECT answer is:
    A. I, IV, V, II, III   B. I, III, II, IV, V   C. IV, I, III, V, II   D. III, I, II, IV, V

16._____

17.
   I. It was only years afterwards that he learned his ancestors were actually accomplished coppersmiths.
   II. He's an old-fashioned current day blacksmith that still practices manipulating metal over hot fires.
   III. This started him on his quest to collect and read any and every book concerning the nature and process of blacksmithing.
   IV. Beginning at age 30, Lee's attraction to metal work lay in creating an object out of such obstinate material such as iron.
   V. While one will probably never read about him in a history book, Mr. Amos Lee contributes mightily to the preservation of America.
   The CORRECT answer is:
   A. II, III, I, IV, V   B. V, II, IV, III, I   C. III, I, V, II, IV   D. I, IV, III, V, II

17.____

18.
   I. After she was stung, she killed the scorpion with a boot, and flushed it down the sink.
   II. My sister once told me about a scorpion that stung her in her bed.
   III. As she recounted her tale of horror, I could only wonder how she remained so calm.
   IV. Later, she realized she should've kept it to figure out what type of scorpion it was.
   V. While she's lucky to be alive, it could've been a deadly scorpion that would've required medical attention immediately.
   The CORRECT answer is:
   A. II, III, I, IV, V   B. II, I, IV, V, III   C. I, IV, II, III, V   D. V, II, III, I, IV

18.____

19.
   I. While the majority of people know this, it was not always the case.
   II. Many laws hold sponsors responsible to participants and courts are full of non-compliance lawsuits on both sides.
   III. Seven months after departure, she arrived at her destination, battered and tired, but the contest sponsors were nowhere to be found.
   IV. For anyone who has ever entered a contest, the rules and disclaimers that go along with each one are well known.
   V. In 1896, a contest motivated a Norwegian immigrant to travel from New York City to the state of Washington.
   The CORRECT answer is:
   A. II, III, V, IV, I   B. V, I, IV, III, II   C. IV, II, I, V, III   D. I, IV, III, II, V

19.____

20.
   I. One thought as to why this happens is due to a person's circadian rhythm being thrown off.
   II. While most people find traveling internationally to be exhilarating, those same people would probably agree that the worst part is the jet lag.
   III. It is considered a sleeping disorder, albeit one that is temporary and not as serious as other sleeping dysfunctions.
   IV. Normally, the body operates on a 24-hour time period in conjunction with the earth's 24-hour cycle of night and day.
   V. When one adds or subtracts time while traveling, a condition known as desynchronosis likely affects them.
   The CORRECT answer is:
   A. I, II, III, IV, V   B. IV, I, III, V, II   C. III, IV, I, II, V   D. II, V, III, I, IV

20.____

21.
I. The consumption rate is due to its ability to create cleaner fuel for electrical power.
II. While cleaner burning fuel is optimal, the usage rate will mean the U.S. only has about a five-year supply of natural gas.
III. Current research studies are showing that Americans use around 20 trillion cubic feet (TCF) on a yearly basis.
IV. It is no wonder, then, that natural gas has become such a controversial and critical topic for politicians, businesses, and consumers.
V. While gasoline is still a crucial energy source, natural gas actually supplies approximately one-fourth of America's energy needs.
The CORRECT answer is:
A. I, IV, II, III, V   B. IV, II, III, V, I   C. V, III, I, II, IV   D. III, V, IV, I, II

21._____

22.
I. Their protection comes from bony plates covered by leathery skin.
II. This desert wanderer has few worries and one can understand why: his "coat" of armor.
III. What would be certain death for most animals, armadillos meander along highway shoulders and remains surprisingly unaffected.
IV. While their shells are not impenetrable, the armadillo can relax knowing that he is safer than many animals who wander the roads of the southwest.
V. While on the smaller side, armadillos are equipped to deal with aggressive and dangerous predators.
The CORRECT answer is:
A. III, II, V, I, IV   B. IV, I, II, V, III   C. I, III, IV, II, V   D. V, IV, I, III, II

22._____

23.
I. Since its discovery in 1930, Pluto has had a troubled history concerning its acceptance as a planet.
II. Anytime there is a controversial topic like this, it is sure to be debated for years to come.
III. Some researchers believe that it is a planet arguing that Pluto is almost 1,000 times bigger than an average comet.
IV. However, others argue that due to its icy composition and irregular orbit, Pluto more likely belongs to the Kuiper Belt, which features sizeable comets.
V. They also argue that any would be planet must be large enough to be pulled into a spherical shape by its own gravity, which like the other eight, Pluto can lay claim to.
The CORRECT answer is:
A. IV, V, I, II, III   B. I, III, V, IV, II   C. III, I, IV, V, II   D. II, IV, V, III, I

23._____

24. I. When I found out I'd be traveling to France, I was so ecstatic.
     II. He told me that studying may be difficult because I will want to meet new friends and see all the landmarks associated with such a beautiful country.
     III. My brother has also been in an exchange before and he had some advice for me.
     IV. Despite his warnings to study hard, I know I would be disappointed if I didn't do any sightseeing at all.
     V. In the fall, I will be participating in a foreign exchange program.
     The CORRECT answer is:
     A. I, V, II, IV, III   B. IV, II, I, III, V   C. III, I, II, IV, IV   D. V, I, III, II, IV

25. I. Well over two hundred years ago, Lewis and Clark set forth on a journey at the request of President Thomas Jefferson.
     II. Their instructions were simple; they needed to find the fastest route across North America.
     III. Throughout it all, including long winters and harsh conditions, the travelers forged west in search of a trade route using only rivers.
     IV. The actual task was much more difficult as it would require them to set a course through dangerous territories replete with hostile natives and ferocious animals.
     V. While land travel ended up being faster, many still credit this group with "breaking through" into the unknown land and launching a movement for westward expansion.
     The CORRECT answer is:
     A. I, II, IV, III, V   B. II, I, III, IV, V   C. V, III, IV, II, I   D. IV, I, III, V, II

KEY (CORRECT ANSWERS)

1.	A	11.	B
2.	B	12.	D
3.	D	13.	B
4.	C	14.	C
5.	D	15.	A
6.	A	16.	D
7.	B	17.	B
8.	C	18.	A
9.	A	19.	C
10.	C	20.	D

21. C
22. A
23. B
24. D
25. A

TEST 2

DIRECTIONS: The sentences listed below are part of a meaningful paragraph, but they are not given in their proper order. You are to decide what would be the BEST order to put sentences to form a well-organized paragraph. Each sentence has a place in the paragraph; there are no extra sentences. *PRINT THE LETTER OF THE CORRECT ANSWER IN THE SPACE AT THE RIGHT.*

1. I. Whenever I start to feel sadness and disgust over a poor hair style, I ask myself why we are so obsessed with the hair on our heads.
    II. The answer always comes to me in a flash.
    III. Soon after this realization, I often cease my crying over how I look.
    IV. It's pure vanity; no other reason explains fully why we worry about how to style, color or cut our follicles.
    V. Instead, I focus on positive, kind thoughts towards myself and others, which usually allows me to overcome any negative feelings I had right after I looked in the mirror.
    The CORRECT answer is:
    A. III, I, V, IV, II   B. I, II, IV, III, V   C. IV, III, II, V, I   D. V, IV, I, II, III

    1.____

2. I. The riverboat director was our captain and our host.
    II. We affectionately watched him with his back toward us, as he stood at the helm, looking toward the sea.
    III. Within all of the Mississippi River, nothing looked nearly as nautical and trustworthy as our pilot as he surveyed the waters before him.
    IV. What we had not realized at the time was that his work was not out there in the estuaries, but rather behind him, within the gloom of the vessel.
    V. We would realize soon enough, however, how difficult the next few days would get, and why he was so ponderous on that ship deck.
    The CORRECT answer is:
    A. III, I, IV, II, V   B. IV, II, III, V, I   C. V, II, I, IV, III   D. I, III, II, IV, V

    2.____

3. I. Ultimately, no new qualities are added to an object, person, or action when it becomes good.
    II. Whenever one examines the word "good", there is always an implied end to be reached.
    III. The good is useful, and it must be used for something.
    IV. However, good is a relative term.
    V. So in that light, whether good is spoken out loud or silently assumed, it is a mental exercise to something else that puts all meaning into it.
    The CORRECT answer is:
    A. V, II, I, IV, III   B. III, I, V, II, IV   C. I, V, IV, III, II   D. II, IV, III, V, I

    3.____

4.
   I. There are specific temperature ranges for petroleum gas, kerosene, oil stocks and also residue.
   II. Called fractional distillation, the oil is heated and drawn off at different points, which leads to the various products.
   III. To start, the oil is heated up to around 600 degrees Celsius, which vaporizes it.
   IV. From there, the vapors cool and condense as they move upwards and eventually turn back into liquid and flows into various tanks.
   V. Crude oil is refined when it is split into different by-products.
   The CORRECT answer is:
   A. II, III, I, V, IV   B. IV, I, IV, III, V   C. V, II, I, III, IV   D. I, IV, II, III, V

5.
   I. With that said, x-ray distortion has more than one use regarding planets.
   II. The higher "bend" in an x-ray would seemingly indicate a larger planet, while lower bending would most likely mean a smaller planet.
   III. Distortion can also help determine how a planet orbits its star.
   IV. Releasing x-rays by distant stars can help reveal the presence of planets orbiting these stars.
   V. The distortion of the x-rays, which is how scientists would tell if planets are near, would be caused by gravitational pull exerted from planets.
   The CORRECT answer is:
   A. IV, V, II, I, III   B. V, IV, III, I, II   C. II, III, I, IV, V   D. I, V, II, III, IV

6.
   I. Some feel that this fact reflects the rise of English as an accepted language of business around the world, and, therefore, that foreign languages are lessening in importance.
   II. Foreign language instruction is dropping in U.S. public high schools.
   III. They feel that this drop is actually a threat to the nation's vitality in what is an ever-increasing multicultural marketplace.
   IV. Others feel that the reduction in language study is a U.S. failure to integrate with the rest of the world.
   V. The question then becomes this, should greater support be given to foreign language programs in U.S. public schools?
   The CORRECT answer is:
   A. V, IV, III, I, II   B. III, IV, V, II, I   C. II, I, IV, III, V   D. IV, II, III, V, I

7.
   I. The owner, Nate, still runs the joint, which means it doesn't usually close until he's served the last customer.
   II. The alley might dissuade visitors from finding this local gem, but if one can get past the masking tape and yellowing paint that line the door, they will be in for a real treat.
   III. The Shack, as the locals call it, is located in a nondescript alley across from beautiful City Park.
   IV. While I'd love for Nate to get more publicity, I'm just fine with knowing that the Shack will have a short line and a great ambience each time I stop in.
   V. Nathan's Crab Shack serves up some of the best sandwiches I've ever eaten.
   The CORRECT answer is:
   A. III, II, V, IV, I   B. I, IV, II, III, V   C. II, V, I, IV, III   D. V, I, III, II, IV

8.
   I. All activity halted, however, at the onset of World War II, so construction did not officially begin until the early 1950s.
   II. In total, it took almost three years to build, cost five men their lives, and cost the state of Michigan more than $40 million.
   III. In the 1930's, the Mackinac Bridge Authority sought funding from the federal government to construct a bridge.
   IV. Even though they were denied, the MBA plotted a route and studied the lake bed and rock below.
   V. Despite numerous setbacks, the Mackinac Bridge opened to traffic on November 1, 1957, and for years it was the longest suspension bridge in the world.
   The CORRECT answer is:
   A. II, I, V, IV, III   B. III, IV, I, II, V   C. V, III, IV, I, II   D. I, II, III, V, IV

8.____

9.
   I. It also teaches them to bargain and trade for cards to complete their sets.
   II. Collecting cards is a rewarding experience not only for kids, but also adults.
   III. It teaches important skills, such as patience and organization.
   IV. Lastly, card collecting is a social activity that encourages the old and the young to swap stories, cards, and knowledge in a fun and engaging way.
   V. For younger collectors, it enhances fine motor skills such as developing a more careful touch.
   The CORRECT answer is:
   A. III, IV, I, II, V   B. II, V, III, IV, I   C. I, II, V, III, IV   D. II, III, V, I, IV

9.____

10.
   I. Spyware can cripple unsecured computers and data around the world.
   II. Even when computer users experience program crashes and warnings about missing system files, they tend to wait until these problems get too ad to manage.
   III. Sometimes it is used for marketing agencies, but just as often there is a more malicious intent behind spyware stored on an unsecured computer.
   IV. Much of the time, the cause of these problems rests with the biggest online threat there is: spyware.
   V. While most people do not realize it, those who use a personal computer to connect to the internet expose themselves to many risks.
   The CORRECT answer is:
   A. II, IV, V, III, I   B. V, II, IV, I, III   C. III, II, I, IV, V   D. V, IV, I, II, III

10.____

11.
   I. When people have parties at their homes, Susan cooks for them, and she is a fabulous cook.
   II. My friend, Susan, owns her own catering business.
   III. Once everything has been planned, Susan will hire servers to wait on the people.
   IV. One of the things that makes her so good is that she asks the customer lots of questions like how many people will be there and what food the customer would like to serve.
   V. All in all, she loves the work involved with her catering business and it does not hurt that she's really good at it.

11.____

The CORRECT answer is:
A. II, I, IV, III, V   B. I, III, V, II, IV   C. IV, II, I, III, V   D. V, IV, I, III, II

12.
I. "To be, or not to be...." is an extremely well-known phrase that has been the source of both mystery and wonderment since the turn of the 16th century.
II. Where did it come from and what does it mean?
III. As for the meaning of the phrase, a complete answer would necessitate a deeper, more comprehensive look into Shakespeare culture and nuance.
IV. The first question is easy enough to answer: from Shakespeare's famous play, *Hamlet*.
V. The issue, however, is that despite the fact that everyone knows the phrase, few actually know the context of this well-worn saying.
The CORRECT answer is:
A. V, I, III, II, IV   B. II, III, IV, V, I   C. I, V, II, IV, III   D. IV, II, I, III, V

12.____

13.
I. For example, it was recently discovered that we were connected to a Civil War ancestor that we previously had not known about.
II. He maintains the records of births, deaths, marriages, and even divorces, and he takes the job very seriously.
III. This ancestor bestowed his beautiful and antique furniture to his children, who then passed the items down to their descendants.
IV. My Uncle Mike is the genealogist of our family.
V. In fact, he will even send out letters to our family whenever something noteworthy occurs.
The CORRECT answer is:
A. II, III, I, IV, V   B. V, IV, II, III, I   C. I, II, IV, V, III   D. IV, II, V, I, III

13.____

14.
I. He was part of a team that performed complicated experiments during the 1940s.
II. However, he is most likely known for his creation of "Murphy's Law."
III. While many Americans do not know the name Edward Murphy, they owe a considerable debt to this member of the Air Force.
IV. This somewhat funny observation has actually inspired similar "laws" such as Hofstadter's Law.
V. This "law" states that "if anything can go wrong, it will."
The CORRECT answer is:
A. I, III, V, II, IV   B. III, IV, V, I, II   C. III, I, II, V, IV   D. V, II, IV, I, III

14.____

15.
I. During winter months, its white coat is ideal to camouflage and the insulation provided by its unbeatable fur lining allows the fox to hunt all winter long.
II. While this strategy could be fruitful, it also carries risk because of the possibility that the polar bear might consume the fox if it catches it.
III. One of the Snow Fox's unique traits is the ability to adapt to extreme weather conditions.

15.____

IV. When food becomes scarce, the Arctic fox can follow polar bears as they attack seals on the sea ice.
V. Often referred to as the "Snow Fox," the Arctic fox is comparable in size to a domestic cat.
The CORRECT answer is:
A. V, III, I, IV, II   B. II, IV, III, I, V   C. III, I, V, II, IV   D. IV, III, II, V, I

16.
I. The venerable professor, aged 85, encouraged his audience to show compassion for the poor and homeless in the city.
II. Students flocked to hear the returning professor, Dr. Willis, give a speech.
III. He abhors opulence and urges people to be charitable through frugality.
IV. Dr. Willis, a kind and empathetic activist for the poor, spoke to a full auditorium on Tuesday.
V. Much of his work is due to his personal memories stemming from the Great Depression.
The CORRECT answer is:
A. I, II, III, IV, V   B. V, IV, III, II, I   C. III, I, IV, II, V   D. II, IV, I, V, III

16._____

17.
I. As some of his friends have noted, this antisocial attitude is an aberration for him, as he is normally quite extroverted and cheerful.
II. Many people have tried to evoke some of his normal geniality, but it has not worked, which is disconcerting.
III. It is now a commonly held belief that the only antidote to Johnny's stressful situation would be complete and total success on his exam.
IV. Upon learning of his pending exam, his roommates have agreed that his current mood is directly correlated to the test.
V. Upon being informed of an upcoming test in statistics, Johnny has started to act aloof and uninterested in social activities.
The CORRECT answer is:
A. I, V, II, III, IV   B. IV, III, I, V, II   C. II, IV, I, III, V   D. V, I, IV, II, III

17._____

18.
I. When viewing a star formation through the Spitzer Space Telescope, a person has a view of disruption.
II. The Spitzer Space Telescope challenges the commonly held thought that smooth gas clouds gracefully facilitate the creation of new stars.
III. The relative few stars can be attributed to the turbulence that these processes bring to the heavens.
IV. Through the telescope's lens, one can see the creation of a star that disrupts nearby space.
V. Recent models of star formation, aided by telescopes like Spitzer, recognize that stars interact with one another in their stellar neighborhood.
The CORRECT answer is:
A. IV, II, I, III, V   B. I, IV, II, V, III   C. III, I, V, IV, II   D. II, V, III, I, IV

18._____

19.
I. In addition, models predicting the placement of electrons within the cloud describe one probability among many, instead of showing planet-like electrons orbiting a sun-like nucleus.
II. Although the majority of us think of an atom's nucleus being orbited by electrons, the reality differs considerably from the stereotypical depiction.
III. Oddly enough, it is mostly composed of empty space: its nucleus, made of protons and neutrons, makes up only about a billionth of the atom itself.
IV. As many people know, the atom is the basic building block of matter.
V. Researchers prefer to describe the electron movement as a "wave-pattern cloud."

The CORRECT answer is:
A. III, I, V, IV, II   B. V, III, IV, I, II   C. IV, III, II, V, I   D. II, V, I, III, IV

20.
I. These buildings were thought to have been constructed upwards in order to thwart would-be attackers.
II. Ancient Yemeni architects created a walled city that they called Shibam.
III. Nowadays, with the planning of mile-high skyscrapers planned for construction, Shibam does not seem as impressive, but given their tools and knowledge at the time, the city will be held in esteem in architecturfal history books.
IV. This wonder of the old world is now dubbed "Manhattan of the Desert".
V. The city was composed of 500 buildings, ranging from five to eight stories high.

The CORRECT answer is:
A. II, IV, V, I, III   B. V, III, I, IV, II   C. IV, V, II, III, I   D. III, I, IV, II, V

21.
I. Almost 2,000 years after being buried by falling ash from a volcanic eruption, the residents of Pompeii do reveal fascinating details about daily life in the Roman Empire.
II. Pompeii's population, roughly 20,000 inhabitants, practiced several different religions.
III. This is evidenced by temples dedicated to Egyptian gods, as well as Jewish temples and worshippers of Cybele.
IV. While radically different in beliefs, Pompeii's citizens practiced all of these religions in peaceful co-existence with followers of the state religion.
V. These people worshipped Jupiter and the Roman emperor.

The CORRECT answer is:
A. I, III, V, II, IV   B. II, IV, I, III, V   C. IV, I, III, V, II   D. III, II, IV, I, V

22.
   I. Instead of driving there, I may just stay home and cook myself a big breakfast with toast, fruit, eggs, and bacon.
   II. I was going to take a jog around the neighborhood to train for my race.
   III. As I woke up today, I realized that it would be yet another rainy day.
   IV. Now, I will have to drive to the gymnasium that is on the opposite side of town.
   V. After I eat, hopefully the rain will have gone away so I can train successfully.
   The CORRECT answer is:
   A. IV, I, II, V, III   B. III, II, IV, I, V   C. II, IV, I, III, V   D. V, III, II, I, IV

23.
   I. Yesterday, he received a call from an H.R. representative of a firm in Chicago.
   II. The H.R. rep asked William to fly out to Chicago for an interview and he even offered to pay for William's plane ticket.
   III. Having received such a generous offer, William could not say no to the interview.
   IV. The interview will take place in one week, so William will spend the next few days researching the company's history.
   V. William has been searching for a full-time job for the last few months.
   The CORRECT answer is:
   A. IV, II, III, I, V   B. V, II, I, IV, III   C. I, II, III, IV, V   D. V, I, II, III, IV

24.
   I. I wonder when I'll feel well enough to go back to work.
   II. I've tried eating chicken soup, drinking orange juice, taking Benadryl since the weekend.
   III. I finally decided to visit the doctor to see if I can get any stronger medicine to help me.
   IV. My allergies have been terrible the last several days.
   V. I've been blowing my nose, sneezing, and coughing the entire time.
   The CORRECT answer is:
   A. V, II, IV, III, I   B. I, III, II, IV, V   C. IV, V, II, III, I   D. II, III, V, I, IV

25.
   I. Myrta is a sophomore in college and she's working on her degree in Special Education.
   II. In order to prepare herself for her career, she works at a camp in the summer.
   III. All of the children who attend this camp have physical and mental disabilities.
   IV. Myrta helps the kids get exercise and increase their social skills.
   V. At the end of each summer, she cannot wait to start her career in Special Education.
   The CORRECT answer is:
   A. V, I, II, III, IV   B. I, II, III, IV, V   C. III, IV, V, I, II   D. V, IV, III, II, I

KEY (CORRECT ANSWERS)

1. B
2. A
3. D
4. C
5. A

6. C
7. D
8. B
9. D
10. B

11. A
12. C
13. D
14. C
15. A

16. D
17. D
18. B
19. C
20. A

21. A
22. B
23. D
24. C
25. B

PREPARING WRITTEN MATERIAL
PARAGRAPH REARRANGEMENT

EXAMINATION SECTION
TEST 1

DIRECTIONS: The sentences listed below are part of a meaningful paragraph, but they are not given in their proper order. You are to decide what would be the BEST order to put sentences to form a well-organized paragraph. Each sentence has a place in the paragraph; there are no extra sentences. *PRINT THE LETTER OF THE CORRECT ANSWER IN THE SPACE AT THE RIGHT.*

Questions 1-3.

DIRECTIONS: Questions 1 through 3 are to be answered on the basis of the following paragraph.

The CDC estimates that food-borne pathogens cause approximately 48 million illnesses, 3,000 deaths, and 128,000 hospitalizations in the United States each year. Contamination with disease-causing microbes called pathogens is usually due to improper food handling or storage. Other causes of food-borne diseases are toxic chemicals or other harmful substances in food and beverages. Food-borne diseases are illnesses caused when people consume contaminated food or beverages. More than 250 food-borne illnesses have been described, according to the United States Centers for Disease Control and Prevention (CDC).

1. When the five sentences are arranged in proper order, the paragraph starts with the sentence that begins:
   A. "Food-borne diseases..."
   B. "More than 250..."
   C. "Other causes of..."
   D. The CDC estimates..."

2. If the above paragraph were correctly organized, which of the following transition words would be appropriate to place at the beginning of the sentence that starts "The CDC estimates..."?
   A. With that said
   B. However
   C. To start off
   D. Ultimately

3. When the above paragraph is properly arranged, it ends with the words:
   A. "...Disease Control and Prevention (CDC).
   B. "...improper food handling or storage."
   C. "...United States each year."
   D. "...in food and beverages."

Questions 4-7.

DIRECTIONS: Questions 4 through 7 are to be answered on the basis of the following passage.

107

Her father, Abraham Quintanilla, who worked in the shipping department of a chemical plant and later opened a restaurant, had fronted a moderately successful band called Los Dinos ("The Guys") as a young man. Among them, her murder evoked an outpouring of grief comparable to that experienced by other Americans after the deaths of such major cultural figures as President John F. Kennedy. Selena had become an icon in the Hispanic community.

Selena Quintanilla was born in Lake Jackson, Texas, near Houston, on April 16, 1971. She had turned into a beloved figure to whom Mexican-Americans attached their aspirations and their feelings about their cultural identities. The violent death of beloved Tejano vocalist Selena on Mach 31, 1995 brought to an end more than just a promising musical career.

4. When arranged properly, the paragraph's opening sentence should start with: 4.____
   A. "Among them…"   B. "The violent death…"
   C. "Her father, Abraham…"   D. "Selena had become…"

5. In the second sentence listed above, "them" refers to 5.____
   A. Selena and her fans   B. other non-Mexican Americans
   C. Selena and John F. Kennedy   D. Mexican-Americans

6. After correctly organizing the paragraph, the author decides to split it into two separate paragraphs. Which of the following would begin the newly made second paragraph? 6.____
   A. "Selena had become…"   B. "Selena Quintanilla was…"
   C. "The violent death…"   D. "Her father, Abraham…"

7. When correctly organized, the final sentence of the paragraph should end end with the words: 7.____
   A. "…as a young man."   B. "…on April 16, 1971."
   C. "…in the Hispanic community."   D. "…a promising music career."

Questions 8-10.

DIRECTIONS: Questions 8 through 10 are to be answered on the basis of the following paragraph.

Whether Death takes the form of a decrepit old man, a grim reaper, or a ferryman, his visit is almost never welcome by the poor mortal who finds him at the door. Such is not the case in "Because I Could Not Stop for Death." Knowing that the woman has been keeping herself too busy in her daily life to remember Death, he "kindly" comes by to get her. Perhaps Dickinson's most famous work, "Because I Could Not Stop for Death" is generally considered to be one of the great masterpieces of American poetry. Here, Death is a gentleman, perhaps handsome and well-groomed, who makes a call at the home of a naïve young woman. The poem begins with a comment upon Death's politeness, although he surprises the woman with his visit. While most people would try to bar the door once they recognized his identity, this woman gives the impression that she is quite flattered to find herself in even this gentleman's favor. Death is personified, or described in terms of human characteristics, throughout literature. Figuratively speaking, this poem is about one woman's "date with death." Dickinson uses the personification of Death as a metaphor throughout the poem.

8. Which of the following sentence beginnings indicate the opening sentence of this paragraph?
   A. "Perhaps Dickinson's most…"
   B. "The poem begins with…"
   C. "Death is personified…"
   D. "Whether Death takes…"

   8.____

9. To whom does "his" refer to in the sentence that starts "While most people would…"?
   A. A gentleman
   B. Death
   C. People trying to avoid death
   D. Ms. Dickinson

   9.____

10. If the paragraph were correctly organized, the second to last sentence would end with:
    A. "…gentleman's favor."
    B. "…a naive young woman."
    C. "…of American poetry."
    D. "…throughout literature."

    10.____

Questions 11-13.

DIRECTIONS: Questions 11 through 13 are to be answered on the basis of the following paragraph.

Reformers such as Jacob Riis, author of *The Children of the Tenements* (1903), and George Creel, who with the assistance of Denver's juvenile court judge, Ben Lindsey, wrote *Children in Bondage* (1913), helped broaden awareness of the conditions under which many of the nation's poor children were reared. At the same time, changes were taking place in the way the childhood years were perceived. More and more Americans began to regard children as a national resource that deserved society's protection and guidance. In sharp contrast to these images of child workers worn down by the toil of their labor were the children of the middle class, who led quite different lives and whose progress was measured not in industrial output, but in ways increasingly seen as being vital to their development as productive citizens. Exhibitions of photographs of children employed in all sorts of economic pursuits, including those considered among the most dangerous and grueling, proved equally successful in pricking the public's conscience. When the United States was a nation of farms, shops, and small mills, the use of children to supplement a family's income was so common that it attracted little notice and even less concern. The nation's rapid and dramatic transformation into an industrialized society, however, changed the environment in which children labored and the conditions to which they were exposed.

11. When organized correctly, the third sentence in the above paragraph would start:
    A. "The nation's rapid…"
    B. "In sharp contrast…"
    C. "At the same time…"
    D. "Exhibitions of photographs…"

    11.____

12. If the author wanted to change the beginning of the topic sentence for this paragraph to "In the past," they would need to change which of the following?
    A. "Reformers such as…"
    B. "Exhibitions of photographs…"
    C. "More and more Americans…"
    D. "When the United States…"

    12.____

13. If the above paragraph was organized correctly, its ending words of the last sentence would be:

    13.____

A. "...as productive citizens."
B. "...and even less concern."
C. "...in pricking the public's conscience."
D. "...poor children were reared."

Questions 14-16.

DIRECTIONS: Questions 14 through 16 are to be answered on the basis of the following paragraph.

Here we outline a unique bivariate flood hazard assessment framework that accounts for the interactions between a primary oceanic flooding hazard, coastal water level, and fluvial flooding hazards. Common flood hazard assessment practices typically focus on one flood driver at a time and ignore potential compounding impacts. The results show that, in a warming climate, future sea level rise not only increases the failure probability, but also exacerbates the compounding effects of flood drivers. Using the notion of "failure probability," we also assess coastal flood hazard under different future sea level rise scenarios. Population and assets in coastal regions are threatened by both oceanic and fluvial flooding hazards.

14. When the sentences above are organized correctly, the paragraph starts with the sentence that begins:
    A. "The results show..."
    B. "Here we outline..."
    C. "Population and assets..."
    D. "Using the notion..."

14._____

15. If the author wanted to add the phrase "To sum up" to the above paragraph, he would insert it in front of the sentence that begins:
    A. "Using the notion..."
    B. "Common flood hazard..."
    C. "Here we outline..."
    D. "The results show..."

15._____

16. Assuming the paragraph were organized correctly, the second to last sentence would end:
    A. "...of flood drivers."
    B. "...level rise scenarios."
    C. "...fluvial flooding hazards."
    D. "...compounding impacts."

16._____

Questions 17-19.

DIRECTIONS: Questions 17 through 19 are to be answered on the basis of the following paragraph.

The adhesive stuck to a pig heart even when the surface was coated in blood, the team reported in the July 28 Science. Li, who did the research while at Harvard University, and colleagues also tested the glue in live rats with liver lacerations. A solution might be found under wet leaves on a forest floor, recent research suggests. For surgeons closing internal incisions, that's more than an annoyance. The right glue could hold wounds together as effectively as stitches and staples with less damage to the surrounding soft tissue, enabling safer surgical procedures. It stopped the rats' bleeding, and the animals didn't appear to suffer any bad reaction from the adhesive. Finding a great glue is a sticky task — especially if you want to attach to something as slick as the inside of the human body. Jianyu Li of McGill University in Montreal and colleagues have created a surgical glue that mimics the chemical recipe of goopy slime that slugs exude when they're startled. Using the glue to plug a hole in the pig heart worked so well that the heart still held in liquid after being inflated and deflated tens of thousands of times. Even the strongest human-made adhesives don't work well on wet surfaces like tissues and organs.

17. The above paragraph, when organized correctly, should begin with the words: 17._____
    A. "Finding a great..."   B. "Using the glue..."
    C. "The adhesive stuck..."   D. "It stopped the rats..."

18. If the author wanted to split the paragraph into two separate paragraphs, the 18._____
    first sentence of the second paragraph would begin:
    A. "For surgeons closing..."   B. "Even the strongest..."
    C. "A solution might be..."   D. "Jianyu Li of McGill..."

19. If the above paragraph were organized correctly, the final sentence would 19._____
    end with:
    A. "...recent research suggests."   B. "...from the adhesive."
    C. "...like tissues and organs."   D. "...thousands of times."

Questions 20-22.

DIRECTIONS: Questions 20 to 22 are to be answered on the basis of the following paragraph.

The signal from the spacecraft is gone, and within the next 45 seconds, so will be the spacecraft," Cassini project manager Earl Maize announced from the mission control center at NASA's Jet Propulsion Lab. The signal that Cassini had reached its destination arrived at Earth at 4:54 A.M., and cut out about a minute later as the spacecraft lost its battle with Saturn's atmosphere. I'm going to call this the end of mission. Project manager, off the net." With that, the mission control team erupted in applause, hugs and some tears. This has been an incredible mission, an incredible spacecraft, and you're all an incredible team. The spacecraft entered Saturn's atmosphere at about 3:31 A.M. PDT on September 15 and immediately began running through all of its stabilizing procedures to try to keep itself upright. Cassini went down fighting. After 20 years in space and 13 years orbiting Saturn, the veteran spacecraft spent its last 90 seconds or so firing its thrusters as hard as it could to keep sending Saturnian secrets back to Earth for as long as possible.

20. In the above paragraph, who does "you all" refer to in the sentence that begins 20._____
    "Congratulations"?
    A. All Americans   B. Cassini
    C. Earl Maize   D. The mission control team

21. If the sentence were organized correctly, the fourth sentence's last words 21._____
    would be:
    A. "...as long as possible."   B. "...this amazing accomplishment."
    C. "...Saturn's atmosphere."   D. "...off the net."

22. When organized correctly, the final sentence would end with the following: 22._____
    A. "...and some tears."   B. "...went down fighting."
    C. "...Jet Propulsion Lab."   D. "...keep itself upright."

Questions 23-25.

DIRECTIONS: Questions 23 through 25 are to be answered on the basis of the following paragraph.

As the first African-American woman to carry mail, she stood out on the trail — and became a Wild West legend. Born Mary Fields in around 1832, Fields was born into slavery, and like many other enslaved people, her exact date of birth is not known. Rumor had it that she'd fending off an angry pack of wolves with her rifle, had "the temperament of a grizzly bear," and was not above a gunfight. Bandits beware: In 1890s Montana, would-be mail thieves didn't stand a chance against Stagecoach Mary. Even the place of her birth is questionable, though historians have pinpointed Hickman County, Tennessee as the most likely location. At the time, slaves were treated like pieces of property; their numbers were recorded in record books, their names were not. But how much of Stagecoach Mary's story is myth? The hard-drinking, quick-shooting mail carrier sported two guns, men's clothing, and a bad attitude.

23. Who does "she'd" refer to in the sentence that begins "Rumor had it..."? 23.____
    A. An anonymous African-American   B. Hickman County
    C. A mail thief   D. Stagecoach Mary

24. If the author were interested in splitting this paragraph into two separate paragraphs, the topic sentence of the second paragraph would begin: 24.____
    A. "At the time…"   B. "Born Mary Fields…"
    C. "Bandits beware…"   D. "As the first…"

25. When organized correctly, the final sentence of the paragraph would end with the words: 25.____
    A. "…their names were not."   B. "…above a gunfight."
    C. "…against Stagecoach Mary."   D. "…a Wild West legend."

KEY (CORRECT ANSWERS)

1.	A	11.	C
2.	D	12.	D
3.	C	13.	A
4.	B	14.	C
5.	D	15.	D
6.	B	16.	B
7.	A	17.	A
8.	C	18.	C
9.	B	19.	B
10.	A	20.	D
21.	C		
22.	A		
23.	D		
24.	B		
25.	A		

TEST 2

DIRECTIONS: Each question or incomplete statement is followed by several suggested answers or completions. Select the one that BEST answers the question or completes the statement. *PRINT THE LETTER OF THE CORRECT ANSWER IN THE SPACE AT THE RIGHT.*

Questions 1-3.

DIRECTIONS: Questions 1 through 3 are to be answered on the basis of the following paragraph.

The majority of people who develop these issues are athletes who participate in popular high-impact sports, especially football. Although most people who suffer a concussion experience initial bouts of dizziness, nausea, and drowsiness, these symptoms often disappear after a few days. Although both new sports regulations and improvements in helmet technology can help protect players, the sports media and fans alike bear some of the responsibility for reducing the incidence of these devastating injuries. These psychological problems can include depression, anxiety, memory loss, inability to concentrate, and aggression. In extreme cases, people suffering from CTE have even committed suicide or homicide. The long-term effects of concussions, however, are less understood and far more severe. Recent studies suggest that people who suffer multiple concussions are at a significant risk for developing chronic traumatic encephalopathy (CTE), a degenerative brain disorder that causes a variety of dangerous mental and emotional problems to arise weeks, months, or even years after the initial injury. Chronic Traumatic Encephalopathy Concussions are brain injuries that occur when a person receives a blow to the head, face, or neck.

1. When organized correctly, the first sentence of the paragraph begins with: 1._____
   A. "Recent studies suggest…" B. "The long-term effects…"
   C. "Although both new…" D. "Chronic Traumatic…"

2. Upon ordering the paragraph correctly, the author wishes to substitute for a word in sentence four that means "progressive irreversible deterioration." Which word does the author wish to replace? 2._____
   A. Anxiety B. Degenerative
   C. Responsibility D. Devastating

3. If put in the right order, the paragraph's last words would be: 3._____
   A. "…to the head, face, or neck."
   B. "…committed suicide or homicide."
   C. "…these devastating injuries."
   D. "…far more severe."

Questions 4-8.

DIRECTIONS: Questions 4 through 8 are to be answered on the basis of the following paragraph.

These controversies were settled by the 1977 treaty, which provided for a twenty-two-year period of U.S. withdrawal and turnover of the canal to Panama. For its first 85 years the canal was operate exclusively by the United States government as an international maritime passage, according to the 1903 Hay-Buneau-Varilla Treaty and the 1977 Carter-Torrijos Treaty that replaced it. Panamanian and other critics pointed out that the United States took unfair advantage of the newly independent republic (separated from Colombia in 1903, with the help of the United States) to impose conditions for near-sovereign ownership; complained that it exceeded its original concession by creating a strategic military complex with fourteen bases and numerous intelligence sites; and asserted that it created a virtual state within a state by establishing public agencies and enterprises in the 500-plus square miles of territory it controlled in the Canal Zone. One of the world's great engineering projects, the canal was controversial because of the method by which the United States gained the concession (by negotiating a treaty with a French shareholder temporarily representing Panama) and its operation of the utility with regard to the interests of Panama. Built between 1904 and 1914, the canal shortened maritime voyages considerably. The Panama Canal is a 51-mile ship canal with six pairs of locks that crosses the Isthmus of Panama and allows vessels to transit between the Caribbean Sea and the Pacific Ocean. Under the latter treaty, the canal was turned over in 1999 to the Republic of Panama, which has operated it ever since.

4. When organized correctly, the sentence AFTERs the topic sentence should begin:
    A. "Built between 1904..." B. "The Panama Canal..."
    C. "These controversies..." D. "Panamanian and other..."

5. If the author ordered the sentences correctly, one sentence that provides evidence of controversy surrounding the Panama Canal would be Sentence
    A. 7 B. 5 C. 1 D. 2

6. When correctly ordered, the last words of the paragraph would be:
    A. "...the canal to Panama." B. "...in the Canal Zone."
    C. "...and the Pacific Ocean." D. "...to the interests of Panama."

7. What "latter treaty" is the sentence that begins "Under the latter treaty..." referring to in the paragraph?
    A. The Treaty of Panama B. The Hay-Buneau-Varilla Treaty
    C. The Carter-Torrijos Treaty D. Both B and C

8. When organized correctly, the sentence that ends "...in the Canal Zone" would be preceded by the sentence that begins:
    A. "The Panama Canal..." B. "These controversies were..."
    C. "For its first..." D. "One of the world's great..."

Questions 9-11.

DIRECTIONS: Questions 9 through 11 are to be answered on the basis of the following paragraph.

Such incidents revolved around many issues, including, among others, job security, wages, occupational safety, and, especially, the eight-hour day. The Haymarket Riot of 1886 grew out of a long string of circumstances that eventually culminated in an unfortunate incident. Not only were skilled craftsmen seeing their professions disappear in the face of machines operated by unskilled labor, but the length of hours in the workday lengthened and could range from ten to twelve and even longer in some specific instances. It was this last issue that was particularly important as the Industrial Revolution truly swept over America. Regardless of who might have been at fault in a labor struggle, each moment of violent upheaval had serious consequences. During the post-Civil War era, there were periods of labor upheaval both in Chicago and across the nation. Each of these topics played an important role in labor unrest as the climate in the country between workers and the state reached fever pitch. At issue were several key points: the continued growth of the Industrial Revolution and its impact on society, the movement for the eight-hour workday, worker dissatisfaction, suppression of labor activities by various government authorities, and the growth of radicalism in the United States.

9. If the author were to put the paragraph in the correct order, the third sentence would begin with the words:
   A. "Each of these..."
   B. "It was this last..."
   C. "Not only were skilled..."
   D. "The Haymarket Riot..."

10. The author has determined that one paragraph is too long, so they wish to split it into two paragraphs and change the start of the new paragraph to "Dating back to". The sentence that the author would need to alter slightly currently begins:
    A. "The Haymarket Riot..."
    B. "Each of these topics..."
    C. "During the post-Civil..."
    D. "Not only were..."

11. When organized correctly, the last sentence of the paragraph would end with the words:
    A. "...an unfortunate incident."
    B. "...some specific instances."
    C. "...in the United States."
    D. "...across the nation."

Questions 12-14.

DIRECTIONS: Questions 12 through 14 are to be answered on the basis of the following paragraph.

Using an experimental design, they find no evidence that the use of Twitter improves students' learning. The authors assess students across three different institutions to see if the use of Twitter improves learning outcomes relative to a traditional Learning Management System. Ever since Becker and Watts (1996) found that economic educators rely heavily on "chalk and talk" as a primary teaching method, economic educators have been seeking new ways to engage students and improve learning outcomes. Recently, the use of social media as a pedagogical tool in economics has received increasing interest.

12. When organized correctly, the paragraph would begin with the words:
    A. "Using an..." B. "Recently, the..."
    C. "The authors..." D. "Ever since..."

13. In the sentence that begins "Using an experimental...", to whom does "they" refer?
    A. Social media users B. Becker and Watts
    C. Economic educators D. Different institutions

14. If the author wanted to start the last sentence with "With that said...", they would be adding it to the sentence that currently starts:
    A. "Using an..." B. "The authors..."
    C. "Recently, the..." D. "Ever since..."

Questions 15-17.

DIRECTIONS: Questions 15 through 17 are to be answered on the basis of the following paragraph.

Teaching the topic of genetics in relationship to ancestry and race generates many questions, and requires a teaching strategy that encourages perspective-based exploration and discussion. We have developed a set of dialogues for discussing the complex science of genetics, ancestry, and race that is contextualized in real human interactions and that contends with the social and ethical implications of this science. This article provides some brief historical and scientific context for these dialogues, describes their development, and relates how we have used them in different ways to engage diverse groups of science learners. The dialogue series can be incorporated into classroom or informal science education settings. After listening to or performing the dialogues and participating in a discussion, students will: (1) recognize misunderstandings about the relationship between DNA and race; (2) describe how DNA testing services assign geographic ancestry; (3) explain how scientific findings have been used historically to promote institutionalized racism and the role personal biases can play in science; (4) identify situations in their own life that have affected their understanding of genetics and race; and (5) discuss the potential consequences of the racialization of medicine as well as other fallacies about the connection of science and race.

15. If the author organized the above paragraph correctly, the fourth sentence would end with the words:
    A. "...connection of science and race."
    B. "...implications of this science."
    C. "...exploration and discussion."
    D. "...science education settings."

16. The author wishes to split the paragraph into two distinct paragraphs. When organized, the last sentence of the first paragraph would begin:
    A. "We have developed..." B. "This article proves..."
    C. "The dialogue series..." D. "Teaching the topic..."

17. When organized correctly, the last sentence would begin with the words: 17.____
    A. "After listening to…" B. "Teaching the topic…"
    C. "We have developed…" D. "This article provides…"

Questions 18-20.

DIRECTIONS: Questions 18 through 20 are to be answered on the basis of the following paragraph.

For example, Canadian Immigration officers have the power to deny persons with OWI convictions from crossing the border into Canada. Individuals who have been acquitted of an OWI can still be stopped at the border and denied entry. Some restrictions, however, are not known to individuals that have been charged with an OWI. In fact, if you have been arrested or convicted for driving under the influence of drugs or alcohol, regardless of whether it was a felony or a misdemeanor, you may be criminally inadmissible to Canada or denied entry. In order to receive an eTA, individuals have to disclose their criminal convictions, which may bar them from entering Canada. The restrictions imposed by an OWI conviction can be quite burdensome. Even if you will not be driving in Canada, you can still be denied entry. This stringent border patrol comes as a surprise to many U.S. citizens. Canadian Immigration Officials have introduced a new entry requirement, known as an Electronic Travel Authorization (eTA).

18. When organized correctly, the topic sentence of the paragraph would begin with 18.____
    the words:
    A. "This stringent border…" B. "In fact, if…"
    C. "Canadian Immigration Officials…" D. "The restrictions imposed…"

19. Once properly ordered, it would make the most sense to insert the words 19.____
    "With that being the case…" in front of the sentence that currently begins:
    A. "The restrictions imposed…" B. "For example…"
    C. "Canadian Immigration Officials…" D. "Even if you will…"

20. If the author were to put the paragraph in correct order, the second to last 20.____
    sentence would end with the words:
    A. "…border into Canada." B. "…from entering Canada."
    C. "…to many U.S. citizens." D. "…to Canada or denied entry."

Questions 21-25.

DIRECTIONS: Questions 21 through 25 are to be answered on the basis of the following paragraph.

Many instructors at the college level require that you use scholarly articles as sources when writing a research paper. Scholarly or peer-reviewed articles are written by experts in academic or professional fields. They are excellent sources for finding out what has been studied or researched on a topic as well as to find bibliographies that point to other relevant sources of information. Peer-reviewed journals require that articles are read and evaluated by experts in the field before they are accepted for publication. Although most scholarly articles are refereed or peer reviewed, some are not. Generally, instructors are happy with either peer-reviewed or scholarly articles, but if your article HAS to be peer-reviewed, you will need to find that information in the front of the journal, or use Ulrich's Periodicals Directory (Reference Z6941 U5) located behind the Reference Desk on the 2nd floor of the library. Look up your title and look for the Document Type: Journal, Academic/Scholarly. Articles that are peer-reviewed will have an arrow to the left of the title.

21. When organized correctly, the introductory sentence would begin with the words:
    A. "They are excellent…"
    B. "Peer-reviewed journals…"
    C. "Many instructors at…"
    D. "Look up your…"

    21.____

22. In the sentence that begins "They are", to what/whom does "They" refer?
    A. Scholarly articles
    B. Instructors
    C. Peers
    D. Library directory

    22.____

23. If the author were interested in splitting up the paragraph into two separate paragraphs, the topic sentence of the second paragraph would begin:
    A. "Many instructors at…"
    B. "Peer-reviewed journals…"
    C. "Generally instructors are…"
    D. "Scholarly or peer-reviewed…"

    23.____

24. When organized correctly, the third sentence of the paragraph would end with the words:
    A. "…a research paper."
    B. "…of the title."
    C. "…of the library."
    D. "…sources of information."

    24.____

25. If the author were to organize the paragraph correctly, the paragraph would end with the words:
    A. "…some are not."
    B. "…a research paper."
    C. "…or professional fields."
    D. "…of the title."

    25.____

KEY (CORRECT ANSWERS)

1. D
2. B
3. C
4. A
5. B

6. A
7. C
8. D
9. A
10. C

11. B
12. D
13. B
14. A
15. D

16. C
17. A
18. D
19. C
20. B

21. C
22. A
23. B
24. D
25. D

PHILOSOPHY, PRINCIPLES, PRACTICES, AND TECHNICS OF SUPERVISION, ADMINISTRATION, MANAGEMENT, AND ORGANIZATION

TABLE OF CONTENTS

	Page
MEANING OF SUPERVISION	1
THE OLD AND THE NEW SUPERVISION	1
THE EIGHT (8) BASIC PRINCIPLES OF THE NEW SUPERVISION	1
I. Principle of Responsibility	1
II. Principle of Authority	2
III. Principle of Self-Growth	2
IV. Principle of Individual Worth	2
V. Principle of Creative Leadership	2
VI. Principle of Success and Failure	2
VII. Principle of Science	3
VIII. Principle of Cooperation	3
WHAT IS ADMINISTRATION?	3
I. Practices Commonly Classed as "Supervisory"	3
II. Practices Commonly Classed as "Administrative"	3
III. Practices Commonly Classed as Both "Supervisory" and "Administrative"	4
RESPONSIBILITIES OF THE SUPERVISOR	4
COMPETENCIES OF THE SUPERVISOR	4
THE PROFESSIONAL SUPERVISOR-EMPLOYEE RELATIONSHIP	4
MINI-TEXT IN SUPERVISION, ADMINISTRATION, MANAGEMENT, AND ORGANIZATION	5
I. Brief Highlights	5
A. Levels of Management	6
B. What the Supervisor Must Learn	6
C. A Definition of Supervision	6
D. Elements of the Team Concept	6
E. Principles of Organization	6
F. The Four Important Parts of Every Job	7
G. Principles of Delegation	7
H. Principles of Effective Communications	7
I. Principles of Work Improvement	7
J. Areas of Job Improvement	7
K. Seven Key Points in Making Improvements	8

	L.	Corrective Techniques for Job Improvement	8
	M.	A Planning Checklist	8
	N.	Five Characteristics of Good Directions	9
	O.	Types of Directions	9
	P.	Controls	9
	Q.	Orienting the New Employee	9
	R.	Checklist for Orienting New Employees	9
	S.	Principles of Learning	10
	T.	Causes of Poor Performance	10
	U.	Four Major Steps in On-the-Job Instructions	10
	V.	Employees Want Five Things	10
	W.	Some Don'ts in Regard to Praise	11
	X.	How to Gain Your Workers' Confidence	11
	Y.	Sources of Employee Problems	11
	Z.	The Supervisor's Key to Discipline	11
	AA.	Five Important Processes of Management	12
	BB.	When the Supervisor Fails to Plan	12
	CC.	Fourteen General Principles of Management	12
	DD.	Change	12
II.	Brief Topical Summaries		13
	A.	Who/What is the Supervisor?	13
	B.	The Sociology of Work	13
	C.	Principles and Practices of Supervision	14
	D.	Dynamic Leadership	14
	E.	Processes for Solving Problems	15
	F.	Training for Results	15
	G.	Health, Safety, and Accident Prevention	16
	H.	Equal Employment Opportunity	16
	I.	Improving Communications	16
	J.	Self-Development	17
	K.	Teaching and Training	17
		1. The Teaching Process	17
		a. Preparation	17
		b. Presentation	18
		c. Summary	18
		d. Application	18
		e. Evaluation	18
		2. Teaching Methods	18
		a. Lecture	18
		b. Discussion	18
		c. Demonstration	19
		d. Performance	19
		e. Which Method to Use	19

PHILOSOPHY, PRINCIPLES, PRACTICES, AND TECHNICS
OF
SUPERVISION, ADMINISTRATION, MANAGEMENT, AND ORGANIZATION

MEANING OF SUPERVISION

The extension of the democratic philosophy has been accompanied by an extension in the scope of supervision. Modern leaders and supervisors no longer think of supervision in the narrow sense of being confined chiefly to visiting employees, supplying materials, or rating the staff. They regard supervision as being intimately related to all the concerned agencies of society, they speak of the supervisor's function in terms of "growth," rather than the "improvement" of employees.

This modern concept of supervision may be defined as follows: Supervision is leadership and the development of leadership within groups which are cooperatively engaged in inspection, research, training, guidance, and evaluation.

THE OLD AND THE NEW SUPERVISION

TRADITIONAL
1. Inspection
2. Focused on the employee
3. Visitation
4. Random and haphazard
5. Imposed and authoritarian
6. One person usually

MODERN
1. Study and analysis
2. Focused on aims, materials, methods, supervisors, employees, environment
3. Demonstrations, intervisitation, workshops, directed reading, bulletins, etc.
4. Definitely organized and planned (scientific)
5. Cooperative and democratic
6. Many persons involved (creative)

THE EIGHT (8) BASIC PRINCIPLES OF THE NEW SUPERVISION

I. Principle of Responsibility
   Authority to act and responsibility for acting must be joined.
   A. If you give responsibility, give authority.
   B. Define employee duties clearly.
   C. Protect employees from criticism by others.
   D. Recognize the rights as well as obligations of employees.
   E. Achieve the aims of a democratic society insofar as it is possible within the area of your work.
   F. Establish a situation favorable to training and learning.
   G. Accept ultimate responsibility for everything done in your section, unit, office, division, department.
   H. Good administration and good supervision are inseparable.

II. Principle of Authority
The success of the supervisor is measured by the extent to which the power of authority is not used.
   A. Exercise simplicity and informality in supervision
   B. Use the simplest machinery of supervision
   C. If it is good for the organization as a whole, it is probably justified.
   D. Seldom be arbitrary or authoritative.
   E. Do not base your work on the power of position or of personality.
   F. Permit and encourage the free expression of opinions.

III. Principle of Self-Growth
The success of the supervisor is measured by the extent to which, and the speed with which, he is no longer needed.
   A. Base criticism on principles, not on specifics.
   B. Point out higher activities to employees.
   C. Train for self-thinking by employees to meet new situations.
   D. Stimulate initiative, self-reliance, and individual responsibility
   E. Concentrate on stimulating the growth of employees rather than on removing defects.

IV. Principle of Individual Worth
Respect for the individual is a paramount consideration in supervision.
   A. Be human and sympathetic in dealing with employees.
   B. Don't nag about things to be done.
   C. Recognize the individual differences among employees and seek opportunities to permit best expression of each personality.

V. Principle of Creative Leadership
The best supervision is that which is not apparent to the employee.
   A. Stimulate, don't drive employees to creative action.
   B. Emphasize doing good things.
   C. Encourage employees to do what they do best.
   D. Do not be too greatly concerned with details of subject or method.
   E. Do not be concerned exclusively with immediate problems and activities.
   F. Reveal higher activities and make them both desired and maximally possible.
   G. Determine procedures in the light of each situation but see that these are derived from a sound basic philosophy.
   H. Aid, inspire, and lead so as to liberate the creative spirit latent in all good employees.

VI. Principle of Success and Failure
There are no unsuccessful employees, only unsuccessful supervisors who have failed to give proper leadership.
   A. Adapt suggestions to the capacities, attitudes, and prejudices of employees.
   B. Be gradual, be progressive, be persistent.
   C. Help the employee find the general principle; have the employee apply his own problem to the general principle.
   D. Give adequate appreciation for good work and honest effort.
   E. Anticipate employee difficulties and help to prevent them.
   F. Encourage employees to do the desirable things they will do anyway.
   G. Judge your supervision by the results it secures.

VII. Principle of Science
Successful supervision is scientific, objective, and experimental. It is based on facts, not on prejudices.
- A. Be cumulative in results.
- B. Never divorce your suggestions from the goals of training.
- C. Don't be impatient of results.
- D. Keep all matters on a professional, not a personal, level.
- E. Do not be concerned exclusively with immediate problems and activities.
- F. Use objective means of determining achievement and rating where possible.

VIII. Principle of Cooperation
Supervision is a cooperative enterprise between supervisor and employee.
- A. Begin with conditions as they are.
- B. Ask opinions of all involved when formulating policies.
- C. Organization is as good as its weakest link.
- D. Let employees help to determine policies and department programs.
- E. Be approachable and accessible—physically and mentally.
- F. Develop pleasant social relationships.

WHAT IS ADMINISTRATION

Administration is concerned with providing the environment, the material facilities, and the operational procedures that will promote the maximum growth and development of supervisors and employees. (Organization is an aspect and a concomitant of administration.)

There is no sharp line of demarcation between supervision and administration; these functions are intimately interrelated and, often, overlapping. They are complementary activities.

I. Practices Commonly Classed as "Supervisory"
- A. Conducting employees' conferences
- B. Visiting sections, units, offices, divisions, departments
- C. Arranging for demonstrations
- D. Examining plans
- E. Suggesting professional reading
- F. Interpreting bulletins
- G. Recommending in-service training courses
- H. Encouraging experimentation
- I. Appraising employee morale
- J. Providing for intervisitation

II. Practices Commonly Classified as "Administrative"
- A. Management of the office
- B. Arrangement of schedules for extra duties
- C. Assignment of rooms or areas
- D. Distribution of supplies
- E. Keeping records and reports
- F. Care of audio-visual materials
- G. Keeping inventory records
- H. Checking record cards and books

I. Programming special activities
J. Checking on the attendance and punctuality of employees

III. Practices Commonly Classified as Both "Supervisory" and "Administrative"
   A. Program construction
   B. Testing or evaluating outcomes
   C. Personnel accounting
   D. Ordering instructional materials

RESPONSIBILITIES OF THE SUPERVISOR

A person employed in a supervisory capacity must constantly be able to improve his own efficiency and ability. He represent the employer to the employees and only continuous self-examination can make him a capable supervisor.

Leadership and training are the supervisor's responsibility. An efficient working unit is one in which the employees work with the supervisor. It is his job to bring out the best in his employees. He must always be relaxed, courteous, and calm in his association with his employees. Their feelings are important, and a harsh attitude does not develop the most efficient employees.

COMPETENCES OF THE SUPERVISOR

I. Complete knowledge of the duties and responsibilities of his position.
II. To be able to organize a job, plan ahead, and carry through.
III. To have self-confidence and initiative.
IV. To be able to handle the unexpected situation and make quick decisions.
V. To be able to properly train subordinates in the positions they are best suited for.
VI. To be able to keep good human relations among his subordinates.
VII. To be able to keep good human relations between his subordinates and himself and to earn their respect and trust.

THE PROFESSIONAL SUPERVISOR-EMPLOYEE RELATIONSHIP

There are two kinds of efficiency: one kind is only apparent and is produced in organizations through the exercise of mere discipline; this is but a simulation of the second, or true, efficiency which springs from spontaneous cooperation. If you are a manager, no matter how great or small your responsibility, it is your job, in the final analysis, to create and develop this involuntary cooperation among the people whom you supervise. For, no matter how powerful a combination of money, machines, and materials a company may have, this is a dead and sterile thing without a team of willing, thinking, and articulate people to guide it.

The following 21 points are presented as indicative of the exemplary basic relationship that should exist between supervisor and employee:

1. Each person wants to be liked and respected by his fellow employee and wants to be treated with consideration and respect by his superior.
2. The most competent employee will make an error. However, in a unit where good relations exist between the supervisor and his employees, tenseness and fear do not exist. Thus, errors are not hidden or covered up, and the efficiency of a unit is not impaired.

3. Subordinates resent rules, regulations, or orders that are unreasonable or unexplained.
4. Subordinates are quick to resent unfairness, harshness, injustices, and favoritism.
5. An employee will accept responsibility if he knows that he will be complimented for a job well done, and not too harshly chastised for failure; that his supervisor will check the cause of the failure, and, if it was the supervisor's fault, he will assume the blame therefore. If it was the employee's fault, his supervisor will explain the correct method or means of handling the responsibility.
6. An employee wants to receive credit for a suggestion he has made, that is used. If a suggestion cannot be used, the employee is entitled to an explanation. The supervisor should not say "no" and close the subject.
7. Fear and worry slow up a worker's ability. Poor working environment can impair his physical and mental health. A good supervisor avoids forceful methods, threats, and arguments to get a job done.
8. A forceful supervisor is able to train his employees individually and as a team, and is able to motivate them in the proper channels.
9. A mature supervisor is able to properly evaluate his subordinates and to keep them happy and satisfied.
10. A sensitive supervisor will never patronize his subordinates.
11. A worthy supervisor will respect his employees' confidences.
12. Definite and clear-cut responsibilities should be assigned to each executive.
13. Responsibility should always be coupled with corresponding authority.
14. No change should be made in the scope or responsibilities of a position without a definite understanding to that effect on the part of all persons concerned.
15. No executive or employee, occupying a single position in the organization, should be subject to definite orders from more than one source.
16. Orders should never be given to subordinates over the head of a responsible executive. Rather than do this, the officer in question should be supplanted.
17. Criticisms of subordinates should, whoever possible, be made privately, and in no case should a subordinate be criticized in the presence of executives or employees of equal or lower rank.
18. No dispute or difference between executives or employees as to authority or responsibilities should be considered too trivial for prompt and careful adjudication.
19. Promotions, wage changes, and disciplinary action should always be approved by the executive immediately superior to the one directly responsible.
20. No executive or employee should ever be required, or expected, to be at the same time an assistant to, and critic of, another.
21. Any executive whose work is subject to regular inspection should, wherever practicable, be given the assistance and facilities necessary to enable him to maintain an independent check of the quality of his work.

MINI-TEXT IN SUPERVISION, ADMINISTRATION, MANAGEMENT, AND ORGANIZATION

I. Brief Highlights

Listed concisely and sequentially are major headings and important data in the field for quick recall and review.

A. Levels of Management
Any organization of some size has several levels of management. In terms of a ladder, the levels are:

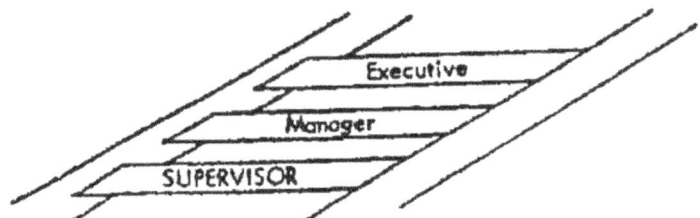

The first level is very important because it is the beginning point of management leadership.

B. What the Supervisor Must Learn
A supervisor must learn to:
1. Deal with people and their differences
2. Get the job done through people
3. Recognize the problems when they exist
4. Overcome obstacles to good performance
5. Evaluate the performance of people
6. Check his own performance in terms of accomplishment

C. A Definition of Supervisor
The term supervisor means any individual having authority, in the interests of the employer, to hire, transfer, suspend, lay-off, recall, promote, discharge, assign, reward, or discipline other employees or responsibility to direct them, or to adjust their grievances, or effectively to recommend such action, if, in connection with the foregoing, exercise of such authority is not of a merely routine or clerical nature but requires the use of independent judgment.

D. Elements of the Team Concept
What is involved in teamwork? The component parts are:
1. Members
2. A leader
3. Goals
4. Plans
5. Cooperation
6. Spirit

E. Principles of Organization
1. A team member must know what his job is.
2. Be sure that the nature and scope of a job are understood.
3. Authority and responsibility should be carefully spelled out.
4. A supervisor should be permitted to make the maximum number of decisions affecting his employees.
5. Employees should report to only one supervisor.
6. A supervisor should direct only as many employees as he can handle effectively.
7. An organization plan should be flexible.

8. Inspection and performance of work should be separate.
9. Organizational problems should receive immediate attention.
10. Assign work in line with ability and experience.

F. The Four Important Parts of Every Job
1. Inherent in every job is the *accountability* for results.
2. A second set of factors in every job is *responsibilities*.
3. Along with duties and responsibilities one must have the *authority* to act within certain limits without obtaining permission to proceed.
4. No job exists in a vacuum. The supervisor is surrounded by key *relationships*.

G. Principles of Delegation
Where work is delegated for the first time, the supervisor should think in terms of these questions:
1. Who is best qualified to do this?
2. Can an employee improve his abilities by doing this?
3. How long should an employee spend on this?
4. Are there any special problems for which he will need guidance?
5. How broad a delegation can I make?

H. Principles of Effective Communications
1. Determine the media.
2. To whom directed?
3. Identification and source authority.
4. Is communication understood?

I. Principles of Work Improvement
1. Most people usually do only the work which is assigned to them.
2. Workers are likely to fit assigned work into the time available to perform it.
3. A good workload usually stimulates output.
4. People usually do their best work when they know that results will be reviewed or inspected.
5. Employees usually feel that someone else is responsible for conditions of work, workplace layout, job methods, type of tools/equipment, and other such factors.
6. Employees are usually defensive about their job security.
7. Employees have natural resistance to change.
8. Employees can support or destroy a supervisor.
9. A supervisor usually earns the respect of his people through his personal example of diligence and efficiency.

J. Areas of Job Improvement
The areas of job improvement are quite numerous, but the most common ones which a supervisor can identify and utilize are:
1. Departmental layout
2. Flow of work
3. Workplace layout
4. Utilization of manpower
5. Work methods
6. Materials handling

7. Utilization
8. Motion economy

K. Seven Key Points in Making Improvements
1. Select the job to be improved
2. Study how it is being done now
3. Question the present method
4. Determine actions to be taken
5. Chart proposed method
6. Get approval and apply
7. Solicit worker participation

l. Corrective Techniques of Job Improvement
Specific Problems
1. Size of workload
2. Inability to meet schedules
3. Strain and fatigue
4. Improper use of men and skills
5. Waste, poor quality, unsafe conditions
6. Bottleneck conditions that hinder output
7. Poor utilization of equipment and machine
8. Efficiency and productivity of labor

General Improvement
1. Departmental layout
2. Flow of work
3. Work plan layout
4. Utilization of manpower
5. Work methods
6. Materials handling
7. Utilization of equipment
8. Motion economy

Corrective Techniques
1. Study with scale model
2. Flow chart study
3. Motion analysis
4. Comparison of units produced to standard allowance
5. Methods analysis
6. Flow chart and equipment study
7. Down time vs. running time
8. Motion analysis

M. A Planning Checklist
1. Objectives
2. Controls
3. Delegations
4. Communications
5. Resources
6. Manpower

7. Equipment
8. Supplies and materials
9. Utilization of time
10. Safety
11. Money
12. Work
13. Timing of improvements

N. Five Characteristics of Good Directions
In order to get results, directions must be:
1. Possible of accomplishment
2. Agreeable with worker interests
3. Related to mission
4. Planned and complete
5. Unmistakably clear

O. Types of Directions
1. Demands or direct orders
2. Requests
3. Suggestion or implication
4. volunteering

P. Controls
A typical listing of the overall areas in which the supervisor should establish controls might be:
1. Manpower
2. Materials
3. Quality of work
4. Quantity of work
5. Time
6. Space
7. Money
8. Methods

Q. Orienting the New Employee
1. Prepare for him
2. Welcome the new employee
3. Orientation for the job
4. Follow-up

R. Checklist for Orienting New Employees   Yes   No
1. Do you appreciate the feelings of new employees when they first report for work?
2. Are you aware of the fact that the new employee must make a big adjustment to his job?
3. Have you given him good reasons for liking the job and the organization?
4. Have you prepared for his first day on the job?
5. Did you welcome him cordially and make him feel needed?

	Yes	No

6. Did you establish rapport with him so that he feels free to talk and discuss matters with you? ___ ___
7. Did you explain his job to him and his relationship to you? ___ ___
8. Does he know that his work will be evaluated periodically on a basis that is fair and objective? ___ ___
9. Did you introduce him to his fellow workers in such a way that they are likely to accept him? ___ ___
10. Does he know what employee benefits he will receive? ___ ___
11. Does he understand the importance of being on the job and what to do if he must leave his duty station? ___ ___
12. Has he been impressed with the importance of accident prevention and safe practice? ___ ___
13. Does he generally know his way around the department? ___ ___
14. Is he under the guidance of a sponsor who will teach the right way of doing things? ___ ___
15. Do you plan to follow-up so that he will continue to adjust successfully to his job? ___ ___

S. Principles of Learning
1. Motivation
2. Demonstration or explanation
3. Practice

T. Causes of Poor Performance
1. Improper training for job
2. Wrong tools
3. Inadequate directions
4. Lack of supervisory follow-up
5. Poor communications
6. Lack of standards of performance
7. Wrong work habits
8. Low morale
9. Other

U. Four Major Steps in On-The-Job Instruction
1. Prepare the worker
2. Present the operation
3. Tryout performance
4. Follow-up

V. Employees Want Five Things
1. Security
2. Opportunity
3. Recognition
4. Inclusion
5. Expression

W. Some Don'ts in Regard to Praise
1. Don't praise a person for something he hasn't done.
2. Don't praise a person unless you can be sincere.
3. Don't be sparing in praise just because your superior withholds it from you.
4. Don't let too much time elapse between good performance and recognition of it

X. How to Gain Your Workers' Confidence
Methods of developing confidence include such things as:
1. Knowing the interests, habits, hobbies of employees
2. Admitting your own inadequacies
3. Sharing and telling of confidence in others
4. Supporting people when they are in trouble
5. Delegating matters that can be well handled
6. Being frank and straightforward about problems and working conditions
7. Encouraging others to bring their problems to you
8. Taking action on problems which impede worker progress

Y. Sources of Employee Problems
On-the-job causes might be such things as:
1. A feeling that favoritism is exercised in assignments
2. Assignment of overtime
3. An undue amount of supervision
4. Changing methods or systems
5. Stealing of ideas or trade secrets
6. Lack of interest in job
7. Threat of reduction in force
8. Ignorance or lack of communications
9. Poor equipment
10. Lack of knowing how supervisor feels toward employee
11. Shift assignments

Off-the-job problems might have to do with:
1. Health
2. Finances
3. Housing
4. Family

Z. The Supervisor's Key to Discipline
There are several key points about discipline which the supervisor should keep in mind:
1. Job discipline is one of the disciplines of life and is directed by the supervisor.
2. It is more important to correct an employee fault than to fix blame for it.
3. Employee performance is affected by problems both on the job and off.
4. Sudden or abrupt changes in behavior can be indications of important employee problems.
5. Problems should be dealt with as soon as possible after they are identified.
6. The attitude of the supervisor may have more to do with solving problems than the techniques of problem solving.
7. Correction of employee behavior should be resorted to only after the supervisor is sure that training or counseling will not be helpful.

8. Be sure to document your disciplinary actions.
9. Make sure that you are disciplining on the basis of facts rather than personal feelings.
10. Take each disciplinary step in order, being careful not to make snap judgments, or decisions based on impatience.

AA. Five Important Processes of Management
1. Planning
2. Organizing
3. Scheduling
4. Controlling
5. Motivating

BB. When the Supervisor Fails to Plan
1. Supervisor creates impression of not knowing his job
2. May lead to excessive overtime
3. Job runs itself—supervisor lacks control
4. Deadlines and appointments missed
5. Parts of the work go undone
6. Work interrupted by emergencies
7. Sets a bad example
8. Uneven workload creates peaks and valleys
9. Too much time on minor details at expense of more important tasks

CC. Fourteen General Principles of Management
1. Division of work
2. Authority and responsibility
3. Discipline
4. Unity of command
5. Unity of direction
6. Subordination of individual interest to general interest
7. Remuneration of personnel
8. Centralization
9. Scalar chain
10. Order
11. Equity
12. Stability of tenure of personnel
13. Initiative
14. Esprit de corps

DD. Change

Bringing about change is perhaps attempted more often, and yet less well understood, than anything else the supervisor does. How do people generally react to change? (People tend to resist change that is imposed upon them by other individuals or circumstances.

Change is characteristic of every situation. It is a part of every real endeavor where the efforts of people are concerned.

1. Why do people resist change?
   People may resist change because of:
   a. Fear of the unknown
   b. Implied criticism
   c. Unpleasant experiences in the past
   d. Fear of loss of status
   e. Threat to the ego
   f. Fear of loss of economic stability

2. How can we best overcome the resistance to change?
   In initiating change, take these steps:
   a. Get ready to sell
   b. Identify sources of help
   c. Anticipate objections
   d. Sell benefits
   e. Listen in depth
   f. Follow up

II. Brief Topical Summaries

   A. Who/What is the Supervisor?
      1. The supervisor is often called the "highest level employee and the lowest level manager."
      2. A supervisor is a member of both management and the work group. He acts as a bridge between the two.
      3. Most problems in supervision are in the area of human relations, or people problems.
      4. Employees expect: Respect, opportunity to learn and to advance, and a sense of belonging, and so forth.
      5. Supervisors are responsible for directing people and organizing work. Planning is of paramount importance.
      6. A position description is a set of duties and responsibilities inherent to a given position.
      7. It is important to keep the position description up-to-date and to provide each employee with his own copy.

   B. The Sociology of Work
      1. People are alike in many ways; however, each individual is unique.
      2. The supervisor is challenged in getting to know employee differences. Acquiring skills in evaluating individuals is an asset.
      3. Maintaining meaningful working relationships in the organization is of great importance.
      4. The supervisor has an obligation to help individuals to develop to their fullest potential.
      5. Job rotation on a planned basis helps to build versatility and to maintain interest and enthusiasm in work groups.
      6. Cross training (job rotation) provides backup skills.

7. The supervisor can help reduce tension by maintaining a sense of humor, providing guidance to employees, and by making reasonable and timely decisions. Employees respond favorably to working under reasonably predictable circumstances.
8. Change is characteristic of all managerial behavior. The supervisor must adjust to changes in procedures, new methods, technological changes, and to a number of new and sometimes challenging situations.
9. To overcome the natural tendency for people to resist change, the supervisor should become more skillful in initiating change.

C. Principles and Practices of Supervision
1. Employees should be required to answer to only one superior.
2. A supervisor can effectively direct only a limited number of employees, depending upon the complexity, variety, and proximity of the jobs involved.
3. The organizational chart presents the organization in graphic form. It reflects lines of authority and responsibility as well as interrelationships of units within the organization.
4. Distribution of work can be improved through an analysis using the "Work Distribution Chart."
5. The "Work Distribution Chart" reflects the division of work within a unit in understandable form.
6. When related tasks are given to an employee, he has a better chance of increasing his skills through training.
7. The individual who is given the responsibility for tasks must also be given the appropriate authority to insure adequate results.
8. The supervisor should delegate repetitive, routine work. Preparation of recurring reports, maintaining leave and attendance records are some examples.
9. Good discipline is essential to good task performance. Discipline is reflected in the actions of employees on the job in the absence of supervision.
10. Disciplinary action may have to be taken when the positive aspects of discipline have failed. Reprimand, warning, and suspension are examples of disciplinary action.
11. If a situation calls for a reprimand, be sure it is deserved and remember it is to be done in private.

D. Dynamic Leadership
1. A style is a personal method or manner of exerting influence.
2. Authoritarian leaders often see themselves as the source of power and authority.
3. The democratic leader often perceives the group as the source of authority and power.
4. Supervisors tend to do better when using the pattern of leadership that is most natural for them.
5. Social scientists suggest that the effective supervisor use the leadership style that best fits the problem or circumstances involved.
6. All four styles—telling, selling, consulting, joining—have their place. Using one does not preclude using the other at another time.

7. The theory X point of view assumes that the average person dislikes work, will avoid it whenever possible, and must be coerced to achieve organizational objectives.
8. The theory Y point of view assumes that the average person considers work to be a natural as play, and, when the individual is committed, he requires little supervision or direction to accomplish desired objectives.
9. The leader's basic assumptions concerning human behavior and human nature affect his actions, decisions, and other managerial practices.
10. Dissatisfaction among employees is often present, but difficult to isolate. The supervisor should seek to weaken dissatisfaction by keeping promises, being sincere and considerate, keeping employees informed, and so forth.
11. Constructive suggestions should be encouraged during the natural progress of the work.

E. Processes for Solving Problems
1. People find their daily tasks more meaningful and satisfying when they can improve them.
2. The causes of problems, or the key factors, are often hidden in the background. Ability to solve problems often involves the ability to isolate them from their backgrounds. There is some substance to the cliché that some persons "can't see the forest for the trees."
3. New procedures are often developed from old ones. Problems should be broken down into manageable parts. New ideas can be adapted from old one.
4. People think differently in problem-solving situations. Using a logical, patterned approach is often useful. One approach found to be useful includes these steps:
   a. Define the problem
   b. Establish objectives
   c. Get the facts
   d. Weigh and decide
   e. Take action
   f. Evaluate action

F. Training for Results
1. Participants respond best when they feel training is important to them.
2. The supervisor has responsibility for the training and development of those who report to him.
3. When training is delegated to others, great care must be exercised to insure the trainer has knowledge, aptitude, and interest for his work as a trainer.
4. Training (learning) of some type goes on continually. The most successful supervisor makes certain the learning contributes in a productive manner to operational goals.
5. New employees are particularly susceptible to training. Older employees facing new job situations require specific training, as well as having need for development and growth opportunities.
6. Training needs require continuous monitoring.
7. The training officer of an agency is a professional with a responsibility to assist supervisors in solving training problems.

8. Many of the self-development steps important to the supervisor's own growth are equally important to the development of peers and subordinates. Knowledge of these is important when the supervisor consults with others on development and growth opportunities.

G. Health, Safety, and Accident Prevention
1. Management-minded supervisors take appropriate measures to assist employees in maintaining health and in assuring safe practices in the work environment.
2. Effective safety training and practices help to avoid injury and accidents.
3. Safety should be a management goal. All infractions of safety which are observed should be corrected without exception.
4. Employees' safety attitude, training and instruction, provision of safe tools and equipment, supervision, and leadership are considered highly important factors which contribute to safety and which can be influenced directly by supervisors.
5. When accidents do occur, they should be investigated promptly for very important reasons, including the fact that information which is gained can be used to prevent accidents in the future.

H. Equal Employment Opportunity
1. The supervisor should endeavor to treat all employees fairly, without regard to religion, race, sex, or national origin.
2. Groups tend to reflect the attitude of the leader. Prejudice can be detected even in very subtle form. Supervisors must strive to create a feeling of mutual respect and confidence in every employee.
3. Complete utilization of all human resources is a national goal. Equitable consideration should be accorded women in the work force, minority-group members, the physically and mentally handicapped, and the older employee. The important question is: "Who can do the job?"
4. Training opportunities, recognition for performance, overtime assignments, promotional opportunities, and all other personnel actions are to be handled on an equitable basis.

I. Improving Communications
1. Communications is achieving understanding between the sender and the receiver of a message. It also means sharing information—the creation of understanding.
2. Communication is basic to all human activity. Words are means of conveying meanings; however, real meanings are in people.
3. There are very practical differences in the effectiveness of one-way, impersonal, and two-way communications. Words spoken face-to-face are better understood. Telephone conversations are effective, but lack the rapport of person-to-person exchanges. The whole person communicates.
4. Cooperation and communication in an organization go hand in hand. When there is a mutual respect between people, spelling out rules and procedures for communicating is unnecessary.
5. There are several barriers to effective communications. These include failure to listen with respect and understanding, lack of skill in feedback, and misinterpreting the meanings of words used by the speaker. It is also common

practice to listen to what we want to hear, and tune out things we do not want to hear.
6. Communication is management's chief problem. The supervisor should accept the challenge to communicate more effectively and to improve interagency and intra-agency communications.
7. The supervisor may often plan for and conduct meetings. The planning phase is critical and may determine the success or the failure of a meeting.
8. Speaking before groups usually requires extra effort. Stage fright may never disappear completely, but it can be controlled.

J. Self-Development
1. Every employee is responsible for his own self-development.
2. Toastmaster and toastmistress clubs offer opportunities to improve skills in oral communications.
3. Planning for one's own self-development is of vital importance. Supervisors know their own strengths and limitations better than anyone else.
4. Many opportunities are open to aid the supervisor in his developmental efforts, including job assignments; training opportunities, both governmental and non-governmental—to include universities and professional conferences and seminars.
5. Programmed instruction offers a means of studying at one's own rate.
6. Where difficulties may arise from a supervisor's being away from his work for training, he may participate in televised home study or correspondence courses to meet his self-development needs.

K. Teaching and Training
1. The Teaching Process
Teaching is encouraging and guiding the learning activities of students toward established goals. In most cases this process consists of five steps: preparation, presentation, summarization, evaluation, and application.

   a. Preparation
   Preparation is two-fold in nature; that of the supervisor and the employee. Preparation by the supervisor is absolutely essential to success. He must know what, when, where, how, and whom he will teach. Some of the factors that should be considered are:
   1) The objectives
   2) The materials needed
   3) The methods to be used
   4) Employee participation
   5) Employee interest
   6) Training aids
   7) Evaluation
   8) Summarization

   Employee preparation consists in preparing the employee to receive the material. Probably the most important single factor in the preparation of the employee is arousing and maintaining his interest. He must know the objectives of the training, why he is there, how the material can be used, and its importance to him.

b. Presentation
In presentation, have a carefully designed plan and follow it. The plan should be accurate and complete, yet flexible enough to meet situations as they arise. The method of presentation will be determined by the particular situation and objectives.

c. Summary
A summary should be made at the end of every training unit and program. In addition, there may be internal summaries depending on the nature of the material being taught. The important thing is that the trainee must always be able to understand how each part of the new material relates to the whole.

d. Application
The supervisor must arrange work so the employee will be given a chance to apply new knowledge or skills while the material is still clear in his mind and interest is high. The trainee does not really know whether he has learned the material until he has been given a chance to apply it. If the material is not applied, it loses most of its value.

e. Evaluation
The purpose of all training is to promote learning. To determine whether the training has been a success or failure, the supervisor must evaluate this learning.
In the broadest sense, evaluation includes all the devices, methods, skills, and techniques used by the supervisor to keep himself and the employees informed as to their progress toward the objectives they are pursuing. The extent to which the employee has mastered the knowledge, skills, and abilities, or changed his attitudes, as determined by the program objectives, is the extent to which instruction has succeeded or failed.
Evaluation should not be confined to the end of the lesson, day, or program but should be used continuously. We shall note later the way this relates to the rest of the teaching process.

2. Teaching Methods
A teaching method is a pattern of identifiable student and instructor activity used in presenting training material.
All supervisors are faced with the problem of deciding which method should be used at a given time.

a. Lecture
The lecture is direct oral presentation of material by the supervisor. The present trend is to place less emphasis on the trainer's activity and more on that of the trainee.

b. Discussion
Teaching by discussion or conference involves using questions and other techniques to arouse interest and focus attention upon certain areas, and by doing so creating a learning situation. This can be one of the most

valuable methods because it gives the employees an opportunity to express their ideas and pool their knowledge.

    c. Demonstration
The demonstration is used to teach how something works or how to do something. It can be used to show a principle or what the results of a series of actions will be. A well-staged demonstration is particularly effective because it shows proper methods of performance in a realistic manner.

    d. Performance
Performance is one of the most fundamental of all learning techniques or teaching methods. The trainee may be able to tell how a specific operation should be performed but he cannot be sure he knows how to perform the operation until he has done so.
As with all methods, there are certain advantages and disadvantages to each method.

    e. Which Method to Use
Moreover, there are other methods and techniques of teaching. It is difficult to use any method without other methods entering into it. In any learning situation, a combination of methods is usually more effective than any one method alone.

Finally, evaluation must be integrated into the other aspects of the teaching-learning process.

It must be used in the motivation of the trainees; it must be used to assist in developing understanding during the training; and it must be related to employee application of the results of training.

This is distinctly the role of the supervisor.

FIRST AID

TABLE OF CONTENTS

	Page
OBJECTIVES	B-2
OVERVIEW	B-3
FIRST AID KIT	B-5
SETTING OF PRIORITIES FOR TREATMENT	B-7
EVALUATION AND TREATMENT OF BLEEDING	B-11
PRACTICE IN CONTROLLING BLEEDING	B-17
MAINTENANCE OF AIRWAY AND RESPIRATION	B-19
PRACTICE IN ARTIFICIAL RESPIRATION	B-25
EVALUATION AND CONTROL OF SHOCK	B-27
PRACTICE IN TREATING SHOCK	B-31
GUIDELINES ON OTHER INJURIES AND CONDITIONS	B-33

OBJECTIVES

1. Set priorities for treating severe injuries.

2. Recognize and treat symptoms of severe bleeding, stoppage of breath, and shock.

OVERVIEW

INSTRUCTOR GUIDELINES	CONTENT

Present local situation in which a student requires first aid on the bus. The driver recognizes symptoms and administers proper treatment. The situation should be severe enough that the child's life is saved.	**BUS DRIVER SAVES A LIFE**
	
	YOUR RESPONSIBILITY TO RENDER FIRST AID*
	
	    The first objective of first aid is to save life. You must know how to apply the principles of first aid. First aid is the immediate and temporary care given to the victim of an accident or sudden illness until the services of a physician can be obtained. A victim will respond much more readily to treatment if he recognizes that a competent person is administering that treatment. Practicing the procedures in this unit will increase your competence in rendering first aid.
	
	    Common sense and a few simple rules are the keys to effective first aid. It is as important to know what not to do, as to know what to do. In case of an emergency, making mistakes could be disastrous to the injured person. You are more likely to act promptly and correctly if you learn only a few simple principles but learn them well.
	
	    Emphasis is placed on problems you may confront on the road. The procedures in this unit include:
	
	    1. Evaluation of injury and setting of priorities for treatment.

INSTRUCTOR GUIDELINES	CONTENT
	2. Evaluation and treatment of bleeding. 3. Maintenance of airway and respiration. 4. Evaluation and control of shock. Other first aid topics that are important but not urgent in the saving of life will be discussed only briefly to provide you with a general knowledge of first aid. Little attention has been given the contents of the first aid kit and its use, because the most important equipment you have is your knowledge of first aid, not the number and types of splints, bandages, and ointments in the first aid kit. Where references are made to bandages or other equipment, use the cleanest materials available but <u>do not delay</u> first aid if clean bandages are not available. However, the first aid kit should contain a supply of 4" x 4" pads and similar clean bandages for covering wounds and stopping bleeding.

FIRST AID KIT

INSTRUCTOR GUIDELINES	CONTENT
Give local details on these three topics. Have trainees take notes.	CONTENTS LOCATION WHERE TO GET NEW SUPPLIES

SETTING OF PRIORITIES FOR TREATMENT

INSTRUCTOR GUIDELINES	CONTENT
	You must make three evaluations in establishing priorities for treatment: condition of scene, types of injuries, and need for immediate treatment. EVALUATION OF THE SCENE Several types of situations require high priority action. For example, if fire is present, the most urgent action is to remove everyone from its danger. Don't give any first aid treatment until everyone is safe. If someone has been electrocuted, the most urgent action for a first aider is to remove him from the electrical source while simultaneously protecting himself and others from also being electrocuted. Use a completely dry stick to lift off an offending wire. Do not touch the injured until he is removed from contact with the electrical source. If a person has drowned or is in the presence of a dangerous gas, such as chlorine or ammonia, do not attempt to rescue him unless you are sure that you can do so without becoming a victim yourself. Often, a few seconds delay will give you enough time to find an alternate, safer way to rescue the person. EVALUATION OF INJURIES At least three types of injuries require prompt attention: 1. *Severe bleeding*. If a person is bleeding profusely, he may be dead in less than two minutes.

INSTRUCTOR GUIDELINES	CONTENT
	2. *Blocked airway or stoppage of breath.* Most people can be saved if they start breathing on their own or artificially within two minutes. If breathing has been stopped for five minutes, there is only a 25 percent chance of saving the victim. It is, therefore, important to note the time at which breathing stopped. 3. *Shock.* In shock the vital body functions are depressed. Death may result if not treated promptly, even though the injury which caused the shock is not severe enough to cause death. PRIORITY FOR TREATMENT A school bus accident may involve injury to a number of people. If several people are injured and the scene permits you to begin treatment promptly, treat severe bleeding first, then move quickly to those who have stopped breathing and still have a chance for survival. Then, move to less urgent injuries. Whenever possible, treat a person where he is found. Before you move any sick or injured person, bleeding should be stopped, breathing should be established, and shock should be treated. If there is great urgency to move an injured person, drag him on the long axis of his body pulling him by his hands (stretched back behind his head), or by the shoulders. If possible, place beneath him a coat or a blanket on which he can ride or be pulled.

INSTRUCTOR GUIDELINES	CONTENT
	There is always the possibility that you may be injured in the accident also. You should, therefore, be able to direct students in first aid practices in the event you are injured. Decide which of your regular passengers might be most capable of assisting you during an emergency.
Add any comments you feel are important before they actually get to the first aid procedures.	NOTES:

B-11

EVALUATION AND TREATMENT OF BLEEDING

INSTRUCTOR GUIDELINES	CONTENT
	Use the following procedures in the evaluation and treatment of bleeding. EVALUATION OF BLEEDING When treating a bleeding injury, determine the type of bleeding and the amount of blood lost. You must be able to recognize three types of external bleeding: 1. *Capillary oozing.* Injuries to capillaries or small veins is indicated by a steady ooze of dark-colored blood. 2. *Venous bleeding.* Bleeding from a vein is indicated by a flow of dark-colored blood at a steady rate. 3. *Arterial bleeding.* Bleeding from an artery is indicated by bright red blood, flowing swiftly in spurts or jets. This may sometimes be mixed with venous bleeding, in which case the blood will be slightly darker in color. When evaluating the severity of bleeding, remember: • Blood dripping slowly from the wound is generally not serious and can be controlled. • Blood flowing in a small, steady stream or in small spurts may be serious and can be controlled. • Blood flowing in a heavy stream or in large spurts indicates a serious condition, and a

INSTRUCTOR GUIDELINES	CONTENT
	first aider must attempt to bring it under control immediately.
	Bleeding needs immediate attention. Even the loss of small amounts of blood will produce weakness and can cause shock. The loss of as much as a pint of blood by a child, or a quart of blood by an adult, may have disastrous results.
	CONTROL OF BLEEDING
	Direct pressure. The main step in controlling bleeding is for the first aider to exert direct pressure over the wound area. This is done by placing the cleanest material available (preferably a pad of sterile gauze) against the bleeding point and applying firm pressure with the hand until a bandage can be applied.
Refer to Figure 1.	To bring bleeding under control, follow these steps:
	1. Apply dressing or pad directly over wound.
	2. Apply direct, even pressure, using bare hand if necessary when bleeding is serious and when dressing is not immediately available.
	3. Leave dressing in place.
	4. Continue pressure by applying bandage.
	5. Secure bandage in place, checking to be sure bandage is not too tight and thus cutting off circulation.
	6. Elevate limb above heart level except when there is a possible broken bone.

To stop bleeding, apply a dressing pad or a bare hand directly over the wound and apply pressure.

Continue the pressure until the bleeding has stopped or slowed to the point that you will be able to apply a bandage. Do not hurry to remove the pressure.

 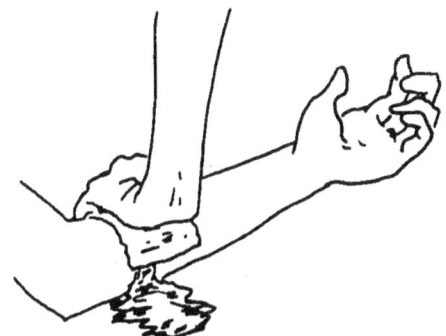

Then apply a bandage over the dressing to continue the pressure and thus control the bleeding. Check the bandage after the knot is tied to be sure it is not too tight and is not cutting off the circulation.

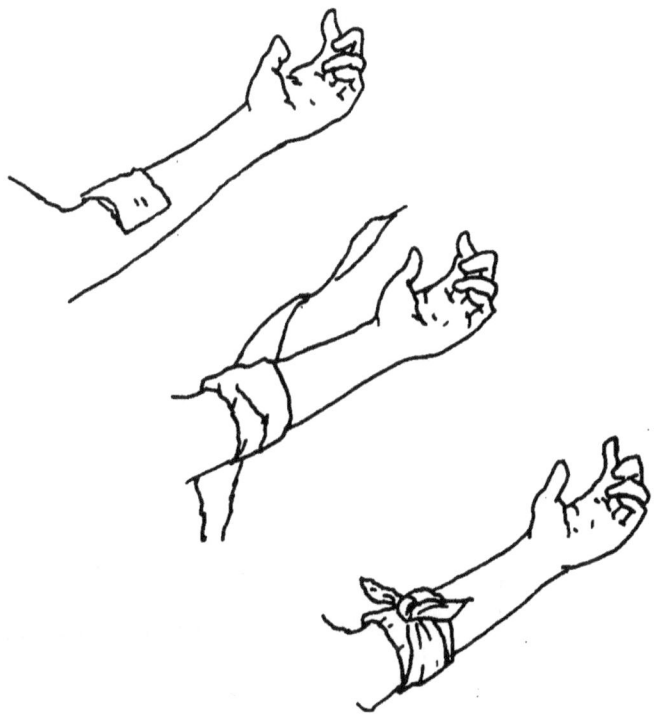

Figure 1. Using Direct Pressure to Control Bleeding*

INSTRUCTOR GUIDELINES	CONTENT
	7. Treat for shock.
	8. If blood soaks through dressing, do not remove but apply more dressings
Answer any questions trainees may ask.	NOTES:
Refer to Figure 2.	*Pressure points*. If direct pressure does not control bleeding, pressure on an artery (pressure point) close to the wound is necessary.
	The point selected must be <u>between</u> the heart and the injury. To control bleeding in this manner, find one of these pressure points:
	1. *Temporal artery*. The temporal artery is located in the hollow just in front of the ear.
	2. *Facial artery*. The facial artery is located in the small crevice about one inch from the angle of the jaw.
	3. *Carotid artery*. The carotid artery is located deep and back on each side of the Adam's apple.
	4. *Subclavian artery*. The subclavian artery is located deep and down in the hollow near the collarbone.
	5. *Brachial artery*. The brachial artery is located on the inner side of the upper arm about three inches below the armpit.

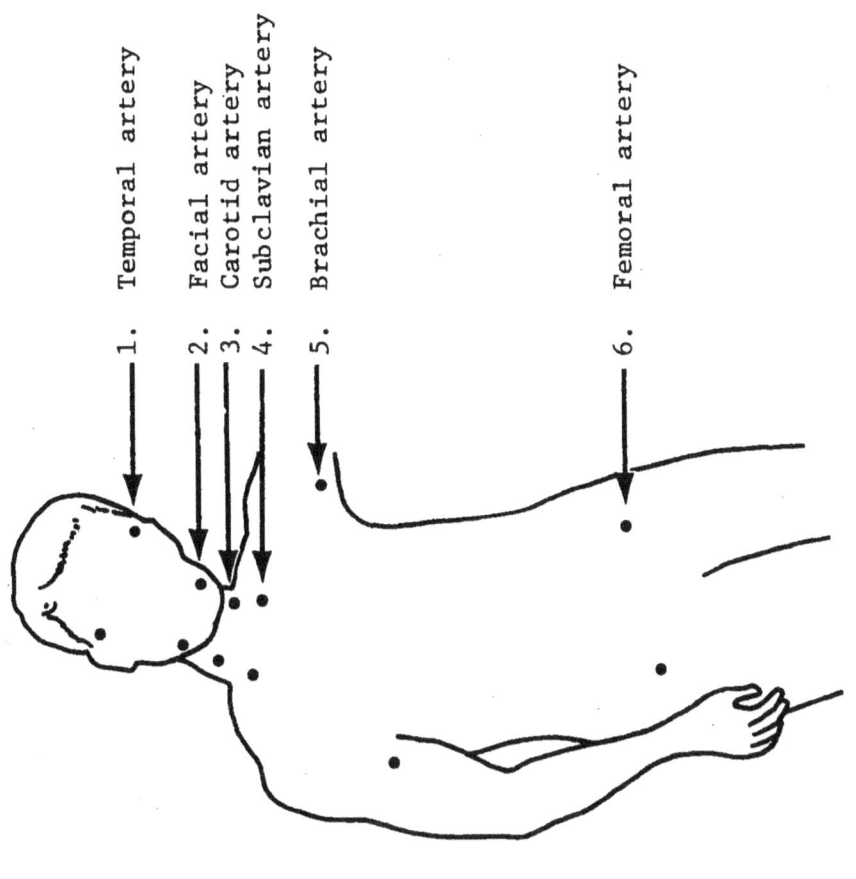

Figure 2. Pressure Points for Applying Arterial Pressure

INSTRUCTOR GUIDELINES	CONTENT
Emphasize. ⟹	6. *Femoral artery.* The femoral artery is located midway in the groin, between the crotch and the hip. *Tourniquet warning.* A tourniquet applied to control bleeding is mentioned here principally to discourage its use. It is dangerous to apply, dangerous to leave on, and dangerous to remove. It will cause tissue injury and stoppage of the entire supply of blood to the part below it. This causes gangrene and, subsequently, could cause loss of limb. A tourniquet is rarely required and should be used only for severe, life-threatening hemorrhage that cannot be controlled with direct pressure or arterial pressure. *Applying the bandage.* After bleeding has been controlled, do not remove the dressing used to apply direct pressure, even though blood may have saturated it. Apply additional layers of cloth to form a good-sized covering; then bandage the wound snugly and firmly. A bandage that is too tight can cause further injury. Therefore, check the bandage periodically. Look for swelling around the wound. If it seems that the bandage is interfering with the circulation of the blood, loosen it. *Treating for shock.* Anyone who has lost much blood will need treatment for shock. Even if the symptoms of shock are not evident, the patient should be kept warm and quiet. NOTES:

PRACTICE IN CONTROLLING BLEEDING

INSTRUCTOR GUIDELINES	CONTENT
Ask for a volunteer from the class to act as the injured person. Demonstrate the direct pressure method and arterial pressure method of controlling bleeding. Explain how to apply and tie bandage. Break class into pairs. Have each pair take turns practicing each method. Assist where necessary. Have them tell you when they feel competent to be checked. Check each method and provide feedback.	Your instructor will first demonstrate the control of bleeding using direct pressure. Watch how he does it. Now observe the location of the six pressure points and how to apply arterial pressure. Now you practice each method on another class member. Suppose you notice a student with severe arterial bleeding at the wrist. Demonstrate what you would do to control bleeding. NOTES:

MAINTENANCE OF AIRWAY AND RESPIRATION*

INSTRUCTOR GUIDELINES	CONTENT
	Breathing may stop for three reasons: 1. The mouth or windpipe is blocked (by the tongue, blood, or mucus). 2. The brain centers that control breathing have stopped (drowning, electrocution, head injury, or poisoning). 3. There is a sucking sound of the chest that prevents the lungs from expanding (obvious by looking at the chest). With the first two, the person may be blue in color and respiration may appear to have stopped, or he may be choking. ARTIFICIAL RESPIRATION Most persons can live about six minutes after breathing stops. Therefore, artificial respiration must begin as soon as possible after natural breathing has been interrupted, or when natural breathing is so irregular or so shallow as to be ineffective. Artificial respiration is a method of getting air into and out of a person's lungs until he can breathe for himself. *Mouth-to-mouth method*. One of the simplest and most effective ways to give artificial respiration is by the mouth-to-mouth (or mouth-to-nose) method. This method is effective for both children and adults and can be used even when there are injuries to the chest and arms. Follow these steps: 1. Place the person who has stopped breathing on his back.

INSTRUCTOR GUIDELINES	CONTENT
	2. Open his mouth and clear out foreign matter (food, dirt, and so forth) with the fingers. If the person has false teeth, remove them.
	3. Tilt his head back so that his chin points upward and tilt his lower jaw beneath and behind so that it juts out. This moves the base of the tongue away from the back of the throat so it does not block the air passage to the lungs. Unless this air passage is open, no amount of effort will get air in.
	4. Blow air into a person's lungs through either his mouth or nose. Open your mouth wide and place it tightly over the person's mouth. Pinch his nostrils shut. Or close the victim's mouth and place your mouth over his nose. With an infant or small child, place your mouth over both his nose and mouth making an airproof seal. Air can be blown into a person's mouth even through clenched teeth.
	5. Blow into the mouth or nose, continuing to hold the unconscious person's lower jaw so that it juts out to keep the air passage open.
	6. Remove your mouth from the patient's mouth. Turn your head to the side and listen for the return outflow of air coming from the patient's lungs. If you hear it, you will know that an exchange of air has occurred.

INSTRUCTOR GUIDELINES	CONTENT
Refer to Figure 3.	7. Continue breathing for the patient. Blow vigorously into his mouth or nose about 12 times each minute. Remove your mouth after each breath and listen for the exchange of air. In the case of an infant or child, blow less vigorously, using shallower breaths about 20 times a minute. 8. If there is not an exchange of air, turn the person on his side and strike him several times between the shoulder blades, using considerable force. This will help dislodge any obstruction in the air passages. Check the position of the head and jaw. Finally, make sure there is no foreign matter in his mouth. Normal breathing may begin again after 15 minutes of artificial respiration. But if it does not, continue the procedure until medical aid arrives. Alternate with other persons, if possible, to maintain maximum efficiency. Cases of electric shock and drug or carbon monoxide poisoning may require artificial respiration for longer periods. The first sign of restored breathing may be a sigh or a gasp. Breathing may be irregular at first, therefore, artificial respiration should be continued until regular breathing resumes. When normal breathing resumes, the person usually recovers rapidly. However, be prepared in case he stops breathing again. NOTES:

A

Before starting any type of artificial respiration be sure that the mouth and throat are completely clear of mucus and foreign objects. Use your fingers to clean the mouth. You may cover fingers with a piece of cloth to help remove mucus and slippery objects.

B

The head must be tipped back to allow a free air passage with the jaw held in a jutting-out position. The more you can achieve the "sword swallower" position the better.

C

Remember – Don't blow too hard. Your mouth and the mouth of the person receiving treatment should be wide open with a complete seal between them. Inhale more than usual before exhaling into person's mouth. In this way he will get more oxygen.

D

Pinching the nostrils prevents air from escaping through the nose. With your right hand be sure to hold the jaw in the jutting-out position. Your fingers, held like a claw, should be hooked behind the jawbone to hold it in the correct position.

E

This is the mouth-to-nose type of respiration with the lips being sealed by the two fingers of the right hand. This would be used when an obstruction in the mouth cannot be removed or a severe mouth injury prevents proper contact.

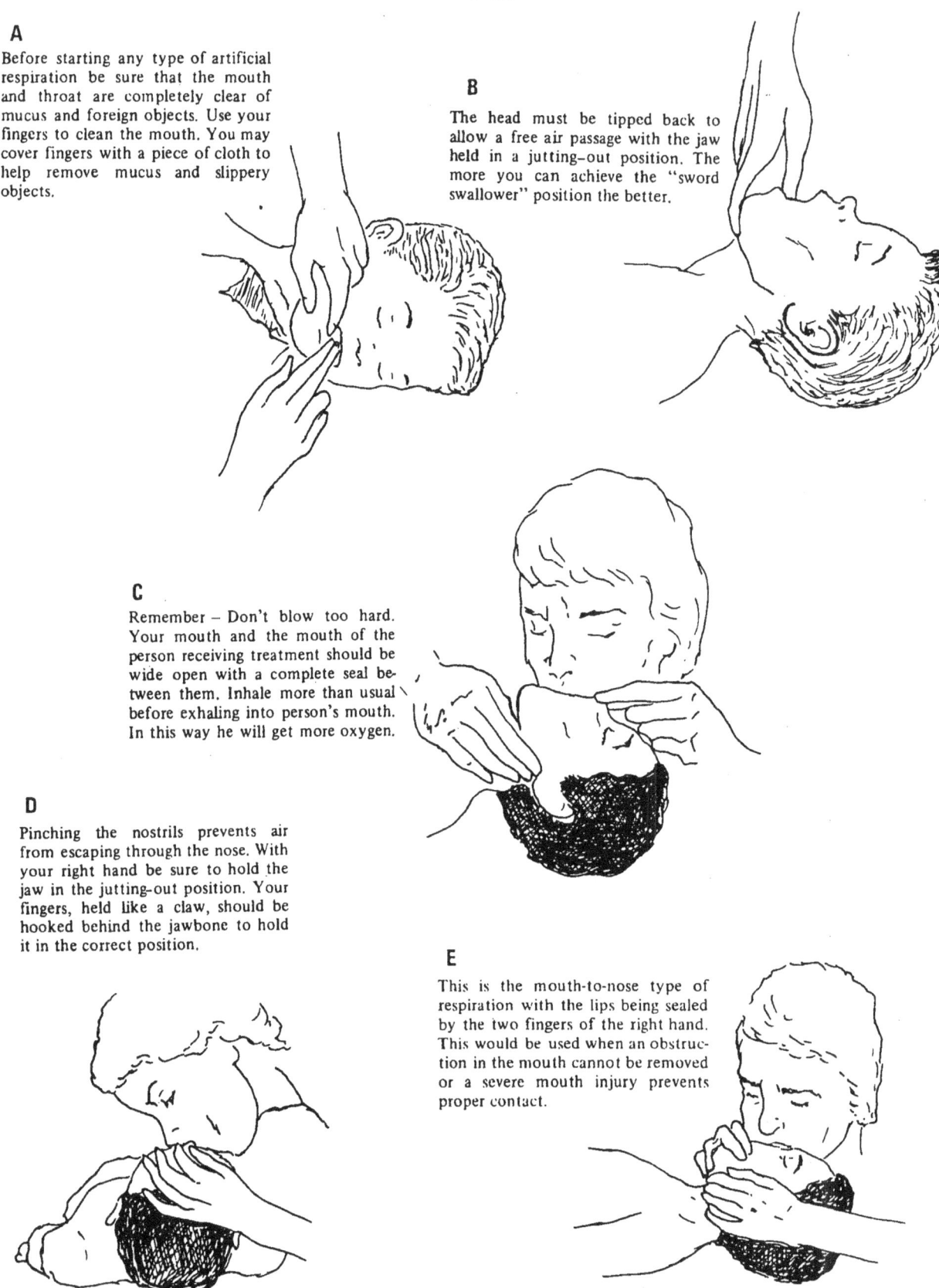

Figure 3. Mouth-to-Mouth and Mouth-to-Nose Method*

INSTRUCTOR GUIDELINES	CONTENT
Refer to Figure 4. Emphasize that this method is not as effective as mouth-to-mouth. Back-pressure method should only be used when mouth injuries, etc., prevent use of mouth-to-mouth method.	*Back-pressure, arm-lift method.* This is the second most desirable method of artificial respiration. It should be used only when injuries to the head or face prevent the use of mouth-to-mouth or mouth-to-nose method. If a person has injuries both to the face and chest so you cannot use either method, one should not hesitate to open the victim's mouth and keep the windpipe clear of blood, mucus, broken teeth, or obstructing tongue. It is better to move a broken jaw, broken nose, or broken teeth and keep the person alive by letting him breathe than to keep the broken bones from moving and have the person die.
Add any comments about artificial respiration you feel are necessary. Answer any questions trainees may ask.	NOTES:

B-24

A This picture shows the correct position of the knee, foot, and hands in the first step of back-pressure arm-lift method. The knee and foot may be alternated to make it less tiring for the person administering this type of artificial respiration.

USE ONLY WHEN MOUTH-TO-MOUTH METHOD IS NOT POSSIBLE

B With hands in correct position the operator starts a rocking forward motion. Note that elbows are straight and stiff. This is when you start the timing. Chant: "Press–Release" – "Lift–Release." Say it in time to your own breathing.

C With arms almost vertical direct pressure is applied to the back. *Do not* use quick, jerking pressure. Use *smooth* even pressure. Release the pressure in the same smooth way. Pull your hands away slowly.

D As the operator rocks back to his original position he grasps each arm just above the elbow. This is the next part of the timing. Chant: "Lift–Release." Slow–Regular–Even.

E The operator continues to rock back lifting the arms up and toward him. This is the end of one cycle. He will next place his hands in correct position on the back and start over again.

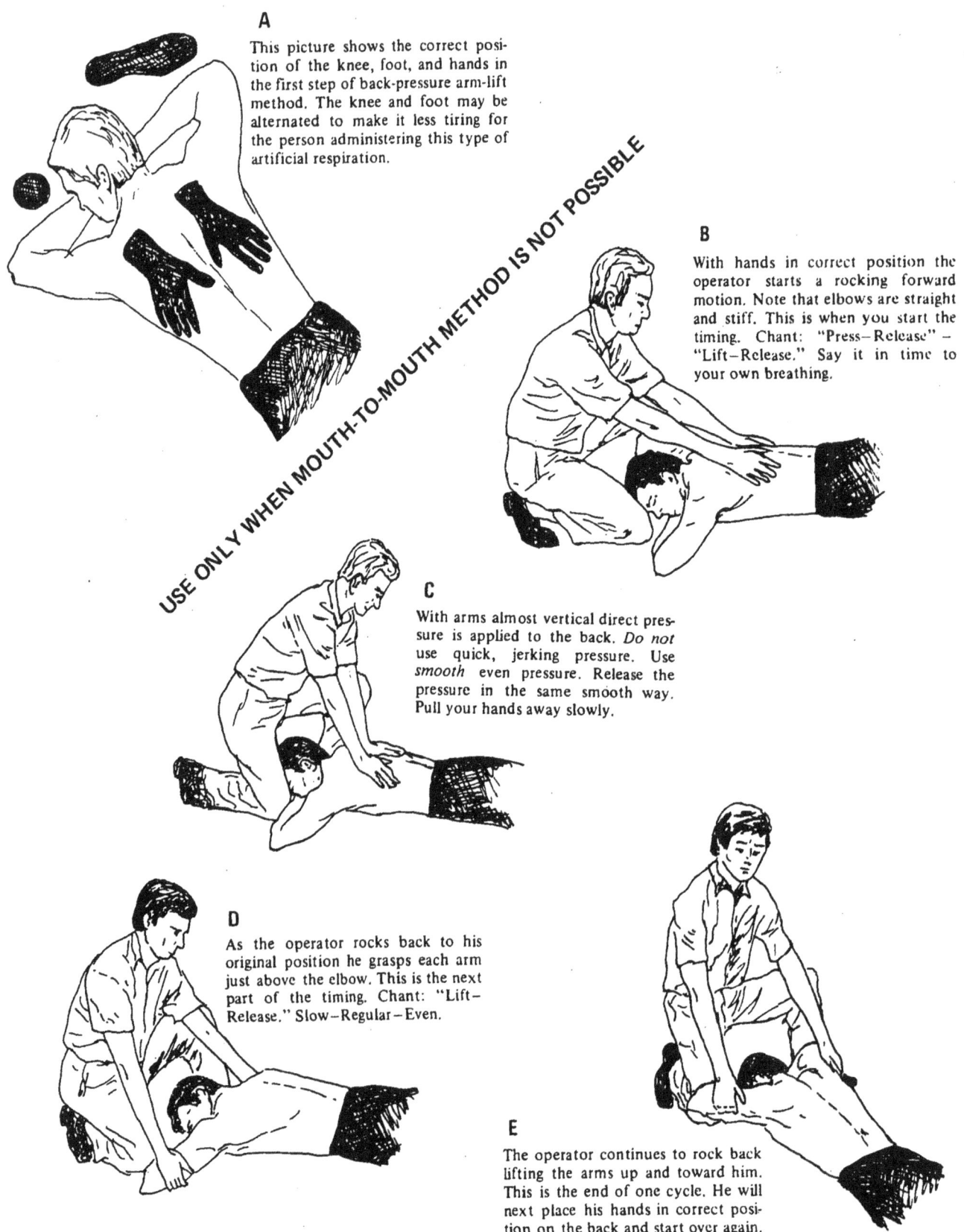

Figure 4. Back-Pressure Arm-Lift Method

PRACTICE IN ARTIFICIAL RESPIRATION

INSTRUCTOR GUIDELINES	CONTENT
If you did not show the film, "First Aid on the Spot," use a volunteer from the class to demonstrate the mouth-to-mouth method of artificial respiration. Also demonstrate the back-pressure arm-lift method. Comment as you go. Break class into pairs. Have each pair take turns practicing each method. Assist where necessary. Have them tell you when they feel competent to be checked. Check each method and provide feedback.	Your instructor will now show you the two methods of artificial respiration. When would you use the back-pressure arm-lift method? How does the mouth-to-mouth method differ when the injured person is a small child? Now you take turns practicing each method with another member of the class. Your instructor will be around to observe. NOTES:

EVALUATION AND CONTROL OF SHOCK

INSTRUCTOR GUIDELINES	CONTENT
It is not recommended that bus drivers attempt to splint a fractured bone. Keeping the person immobile, comfortable, and treating him for shock are usually the best actions until medical help arrives.	Shock may cause death if not treated promptly, even though the injury which caused it may not itself be enough to cause death. The three most common causes of severe shock are inadequate breathing, excessive bleeding, and unsplinted fractures. Correction of these will do much to correct the shock. RECOGNIZING SHOCK Shock is easily recognized: The skin is pale and clammy with small drops of sweat particularly around the lips and forehead; the person may complain of nausea and dizziness; the pulse may be fast and weak and the breathing shallow and irregular; the eyes may be dull with enlarged pupils. A person may be unconscious or unaware of the seriousness of the injury, and then suddenly collapse. 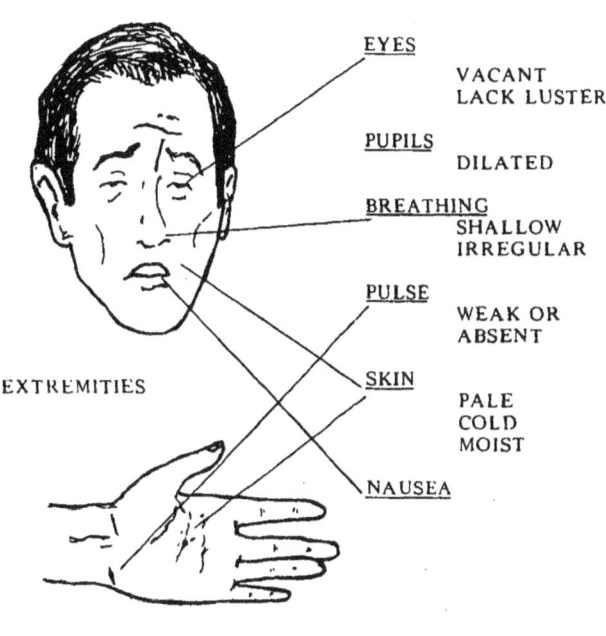

INSTRUCTOR GUIDELINES	CONTENT
	You should treat all seriously injured persons for shock, even though all of these symptoms have not appeared and the person seems normal and alert.
	CONTROL OF SHOCK
	When treating for shock, follow these steps:
	1. Have the injured person lie down.
	2. Elevate his feet and legs 12 inches or more. This helps the flow of blood to his heart and head. If the person has received a head or chest injury, or if he has difficulty breathing, elevate his head and chest rather than his feet.
Usually a first aider would use a blanket, but drivers must use what is available on the bus.	3. Keep the person warm, but not hot. Place a coat, jacket, newspapers, or any available covering <u>under</u> him. Depending on the weather, also cover him. Avoid getting him so hot that he perspires, because this draws blood to the skin and away from the interior of his body where it is needed. On warm days or in a hot room, no covering is necessary.
Feet may be elevated by placing the child on the floor of the bus with his feet raised up to rest on a bus seat.	

INSTRUCTOR GUIDELINES	CONTENT
Generally, water won't be available on the bus. De-emphasize this point. In any case, don't send other students to search for water. It's better to keep them on the bus and do without the water until help arrives.	4. If water is available, give him some every 15 minutes in small amounts if his condition permits. If he is unconscious, do not attempt to give anything to drink. If he vomits or is nauseated, postpone giving liquid until the nausea disappears. 5. Keep the person quiet. See that bleeding is controlled and injured parts are kept still. Assure him that he will get the best care you can give. Reassurance is a potent medicine.
Add any comments you may have on the treatment of shock. Answer any questions trainees may ask.	NOTES:

PRACTICE IN TREATING SHOCK

INSTRUCTOR GUIDELINES	CONTENT
Demonstrate how to check for symptoms of shock, using a volunteer from the class. Demonstrate how to treat shock. Comment and question trainees on when you should elevate the feet and when you should elevate the head and shoulders. Break class into pairs and have each member "treat" the other for shock. Observe each pair, and provide feedback.	Your instructor will now show you how to treat an injured person who has gone into shock (or who is in danger of going into shock). Now, you practice the treatment on another class member. NOTES:

GUIDELINES ON OTHER INJURIES AND CONDITIONS

INSTRUCTOR GUIDELINES	CONTENT
Federal Standards recommend that school bus drivers take a Standard American Red Cross First Aid course. Therefore, procedures for other injuries and conditions are not included here. However, you may want to include procedures for certain injuries that are more likely in your area (for example, snake bites and scorpion bites). Or, your local policy may advise that drivers who have not yet taken Red Cross courses must know how to treat eye injuries, burns, etc., before they transport children. Expand this section to fit your own needs. Insert extra pages if necessary. Administer Unit Review Questions. Provide feedback. Provide remedial review and practice for anyone who does not meet criterion.	Can you think of any injuries or conditions that have not been covered?

MENTAL DISORDERS AND TREATMENT PRACTICES

This section reviews eight areas that are usually tested on examinations:

- The Characteristics of Various Psychiatric Disorders
- The Needs of Special Groups (Children, Geriatrics)
- The Influences of Environment, Society, and Family on Psychiatric Disorders
- Psychotropic Drugs (Reactions and Uses)
- The Assessment and Evaluation of Patients
- The Functions and Purposes of the Treatment Team
- The Development and Implementation of the Treatment Plan
- Methods for Handling People with Various Emotional or Psychiatric Disorders

THE CHARACTERISTICS OF VARIOUS PSYCHIATRIC DISORDERS

It is often difficult to assign labels to human behavior with any large degree of accuracy. Behavior sometimes changes rapidly, and the interpretation of what behavior a label actually represents can vary greatly from one person to the next. One can often learn a great deal more about a person by observing their behavior than by reading a diagnostic label about that person. Regardless, diagnostic labels can be helpful to members of a treatment team as a shorthand method of describing a group of behaviors one might expect from certain individuals. They are also required for many insurance forms. A diagnosis may be useful as long as one views the diagnosis as an ongoing process, and can continue to look at the patient with *new eyes*.

The Difference Between Neurosis and Psychosis

People suffering from a neurosis are usually able to manage with the concerns of daily life, although there is often some distortion in their concept of reality. Those suffering from a neurosis may feel inferior, unloved, or have a long-term feeling of fear or dread. They may have obsessions, compulsions or phobias, but they are rarely dangerous to themselves or others. They usually have some insight into their problems, and except in severe cases, don't require hospitalization. Many go through life without obtaining any help for their problems. Those who experience a psychosis, however, are out of touch with reality and live in an imaginary world. They may hear voices, feel that they are being persecuted, or experience very deep depressions. There is a very definite split between the reality of those suffering from psychoses and the reality of the world. Unlike those suffering from neuroses, those suffering from psychoses often lose track of time, person, and place, and they have little insight into the nature of their behavior. They usually require hospitalization and their behavior is sometimes injurious to other people or themselves, although they may insist that there is nothing wrong with them.

Categories of Neurosis

It is important to keep in mind that rarely will all of a patient's symptoms fall into any one category, and that symptoms may change over time from one category to another. *Anxiety Neuroses* constitute approximately 35% of all neurotic disorders. Those suffering from anxiety neuroses have a tendency to view the world as hostile and cruel, and may frequently restrict daily activities in order to feel safer in their environment. They often feel tense, worried, and anxious, but are unable to articulate exactly why they feel this way. Many anxious individuals are very uncertain of themselves in even minor stress producing situations, and they may have real difficulties in concentrating because of their high anxiety levels.

Other symptoms may include strong anxiety reactions with difficulty catching one's breath, perspiration, increased heart beat, dizziness, and feeling that they are dying. They may come to the Emergency Room of a hospital complaining of a heart attack or heart troubles. It is important to keep in mind that many elements of the anxiety reaction are seen in patients with other neurotic disorders.

Conversion Reactions or *Hysteria* involve the loss of ability to perform some physical function that the person could previously perform, which is psychogenic in origin. This reaction is an attempt by the individual to defend herself or himself from some anxiety producing situation by developing physical symptoms that have no organic or physical cause. These reactions are not common, and constitute less than five percent of neurotic disorders. The lost function is often symbolically related to a situation which has produced stress or anxiety, and is often an attempt to escape from that situation. The person may lose the ability to hear or speak, have unusual bodily sensations, or lose control of some motor function. Since there is no physical cause of dysfunction, some people assume that the pain or paralysis is not real, or that this type of person is faking. *Dissociative Reactions* also serve to protect the individual from particularly stressful situations. Amnesia, fugue, and multiple personalities are the major categories of dissociative reactions. Despite the prevalence of *amnesia* on soap operas, dissociative reactions account for less than five percent of all neurotic disorders. Amnesiacs usually forget specific information for a specified but variable period of time. The patient does not, however, forget his or her basic lifestyle or habits. In *fugue,* the person combines the amnesia with flight, and leaves the area where the stressful situation is. Usually the person is unaware of where he or she has been, or where he or she is going. There are very few cases of *multiple personalities.* In this disorder, the person shows different ways of responding to the environment. Each individual personality within the person is a complete personality system, and may dominate the person's reactions to his or her environment, depending upon the situation.

Obsessive-Compulsive Reactions involve either the inability to stop thinking about something the person does not want to think about, or the obligatory performance of a repetitive act. People experiencing these reactions often recognize they are irrational, but are unable to stop doing them. They often attempt to rearrange their environment, which they may perceive as threatening, in an attempt to impose control and structure, so they can control their environment and feel safer. Those suffering from compulsive reactions feel a strong need to perform or repeat certain behaviors, often in order to prevent something terrible from happening to them. (This might involve pre-determined ways to enter a room, brush their teeth, get into bed, begin conversations, etc.) Of course, many people may exhibit aspects of this behavior. Observing some professional baseball players before they pitch or take a pitch can certainly demonstrate this point. There is little cause for concern if the patterns are relatively temporary and help the person in some way obtain their goal. When the behaviors begin to unduly restrict a person's activities, then the situation becomes more serious. People exhibiting this behavior are often unable to make decisions effectively, are often perfectionists, have a strong need for structure, and are fairly rigid. Those who are obsessed with unwanted thoughts may have quite a variety of areas that they think about. The most common areas, however, concern religion, ethical concerns (something being absolutely right or wrong), bodily functions, and suicide.

Phobic Reactions involve a strong, persistent irrational fear of an object, condition, or place. It is believed that phobias usually involve a displacement of anxiety from the original cause to the phobic object. The phobia serves to assist the individual in avoiding the anxiety-causing situation. Some of the most common phobias include fear of crowds, being alone, darkness, thunderstorms, and high places. It is often very difficult to discover the symbolic significance of a particular phobia.

Neurotic Depressive Reactions involve an intensification of normal grief reactions. Research has indicated that those suffering from this reaction are unable to *bounce back* from upsetting or discouraging events. People who suffer from this reaction tend to have a poor self-concept, exaggerated dependency needs, a tendency to feel guilty about almost anything, and to turn those guilt feelings against themselves in a highly punitive way. The possibility of suicide should be kept in mind when working with these patients.

Categories of Psychosis

Psychoses are generally divided into two categories, *functional psychoses* and *organic psychoses*. Functional psychoses are caused by psychological stress, while organic psychoses are caused by a disorder of the brain for which physical pathology can be demonstrated. A third category, *toxic psychoses,* is sometimes used to refer to psychotic reactions caused by toxic substances such as drugs or poisons.

Schizophrenia accounts for approximately 25 percent of all first admissions to mental institutions, and is the largest single diagnostic group of psychotic patients. The *paranoid schizophrenic* shows a great deal of suspiciousness and hostility, and may be very aggressive. The *simple type schizophrenic* is shy and withdrawn, and shows interest in his or her environment. The *hebephrenic schizophrenic* often has bizarre mannerisms and may appear quite manic. He or she may laugh and giggle inappropriately, and become preoccupied with unimportant matters. The *catatonic schizophrenic* may remain motionless for days or hours, and may refuse to eat. The two phases of catatonia are the *stuporous phase* where the person is motionless and *catatonic excitement* where the person is over-active and appears manic. While the catatonic schizophrenic may alternate between these two phases, most show a preference for just one. Someone suffering from *schizoaffective schizophrenia* will have significant thought disorders and mood variations. They may initially appear to be depressed or manic, but a basic personality disorganization also exists. These are the major categories of schizophrenia you should need for the exam. Since the exam announcement states basic knowledge is required, it is very possible some of the above categories may be too specific. We have included them just in case, however.

The general symptoms of schizophrenia include an inability to deal with reality, the presence of hallucinations or delusions, inappropriate emotions, autism and various other unusual behaviors. There is often a very noticeable inability to organize thoughts. Schizophrenic reactions that occur suddenly are referred to as *acute* schizophrenic reactions, while those that develop slowly over a rather lengthy period are called *chronic* schizophrenic reactions.

Paranoid Reactions in people account for less than one percent of psychiatric admissions. Those with this behavior usually mistrust the motives of everyone, are very resentful, and often hostile. They may show signs of grandiosity or persecution. The person often believes that whatever happens is related to him or her. The major difference between paranoid patients and paranoid schizophrenics is that the paranoid patient usually has better control of his or her thought processes, and is able to make more appropriate responses to situations. They are usually more reality-oriented, and able to state their feelings more effectively.

Affective Reactions are those that represent a change in the normal affect, or mood, of a person. There are two major categories of affective disorders: *manic-depressive reactions* and *involutional psychotic reactions.* In the manic-depressive reaction, the manic and depressive states alternate. In the manic phase, the person may be extremely talkative, agitated or elated, and demonstrate a great deal of physical and verbal activity. They may also exhibit some grandiosity. In the depressive phase, the person is joyless, quiet, and inhibited. The manic reactions are often divided into three degress of severity, each category representing a more severe degree of manic reaction. *Hypomania* is the least severe, *acute mania* is the next, and *delirious mania* is the most severe state. The term *involutional psychosis is* usually related to a patient's age. For women, the involutional age is considered to be somewhere between 40 and 55, and the involutional period for men is somewhere between 50 and 65. It seems that stresses are greater for men and women during these periods, and that these stresses may trigger psychotic reactions which are generally transient. These people generally have a long history of feeling guilty and very anxious, have little diversity of activity, and few sources of satisfaction in their lives.

Selected Personality Disorders

This category includes behavior which is maladaptive, but neither psychotic nor neurotic. This group includes *antisocial reactions,* the *abuse of alchol and other drugs,* and *sexual deviations.* The *antisocial* or *sociopathic* personality type fails to develop a concern for others and uses relationships to get what he or she wants. There is little or no concern about what effect their behavior might have on others, and they seldom feel remorse or guilt. They are often likable, friendly, intelligent people. Their relationships with others tend to be superficial, however, because they lack the capacity for deep emotional responses. The sociopath is often impulsive and seeks immediate gratification of his or her wants. He or she often is unreliable, untruthful, undependable and insincere. A large number of people have sociopathic traits which, as with most other characteristics, vary in severity and number. Sociopaths are found in all professions, although many are able to control their acting out behaviors or channel them in more socially acceptable ways. They avoid acting out not because of internal values, but because they do not wish to get caught. Sociopaths usually have a low frustration tolerance, are easily bored, and continually seek excitement. The sociopath most frequently comes to treatment because he or she has been *caught* doing something or been required to seek help by an employer or family member.

Sexual Deviations occur in those who fail to develop what their society considers appropriate sexual behavior. The major sexual deviations include child molestation, rape, sadism, masochism, voyeurism, fetishism, transvestism, exhibitionism, pedophilia, and incest. As you can see, some of these behaviors are much more harmful to other people than others are.

PSYCHOTROPIC DRUGS (REACTIONS AND USES)

The two major classifications of the psychotropic drugs are the tranquilizers, which are further divided into major (or anti-psychotic) and minor (or antianxiety) groups, and the antidepressants. Other drugs used include anticonvulsants, sedatives, hypnotics, and antiparkinsons.

Tranquilizers are meant to calm disturbed patients, and free them from agitation or disturbance. Drugs designed as *antipsychotic,* or *major tranquilizers,* also help to reduce the frequency of hallucinations, delusions, thought disorders, and the type of withdrawal seen in catatonic schizophrenia. It may take several days of drug therapy before the symptoms begin to subside, but during this time the patient becomes less fearful, hostile and upset by his disturbed sensory perceptions. The *phenothiazine derivatives* are the largest group of antipsychotic drugs. All the drugs in this group have essentially the same type of action on the body, but vary according to strength and the type and severity of their side effects. These drugs include:

Thorazine	Trilafon	Taractan
Mellaril	Compazine	Navane
Stelazine	Dartal	Sordinal
Prolixin	Proketazine	Haldol
Sparine	Tindal	Loxitane
Vesprin	Repoise	Moban

Serious side effects are very important to watch for. For these drugs, the phenothiazine derivatives, there are three major types of extrapyramidal symptoms (EPS): (1) akinesia - inability to sit still, complaints of fatigue and weakness, and continuous movement of the hands, mouth, and body; (2) pseudoparkinsonism -restlessness, mask-like facial expressions, drooling, and tremors; (3) tardive dyskenesia - lack of control over voluntary movements. Symptoms may include involuntary grimacing, sucking and chewing movements, pursing of the tongue and mouth, jerking of the hands, feet and neck, and drooping head. Immediate action must be taken to combat these side effects. The administration of antiparkinson drugs usually produces a dramatic reduction in symptoms. Unless spotted and treated early, however, these can become permanent.

Other side effects may include muscle spasms, shuffling gait, skin rash, eye problems, trembling hands and fingers, fainting, wormlike tongue movements, sore throat and fever, yellowing of skin or eyes, dry mouth, constipation, excessive weight gain, edema, a drop in blood pressure when moving from a lying to standing position, decreased sexual interest, sensitivity to light and prone to sunburn and visual problems, blurred vision, drowsiness, and increased perspiration. Just about any physical symptom or behavior could be caused by a reaction to a drug.

Special Considerations: Patients receiving a high dose of a phenothiazine drug should have their blood pressure checked regularly. Long exposures of skin to sunlight should be avoided (a wide-brimmed hat and long-sleeved clothing can also help). If a patient receiving phenothiazines is lethargic and wants to sleep a great deal, the dose of the drug may be too high and need adjustment. Patients on phenothiazines should not drive or use dangerous equipment. These drugs greatly increase the effects of alcohol. In the first three to five days, a person may feel drowsy and dizzy upon standing. Antipsychotic drugs tend to mask the symptoms of diseases and dictate that patients receiving them undergo thorough physical examinations every six months.

The *Minor Tranquilizers,* or *antianxiety drugs,* reduce anxiety and muscle tension associated with it. They are useful primarily with psychoneurotic and psychosomatic disorders. When given in small doses, they are relatively safe and have few side effects. Unlike the antipsychotic drugs, some of the antianxiety drugs tend to be habit-forming. If the drug is discontinued, the person may experience severe withdrawal symptoms, such as convulsions or delirium. These drugs include:

Librium	Milpath	Frienquel
Azene	Deprol	Phobex
Tranxene	Milprem	Softran
Valium	Miltown	Atarax
Ativan	Robaxin	Vistaril
Serax	Solacen	Trancopal

Side effects may include rashes, chills, fever, nausea, headaches, poor muscle coordination, some inability to concentrate, and dizziness. Excessive amounts of these drugs may lead to coma and death; however, death is less likely with an overdose of minor tranquilizers than with an overdose of barbituates. Patients taking these should be cautioned against driving or performing tasks that require careful attention to detail and mental alertness.

Antidepressants, such as the *Tricyclic Antidepressants,* are used to elevate the patient's mood, and increase appetite and mental and physical alertness. Drugs in this group tend to take one to four weeks of use before significant changes occur in the patient's outlook. Since these drugs sometimes excite patients instead of sedating them, patients must be observed closely for reactions. These drugs include:

Elavil	Sinequan
Endep	Tofranil
Asendine	Aventyl
Morpramin	Vivactil
Adapin	Marplan
Presamine	Janimine

Common side effects include dry mouth, fatigue, weakness, nausea, increased appetite, increased perspiration, heartburn, and sensitivity to sunlight. *Serious side effects* include blurred vision, constipation, irregular heartbeat, problems urinating, headache, eye pain, fainting, hallucination, vomiting, unusually slow pulse, seizures, skin rash, sore throat and fever, and yellowing of eyes and skin.

Serious side effects include blurred vision, constipation, irregular heartbeat, problems urinating, headache, eye pain, fainting, hallucination, vomiting, unusually slow pulse, seizures, skin rash, sore throat and fever, and yellowing of eyes and skin.

Monoamineoxidose Inhibitors (MAO Inhibitors) are sometimes used for depression, but can have *very* serious side effects, and can also lead to serious hypertensive crisis. Their use must be very closely monitored. Their use with some over-the-counter drugs can be very serious. Foods containing Typtophen or Tyramine (some examples: caffeine, chocolate, herring, beans, chicken liver, cheese, beer, pickles, wine) should be avoided also. *Side effects* to watch for include severe headaches, stiff neck, nausea, vomiting, dilated pupils, and cold, clammy skin. A hypertensive crisis requires *immediate* treatment. These drugs include: Marplan, Nardil, Parnate, and Ludiomil.

In addition to the above psychotropic drugs, sedatives, hypnotics, anticonvulsants, and antiparkinsons drugs are also used. Since the exam announcement includes uses and reactions of only the psychotropic drugs, we will not review the non-psychotropic drugs. We will mention, however, the use and reactions of *Lithium Carbonate* (also known as Eskolith, Lithane,

Lithobid, and Lithonate). This drug is primarily used in the treatment of manic depressive psychoses since it is effective in decreasing excessive motor activity, talking, and unstable behavior by acting on the brain's metabolism. It also decreases swings in mood. The correct dose is close to the overdose level for this drug, so it is important to watch closely for symptoms and to report them immediately. *Common side effects* include dry mouth, metal taste, slightly increased urination, hand tremors, increased appetite, and fatigue. *Serious side effects* include greatly increased urination, nausea, vomiting, diarrhea, loss of muscle coordination, muscle cramps or weakness, irritability, confusion, slurred speech, blackout spells, and coma. These side effects require medical attention. *Special Considerations:* This drug must sometimes be taken from one to several weeks before the resident feels better. Hot weather, hot baths, and too much exercise can be dangerous, as too much perspiring can lead to an overdose. The person should drink two to three quarts of fluid a day, but should not drink large quantities of caffeine-containing beverages like coffee, tea, or colas.

MANAGEMENT OF THE EMOTIONALLY DISTURBED

Unit 1. Emotional Aspects of Illness and Injury   1

    Responses of Patients to Illness and Injury   1
    Responses of the Family, Friends, or Bystanders   2
    Responses of the Paramedic   2
    Responses of Patients and Bystanders to Mass Casualties   3
    Death and Dying   4

Unit 2. Psychiatric Emergencies   5

    Patient Assessment and General Principles of Management   5
    Specific Psychiatric Emergencies   8

Unit 3. Techniques of Management: Patient Interviewing   13

MANAGEMENT OF THE EMOTIONALLY DISTURBED

Unit 1. Emotional Aspects of Illness and Injury

Everyone involved in a critical illness or injury situation--the patient, the family, bystanders, health professionals--responds to stresses that naturally occur in such emergencies. Emergency Medical Technicians-Paramedics (EMT-P's) can deal effectively with these responses, both in others and in themselves, only if they can understand and anticipate such responses.

Responses of Patients to Illness and Injury

Although patients' reactions to critical illness or injury are largely determined by mechanisms they already have developed to deal with stressful situations, most of these reactions will follow common patterns. Patients usually become aware of painful or unpleasant sensations, and sometimes decreased energy and strength, with the onset of illness. The coon response to this awareness is anxiety. Some patients will attempt to deny or minimize their symptoms at this point, while others will become irritable and angry. The paramedic must be aware that once patients begin to see themselves as ill or to realize they have been injured, the following reactions may occur:

- Realistic fears. Patients may fear pain, disability, death, or financial problems. Such fears are normal and reasonable in ill or injured patients.
- General anxiety. Feelings of loss of control are common among ill or injured patients. They may feel helpless knowing they are completely dependent on someone else, often a stranger, whose knowledge of medical care and ability they cannot evaluate easily. Patients whose self-esteem depends on being active, independent, and aggressive are particularly prone to anxiety in these situations.
- Depression. Depression is a natural response by some patients to the loss of some bodily function as well as to feelings of loss of control over his or her own destiny.
- Regression. Patients may return to earlier or more primitive modes of behavior. Their behavior may appear childlike. This is natural as ill or injured patients, like children, must depend on others for their survival.
- Denial. Many patients try to deny or ignore the seriousness of their illness or injury because it causes them anxiety. Denial often is seen as a tendency to dismiss all symptoms with words like "only" or "a little." When a patient uses this mechanism, the paramedic may need to find an informant among the patient's family or friends from whom a more accurate history can be obtained.
- Displacement of anger. Patients often respond to discomfort or limitations of activity by becoming resentful and suspicious of those around them. They may vent this anger on the paramedic by becoming impatient and irritable or excessively demanding. It is important for the paramedic to realize that the patient's anger stems from fear and discomfort and is not really directed at the paramedic.
- Confusion. Illness or injury can cause disorientation among patients, especially the elderly. Such confusion is increased by the presence of unfamiliar people and equipment. In these cases, it is important for paramedics to explain carefully who they are and what they plan to do and to explain treatment steps as they are being performed.

In addition, patients usually will have uncomfortable feelings about being examined. Ordinarily, undressing in front of another person is done in situations of intimacy and trust. Thus, every patient will feel some anxiety about having a stranger perform a physical examination. Some patients may consider the physical exam a humiliating invasion of privacy. Therefore, the paramedic always should try to establish a relationship with the patient during an initial interview and then conduct the physical examination. Furthermore, the paramedic always should be aware of the unclothed patient's probable embarrassment and shame and make sure that the patient is properly draped or shielded from the stares of curious bystanders. The EMT-P should conduct the examination in an efficient, businesslike manner and continue talking with the patient during the entire procedure.

Responses of the Family Friends or Bystanders

Those at the scene with the patient also may show many of the responses described above. Family members may be anxious, panicky, or angry. Their anger often results from their feelings of guilt. As a means of coping with their own anxiety, they may demand immediate action, or they may pressure the paramedic to move the patient to the hospital before appropriate examination and stabilization have been completed. They may state or imply that the paramedic is not competent to handle the situation ("Get him to the hospital so he can be seen by a doctor."). No matter how upsetting this may be, a paramedic must realize that the patient's family and friends are concerned and that their behavior, however irritating to the paramedic, arises from distress. The paramedic should remain calm and sympathetic and explain treatment activities to friends and family members. They should be reassured that paramedics are in radio contact with physicians at all times and are acting under a physician's direction to help the patient.

Responses of the Paramedic

Health professionals are not immune to the stresses of emergency situations. When dealing with the critically ill and injured, they may experience a wide range of feelings, some of which are unpleasant. The paramedic may feel irritated by the family or the patient's demands, be anxious when faced with life-threatening injuries, become defensive at implications that he or she is not competent to handle emergencies, and become sad in response to tragedy. Although these feelings are natural, it is best for the paramedic not to express them during an emergency. Furthermore, if the EMT-P gives an outward appearance of calmness and confidence, it will help to relieve the anxiety of those on the scene. Helping others to remain calm is part of the paramedic's therapeutic role.

Another common reaction among health professionals is irritation with the patient who does not appear particularly ill. This reaction can be a special problem of emergency personnel, who are prepared to deal with life-threatening problems and may regard minor complaints as burdensome and annoying. It should be remembered, however, that people call for help only if they are worried about something. Patients may be worried about injuries, pains, disturbing feelings, or bodily functions that they think are abnormal. It is not the duty of the EMT-P to judge whether such complaints are real or imagined. These complaints are always real to the patient. Although it is more dramatic to rescue the multiple trauma victim than to reassure the patient with a minor cold, both patients have indicated that they are distressed and want help. In both cases, the EMT-P must be supportive and nonjudgmental and render whatever care is needed.

Responses of Patients and Bystanders to Mass Casualties

When there are multiple casualties--as in an automobile accident with several victims or a natural disaster (tornado, flood, earthquake)--both victims and bystanders may become dazed, disorganized, or overwhelmed. The American Psychiatric Association has identified five possible types of reactions in such situations:

- Normal reaction. In multiple casualty situations, the normal reaction consists of symptoms of extreme anxiety, including sweating, shaking, weakness, nausea, and sometimes vomiting. Individuals experiencing this type of response may recover completely within a few minutes and can be helpful if given clear instructions.
- Blind panic. In this type of reaction, the individual's judgment seems to disappear completely. Blind panic is particularly dangerous because it may lead to mass panic among others present.
- Depression. The individual who remains motionless and looks numbed or dazed is depressed. It is important to give such a person a task to perform in order to bring him or her back to reality.
- Overreaction. The person who talks compulsively, jokes inappropriately, and races from one task to another, usually accomplishing little, is overreacting to a situation.
- Conversion hysteria. The person's mood may shift rapidly from extreme anxiety to relative calmness. The person may convert anxiety to some bodily dysfunction. This reaction can result in hysterical blindness, deafness, or paralysis.

Paramedics should observe the following guidelines in dealing with mass casualty situations:

- Identify themselves and take command of the situation. Strive to remain self-assured and sympathetic, and conduct themselves in a businesslike manner.
- Treat serious physical injuries immediately, and reassure anxious patients or bystanders.
- Keep spectators away from the patients, but do not leave the patients alone. If all rescue personnel are busy dealing with physical injuries, assign a responsible bystander to stay with any person showing unusual behavioral symptoms.
- Assign tasks to bystanders to keep them occupied. Feeling that they are useful and responsible will lessen their anxiety greatly.
- Respect the right of patients to have their own feelings. Let the patients know that the paramedics are trying to understand their feelings so they can help. Paramedics should not try to tell the patients how they should feel.
- Accept patients' physical and emotional limitations. Fear and panic are as disabling as physical injuries, and some people are able to deal with anxiety better than others. Do not try to force patients to deal with more than they seem able to cope with. Help patients to recognize and use their remaining strength and lessen their anxiety.
- Employ sedatives only as a last resort. In most cases, they only add to the patient's confusion. In the physically injured, they may mask important symptoms. The calm, reassuring attitude of the paramedic is better, more effective therapy.
- Accept personal limitations. In mass casualty situations realize that there are limits to what can be done. Avoid overextending themselves and provide more effective care by establishing care priorities.

Death and Dying

The paramedics' contacts with the dying usually will be confined to the seriously ill or injured patient who is slipping in and out of consciousness. Occasionally, however, paramedics will encounter dying patients who are conscious and aware of their condition. Although everything possible should be done to attend to the patients' physical needs, paramedics should not neglect the emotional and religious needs of dying patients. In such situations, paramedics can reduce the apprehension of the dying to some degree by being as reassuring as possible. Patients can be told that every effort is being made to transport them quickly to the hospital where expert help is available.

Many patients will be anxious about their family members and may express the desire to communicate with them. Paramedics may be able to reduce the anxiety of these patients by offering to make themselves available to the family and to convey any important messages to them. Such communications, since they may have later legal implications, should be noted carefully. Survivors at the scene who are aware of the dying patient's condition should be reassured that everything will be done to save the patient at the scene and at the hospital.

Paramedics must be aware of and master their own feelings concerning death. Contact with dead and dying patients causes anxiety in all health professionals. If paramedics are aware that such normal reactions affect everyone, there will be less chance that their own feelings about death will interfere with proper treatment of dying patients.

Unit 2. Psychiatric Emergencies

Psychiatric emergencies are situations in which patients display disorders of mood, thought, or behavior that are dangerous or disturbing to themselves or others. Almost all disturbed behavior represents the individual's effort to cope with internal or external stress (anxiety). Such behavior often disappears when normal psychological defense mechanisms are mobilized properly.

Most psychiatric emergencies are emergencies because the patients' disturbed behavior makes them, their families, or bystanders feel anxious or panicky. Patients and others will feel they are in a situation that is out of their control and may demand that paramedics take control by pressuring them to "do something" immediately. It is important to remember that the general excitement in such situations results from feelings of fear and loss of control. These feelings can be lessened when the EMT-P maintains a calm, self-assured attitude.

It is important to recall that <u>abnormal behavior may be due to conditions other than mental illness.</u> Diabetes, seizure disorders, severe infections, metabolic disorders, head injury, hypertension, stroke, alcohol, and other drugs all may cause disturbed behavior. Disturbed behavior is caused by intoxication with alcohol or another drug in more than half of the patients who demonstrate such behavior. These other possible causes should be remembered whenever a patient with apparent emotional disturbance is evaluated.

Primary emotional disorders are a response to personal crisis. When individuals' basic needs are threatened, they face crises that vary in severity depending on their ability to deal with their feelings. People in crisis have two alternatives: They can cope with the situation by finding ways to alter it, or they can attempt to decrease the discomfort by escaping from the situation. Escape takes many forms, including the use of alcohol or other drugs, suicide, or the manifestation of psychiatric symptoms. Such symptoms are a compromise for the patient and reduce the anxiety produced by the inner crisis.

Patient Assessment and General Principles of Management

The patient exhibiting bizarre or unusual behavior usually is in the midst of an emotional crisis. Such a patient may need immediate attention to lessen emotional distress. While attempting to alleviate the patient's anxiety, the paramedic also must prevent injury to the patient or others at the scene and attempt to bring a measure of calm to a stressful situation.

The in-depth counseling necessary to deal with a severe psychiatric reaction may not be feasible in field situations. In some cases, a crisis worker, contacted through appropriate local resources, may be more capable of managing the crisis than is the paramedic. Ideally, if the dispatcher anticipates an emotional problem, the appropriate crisis intervention team can be contacted prior to the arrival of the Emergency Medical Services (EMS) team at the scene. However, if the EMS team arrives at the scene without prior warning, paramedics must be prepared to deal with the situation within the limits of their training in crisis counseling and as best as can be expected in a field situation.

Once the paramedics arrive at the scene, they should notify the dispatcher of the presenting conditions and notify support services, such as crisis intervention teams.

Patient assessment and principles of management are presented together because the two are inseparable in dealing with emotional problems. The process of communicating with the patient through which paramedics obtain a history is therapeutic. Therefore, the approach to the disturbed patient and some specific parts of patient assessment will be discussed.

The following general guidelines are recommended to help EMT-P's with emotionally disturbed patients. Paramedics must:

- Be prepared to spend time with disturbed patients and not hurry. A lengthy discussion may be required if it provides the patients with emotional relief. Such individuals require patient, concerned attention.
- Be calm and direct. Disturbed patients often are frightened of losing self-control. Remain calm and undisturbed, thus indicating to the patients that the paramedics are confident that the patients can stay in control. Indeed, one major purpose of the interview is to help a patient regain control. Showing anxiety or panic serves only to increase a patient's belief that the situation is overwhelming.
- Clearly identify themselves. Tell the patients who the EMT crew is and what it is trying to do for them.
- Assess the patients at home or wherever the emergency occurs. Do not rush off to the hospital, which is strange and intimidating for a patient. Hurrying to the hospital also can reinforce the belief that something is terribly wrong. Let patients recover their bearings in familiar surroundings.
- Interview the patients alone, if possible. Ask relatives or bystanders to go into another room, where another EMT-P can obtain their stories.
- Sit down to interview patients. Never tower over them.
- Let the patients tell what happened in their own way. Do not attempt to direct the conversation, but allow the patients to air their feelings.
- Be interested in the patients' stories but not overly sympathetic. If a paramedic overwhelms a patient with pity, the paramedic will convince the patient that the situation is indeed hopeless. Treat a patient as someone expected to get better.
- Maintain a nonjudgmental attitude. Accept the patients' right to have their own feelings, and do not blame or criticize them for feeling as they do.
- Provide honest reassurance. Let the patients know what is expected from them and what they can expect of a paramedic.
- Present a definite plan of action. This makes patients feel that the paramedics are doing something to help and relieves their anxiety. People in crisis need direction. Do not confront patients with questions ("Do you want to go to the hospital?") but rather with statements ("I think it is important for you to go to the hospital. There are doctors there who can help you.").
- Encourage purposeful movement, as this often helps relieve anxiety. If patients will be going to the hospital, encourage them to gather up the belongings they want to bring with them. Letting patients do as much as possible for themselves can reinforce their feelings that the paramedics expect them to get better.
- Stay with the patient at all times. Having responded to the emergency, the paramedics are responsible for the patients' safety.
- Never assume they cannot talk with any patient until they try.

The assessment should begin as soon as the EMT-P begins talking with the patient. The patient's general appearance and clothing should be noted, and it should be observed whether the patient appears neat or disheveled. The patient's rate of speech also should be noted. If it is slowed, it may suggest depression or some kind of intoxication. If it is rapid and pressured, it may suggest mania or the presence of amphetamines. The following questions should be kept in mind when assessing these patients:

- Is the patient easily distracted?
- Are the patient's responses appropriate?
- Is the patient alert and able to communicate coherently?
- Is the patient's memory intact?
- What is the patient's mood?
- Does the patient seem abnormally depressed, elated, or agitated?
- Does the patient appear fearful or worried?
- Does the patient show evidence of disordered thought, such as disturbances in judgment, delusions (false ideas), or hallucinations (seeing or hearing things that are not there)?

Initial questions should be direct and specific to establish whether the patient is alert, oriented, and able to communicate. Only information that is crucial to immediate management should be collected. Paramedics should ask the patient's full name, age, and marital status; find out what kind of work the patient does and where and with whom the patient lives; and inquire about past medical and psychiatric problems. After this, questions should be open ended, beginning with words like "What," "How," or "When." Try not to begin questions with the word "Why." ("Why did you lock everyone out of your room?"). Patients may think they are being criticized by such questions. Let them tell their stories in their own ways.

After talking with patients and gaining their confidence, paramedics should gauge the patient's ability to tolerate a physical examination. If at all possible, they should take vital signs and perform a quick neurological examination, although this may not be possible with violent or extremely fearful patients. Paramedics should do as much as they can without increasing the patient's distress. Conversation should be continued throughout the physical examination.

In general, seriously disturbed patients should be seen by a physician who can decide whether they need to be hospitalized. In most areas, there are four ways to admit patients for psychiatric care. There is "voluntary admission," in which patients sign themselves into the hospital and can leave whenever they want to. Another kind of admission is "voluntary commitment," in which patients agree to be admitted to the hospital but cannot leave until their commitment period ends. Voluntary commitments usually last 10 to 30 days, unless the patients extend the commitment.

Patients who will not agree to come to the hospital usually can be involuntarily detained and brought to the hospital by the police or family members. During this "emergency detention," the patient is examined by a psychiatrist. If the psychiatrist feels that the patient will be dangerous, he or she can authorize hospitalization for a short time, usually about 10 days. In some areas, the psychiatrist must provide evidence to the county mental health authorities to show that the patient needs to be admitted to the hospital and must obtain their permission for an emergency detention.

Many states have a procedure *known as* "court commitment," in which psychiatrists must give evidence in court that patients are mentally ill and need treatment. Some States also require that patients be considered dangerous to themselves or others before they can be committed against their will.

Involuntary commitment deprives people of their civil liberties; and, for this reason, it should not be undertaken lightly. It is not always easy, even for an experienced psychiatrist, to determine whether patients' behaviors justify removing them from society and whether they are dangerous to themselves or others. Laws on involuntary detainment vary considerably from State to State, so paramedics should become familiar with the laws in their communities. In general, patients who are conscious and alert can be taken to the hospital only with their consent. If they do not consent, patients can be taken against their will only at the request of the police. The same applies to forceful restraint. When these measures are necessary, law enforcement officers must be called. Each ambulance service should have clearly defined protocols for dealing with patients who require involuntary commitment.

Specific Psychiatric Emergencies

Psychiatric emergency situations that the paramedic is likely to encounter include those caused by depression, suicide, violent behavior, paranoia, anxiety and phobias, disorganization and disorientation, and alcohol or other drugs.

Depression. Depression can lead to a psychiatric emergency such as suicide and may cause other psychological disorders. Depressed patients may be recognized by their sad appearance, crying spells, and listless or apathetic behavior. These patients feel worthless, guilty, and extremely pessimistic. They often express the desire to be left alone, asserting that no one understands or cares about them and that their problems cannot be solved. Their speech may be halting and retarded, as if they hardly have enough energy to talk. If these patients are able to give a history, they may report that they wake at 3 or 4 a.m. and cannot get back to sleep. They also may note that they feel worse in the morning but improve during the day. Some depressed patients, however, do not feel like talking. In such cases, it may help for paramedics to confront the patients with their own observations. A comment, such as "You look very sad," often encourages patients to talk about their depressed feelings. Such patients may burst into tears and should be permitted to "cry themselves out." Patients should not be encouraged to stop crying; paramedics simply can maintain a sympathetic silence.

Every depressed patient should be questioned directly about suicidal thoughts. The paramedic might ask, for example, "Have you ever wished you were dead or thought about killing yourself?" If the response is yes, the paramedic should ask the patient how he or she would do this and determine whether the patient has made any concrete plans for suicide. Evaluating the seriousness of suicidal intentions in this way can help the paramedic decide whether the patient needs to be hospitalized.

Depressed patients need sympathetic attention and reassurance. They need to know that the paramedic is concerned about them. It usually is best if a single member of the rescue team interviews these patients in private, as the presence of several people may make depressed patients uncomfortable. Patients should be told that many people have periods of unhappiness but that they can be helped to feel better. At this point, the paramedic can mention community sources where such help can be found.

Suicide. Suicide is defined as any willful act designed to end one's own life. Suicide is most common in men, especially those who are single, widowed, or divorced. Suicide also occurs more frequently in depressed persons and alcoholics. At least 60 percent of all suicide victims attempted suicide previously, and 75 percent clearly warned that they intended to commit suicide.

Suicide attempts typically occur when close emotional attachments are in danger or when the individual loses a significant family member or friend. Suicidal people, in addition, often feel unable to manage their lives. Frequently, they lack self-esteem.

<u>Every suicidal act or gesture should be taken seriously, and the patient should be evaluated by a psychiatrist.</u>

Many people will make last minute attempts to communicate their suicidal intentions. When an individual phones to threaten suicide, someone should stay on the line with that person until the rescue squad reaches the scene. When the EMS team arrives, the area should be surveyed quickly for instruments that the individual might use to injure himself or herself; the paramedic should remove them discreetly. The EMT-P's should talk quietly with patients and encourage them to discuss their situation. Paramedics should not be afraid to ask the patients directly about suicidal thoughts. The EMT-P's should find out the following information from these patients: Have they ever attempted suicide before? Have they made any concrete plans as to how they would kill themselves? Has anyone in their families ever committed suicide? Patients who have made previous attempts, who have detailed suicide plans, or whose close relatives have attempted suicide are more likely to attempt suicide. These patients must be reassured and brought to the hospital. These patients must not be left alone under any circumstances.

When patients attempt suicide, their <u>medical</u> treatment has priority. Drug overdoses must be managed for possible respiratory depression or circulatory collapse. Patients with slashed wrists must have their bleeding controlled. Nevertheless, if patients are conscious, the EMT-P should try to talk with them and encourage them to speak about their situation. In drug overdoses, the paramedic should collect any medication containers, pills, or other drugs found near the patients and bring these with the patients to the emergency department.

<u>Rage, hostility, and violent behavior.</u> The angry, violent patient is ready to fight with anyone who approaches and may be difficult to control. It *should* be remembered that anger can be a response to illness and that aggressive behavior may be the patient's way of coping with feelings of helplessness. Paramedics should avoid responding with anger and defensiveness to the patient's behavior. If a possibility of danger exists, the patient should be interviewed with another member of the EMT crew present. Violent patients should be told briefly and honestly what they can expect from the paramedic and what the paramedic expects from them. Many angry or violent patients can be calmed by a trained person who appears confident that the patient will behave well. It also is useful to ask such patients directly about the cause of their anger with a statement such as, "I'm not sure I understand why you are angry." The patients should be reassured that the EMT-P is there to help them and is not going to punish them for their violence or anger. Such patients should be told also that talking to a doctor may help them to feel better.

A more difficult situation arises when a patient is violent and out of control. Paramedics cannot take patients to the hospital against their will. Even if this were possible, two or three paramedics might not be enough to subdue such a patient. If no one is able to communicate with these patients and it seems that they are or will be dangerous to themselves or others, paramedics must notify the police. The ENT crew can transport patients only at their own request, or when authorized by the police.

If police have authorized the transport of a violent patient to the hospital against his or her will, paramedics may need to use restraints. Restraints also require police authorization. Restraints should be padded so that they will not injure patients if they struggle against them. When paramedics apply restraints, they always should explain what they are doing, even if the patients do not appear to be listening. The patients can be told that the restraints are to protect them and others from injury. To restrain a violent patient, the paramedic should:

- Place the patient in a supine position (assuming there are no injuries).

- Apply one cravat to each wrist and ankle with a clove hitch.
- Tie the wrists and ankles together with two or more cravats.
- Secure the tails of the extremity cravats to opposite sides of the stretcher frame.
- Secure the body with two or three straps placed around the chest, waist, or upper legs. Make sure none of the straps are unduly tight or will constrict the patient's breathing.

Once restraints are applied, they must not be removed en route. Paramedics must not bargain with patients and agree to remove restraints if they promise to behave well.

If potentially violent patients are transported without restraints, the EMT-P's should make sure that patients lie down and must watch them at all times. The paramedics should position themselves between patients and the door in case a rapid exit is necessary. They should restrain patients en route if they become dangerous to themselves or others.

If a patient is suspected of being potentially homicidal, paramedics should not attempt restraint. In such situations, the paramedics' responsibilities only should involve contacting the police and removing bystanders from the scene.

Paranoia. Paranoid patients are suspicious and distrustful. They often are hostile and uncooperative and usually have delusions that people are out to get them. They tend to brood over real or imagined injustices, carry grudges, and recall wrongs experienced years before. Many paranoid patients also are excitable and unpredictable and have outbursts of bizarre or aggressive behavior. Their personalities often make others dislike them or feel angry with them.

When dealing with paranoid patients, paramedics must identify themselves clearly and explain what they are trying to do. The person who is paranoid may be suspicious of warmth and reassurance, so the EMT-P should maintain a friendly, but somewhat distant, neutrality. Paramedics should:

- Avoid becoming angry at the patient's anger
- Behave in a consistent manner
- Agree or disagree with the paranoid patient's statements honestly
- Use tact and firmness to persuade the patient to come to the hospital
- Gain the confidence of the patient by showing authority, self-assurance, and a genuine desire to help the individual

Paramedics should not:

- Go along with the delusions of such patients in order to pacify them.
- Interview family or friends in the patient's presence. Taking a relative aside and speaking in hushed tones only reinforces the paranoid patient's delusion that people are plotting against him or her.

Anxiety and phobias. Patients having anxiety attacks show evidence of intense fear. They are tense and restless and often pace and wring their hands. Tremors, tachycardia, dyspnea, sweating, and diarrhea also frequently occur. These patients feel overwhelmed and cannot concentrate. Sometimes they will hyperventilate and develop all the symptoms of that syndrome, including dizziness, tingling around the mouth and fingers, and carpopedal spasms (spasms of the hands and feet). Furthermore, the behavior of these patients creates anxiety in those around them; therefore, they may be surrounded by a horde of anxious and excited people when the EMT crew arrives.

The first step in managing such patients is to separate them from the excited people around them. Paramedics should identify themselves and tell these patients clearly and confidently that effective treatment is available for their problems. They should be firm but supportive. They should explain what they are doing and not leave the patients alone. En route to the hospital, the paramedics should continue to reassure such patients.

Patients with phobias focus all their anxieties on one situation in the form of intense fears. Examples of phobic reactions include intense fears of high places, enclosed places, animals, weapons, and public gatherings. When these patients confront the feared situation, their anxiety becomes unbearable. When dealing with phobic patients, the paramedic must explain carefully each step involved in transporting patients to the hospital and go through each step in detail beforehand ("Then we will walk down the stairs, and I will hold your arm; then we will get into the back of the ambulance. You will sit on a bench in the ambulance, and I will be beside you."). Then the EMT-P should repeat the descriptions as the actions occur ("Now we are going down the stairs."). Such explanations will help to lessen these patients' fears.

Disorganization and disorientation. Disorganized patients are characterized by uncontrolled, disconnected thoughts. Their speech is usually incoherent or rambling, but they may be oriented to person and place. Often, such patients are found wandering aimlessly down the middle of a street, dressed peculiarly, and uttering meaningless words and sentences. Such patients need structure. The paramedic should explain what will be done and exactly 'what the patient will be expected to do. Simple, consistent, firm directions should be given. It may be impossible to get a detailed history, but the EMT-P should try to obtain the patient's name and address. These patients can be told that they need to see a doctor and that the EMT crew is planning to take them to a hospital where they can be helped.

Disoriented patients do not know where they are or what day it is and may not even know their names. This disturbance is more common among the elderly who may lapse back into memories and behave as though they were still living during an earlier period. Disorientation also can result from physical problems, including head injury, alcohol or other drug ingestion, and metabolic disorders such as diabetes. The paramedics must try to keep disoriented patients aware of the time, place, person, and situation. Patients should be told who the paramedics are and what they are doing. This may have to be repeated several times en route. The paramedics should reassure patients by such actions as pointing out landmarks that will help to orient them during the trip to the hospital.

Psychiatric emergencies caused by alcohol and other drugs

As mentioned previously, alcohol and other drugs often cause disturbed behavior. In this section, psychiatric emergencies caused by alcohol and drug use will be discussed.

Acute alcohol intoxication occurs when individuals consume enough alcohol to raise their serum alcohol levels above 150 milligrams per 100 milliliters. Signs of alcohol intoxication include poor impulse control, drowsiness, lack of coordination, slurred speech, and sometimes combativeness. If individuals are not combative, they simply should be allowed to sleep until the alcohol wears off. If they are combative, the physician may order chlorpromazine or paraldehyde to sedate them. Paramedics must remember, however, that the person who appears intoxicated may be suffering from the effects of a more serious medical problem. Therefore, these patients should be checked carefully for signs of illness or injury.

Narcotic withdrawal occurs when individuals stop taking substances to which they are physically addicted. They may develop symptoms, including restlessness, tossing sleep, yawning, watery eyes and nose, sweating, dilated pupils, goose pimples, nausea, and vomiting. Narcotic withdrawal usually is not dangerous in otherwise healthy individuals. Patients should be transported to the hospital, where withdrawal symptoms can be suppressed with narcotics and patients can be withdrawn slowly from addicting drugs. Usually the paramedic should not attempt to suppress narcotic withdrawal symptoms with morphine or meperidine in the field unless so ordered by the physician who feels that the patient may have an underlying disease that may make narcotic withdrawal dangerous. Giving narcotics to addicts in the field also can suggest to other addicts that they can obtain narcotics from the paramedic.

Barbiturate and sedative drug withdrawal symptoms resemble those of alcohol withdrawal. <u>Barbiturate withdrawal can be fatal.</u> Therefore, the physician may order the paramedic to give intravenous diazepam or phenobarbital to suppress symptoms until the patient feels drowsy. The total initial dose must be recorded accurately, since later sedative dosages given during slow withdrawal in the hospital will be determined from the initial dose. Seizures that can occur during barbiturate withdrawal can cause death. If seizures occur, they should be treated in the same manner as seizures from other causes.

Withdrawal symptoms also can occur when patients stop taking commonly prescribed sedative drugs like meprobamate, chiordiazepoxide, and diazepam. These drugs can cause withdrawal symptoms, including insomnia, anxiety, loss of appetite, vomiting, tremors, muscle twitching,, and seizures. Seizures from sedative withdrawal are treated in the same way as seizures from other causes.

The paramedic's manner and attitude during the initial contact with the patient are the most important factors in determining later events. By striving to maintain an attitude of calmness, self-confidence, sympathy, and firmness, the EMT-P often can make the difference between success and failure in handling a psychiatric emergency.

Unit 3. Techniques of Management Patient Interviewing

After the paramedic obtains basic identifying information about the patient (name, age, address), a limited interview can be conducted even in field situations. The situation will dictate the scope of the interview. Only information critical to field management should be collected, unless volunteered by the patient. The interview should be open-ended; that is, patients should not be directed but rather should be allowed to tell their stories in their own way.

To make the interview easier, the paramedic should:

- Begin the interview with an open-ended question ("What problems have you been having?").
- Give patients the floor. Do not be afraid of silences, even though they may. seem intolerably long sometimes. Maintain an attentive, relaxed attitude. It is especially important to be silent when patients stop speaking because they are overwhelmed by emotion. Avoid the temptation to soothe patients and to prevent such expressions of emotion as crying. Expressions of emotion often are therapeutic, and patients usually will express themselves more easily after their intense emotions are released. Silence also allows the patients to gain control of themselves in their own way.
- Encourage patients to communicate by making gestures such as nodding the head or using noncommittal words or phrases ("Go on" or "I see"). This technique, called facilitation, also can be used to return patients to topics for which more information is needed. For example, a patient may have referred briefly to suicidal thoughts and then moved on to another subject. When he or she finishes with the new subject, the paramedic might say, "You say you have thought of suicide?" This suggests to the patient that the paramedic is interested in what the patient has said and would like to learn more.
- Point out to the patients something of interest in their conversation or behavior of which they may not be aware. This technique, known as confrontation, describes how patients appear to the interviewer, based on the interviewer's observations, not judgments. For example, the interviewer might remark, "You seem worried," or "You sound very angry." Such comments often lead to freer expressions of feelings. They must be made, however, in a way that is neither critical nor condescending.
- o If necessary, ask questions to keep the interview moving, but make them as nondirective as possible. Avoid questions that can be answered with a simple yes or no. "How" and "what" questions are better.
- Provide support and reassurance through actions that demonstrate interest in the patient throughout the entire interview. Reassurance should never be unrealistic or foster unreasonable expectations ("You have nothing at all to worry about.") Instead, identify the patient's strengths and reinforce them ("Despite all the troubles you have had, you seem to have done a very good job at work.").

It should be noted that some patients find it difficult to deal with the lack of structure in nondirective questioning. This is true particularly of adolescents, severely depressed patients, and confused or disorganized patients. In such cases, when open-ended questions are met with uncomprehending silence, a more structured interview may produce better results.

GLOSSARY OF MENTAL HEALTH TERMS

A

Access
The extent to which an individual who needs care and services is able to receive them. Access is more than having insurance coverage or the ability to pay for services. It is also determined by the availability of services, acceptability of services, cultural appropriateness, location, and hours of operation, transportation needs, and cost.

Accessible services
Services that are affordable, located nearby, and open during evenings and weekends. Staff is sensitive to and incorporates individual and cultural values. Staff is also sensitive to barriers that may keep a person from getting help. For example, an adolescent may be more willing to attend a support group meeting in a church or club near home than to travel to a mental health center. An accessible service can handle consumer demand without placing people on a long waiting list.

Accreditation
An official decision made by a recognized organization that a health care plan, network, or other delivery system complies with applicable standards.

Activity Therapy
Includes art, dance, music, recreational and occupational therapies, and psychodrama.

Addition
The number of persons admitted, readmitted, or transferred to a specified service during the reporting period.

Administrative Costs
Costs not linked directly to the provision of medical care. Includes marketing, claims processing, billing, and medical record keeping, among others.

Alternative Therapy
An alternative approach to mental health care is one that emphasizes the interrelationship between mind, body, and spirit. Although some alternative approaches have a long history, many remain controversial.

Alzheimer's disease (AD)
A slowly progressive form of dementia, which is a progressive, acquired impairment of intellectual functions. Memory impairment is a necessary feature for the diagnosis. Change in one of the following areas must also be present for any form of dementia to be diagnosed: language, decision-making ability, judgment, attention, and other related areas of cognitive function and personality. The rate of progression is different for each person. If AD develops rapidly, it is likely to continue to progress rapidly. If it has been slow to progress, it will likely continue on a slow course. The cause of Alzheimer's disease (AD) is not known, but it is not a part of normal aging. Prior theories regarding the accumulation of aluminum, lead, mercury, and other substances in the brain have been disproved. A diagnosis of AD is made based on characteristic symptoms and by excluding other causes of dementia. It can be confirmed by microscopic examination of a sample of brain tissue after death. By causing both structural and chemical problems in the brain, AD appears to disconnect areas of the brain that normally work together. There are two types of AD — early onset and late onset. In early onset AD, symptoms first appear before age 60. Some early onset disease runs in families and involves autosomal dominant, inherited mutations that may be the cause of the disease. So far, three early onset genes have been identified. Early onset AD is less common, resulting in about 5-10% of cases. Late onset AD, the most common form of the disease, develops in people 60 and older and is thought to be less likely to occur in families. Late onset AD may run in some families, but the role of genes is less direct and definitive. These genes may not cause the problem itself, but simply increase the likelihood of formation of plaques and tangles or other AD-related pathologies in the brain. In the early stages, the symptoms may be very subtle. Symptoms may often include: repeating statements frequently, frequently misplacing items, trouble finding names for familiar objects, getting lost on familiar routes, personality changes, becoming passive and losing interest in things previously enjoyed. AD cannot be

cured and the impaired functions cannot be restored. Currently, the progression can be slowed but not stopped. Treatment focuses on attempting to slow the progression; managing the behavior problems, confusion, and agitation; modifying the home environment; and most importantly, supporting the family. As the disease progresses, it may take a greater toll on the family than the patient.

American Indian or Alaska Native
A person having origins in any of the original peoples of North and South America (including Central America), and who maintains tribal affiliations or community attachment.

Anorexia
An eating disorder characterized by refusal to maintain a minimally accepted body weight, intense fear of weight gain, and distorted body image. Inadequate calorie intake or excessive energy expenditure results in severe weight loss. The exact cause of this disorder is not known, but social attitudes towards body appearance and family factors are believed to play a role in its development. The condition usually occurs in adolescence or young adulthood. It is more common in women, affecting 1-2% of the female population and only 0.1-0.2% of males. Anorexia is seen mainly in Caucasian women who are high academic achievers and have a goal-oriented family or personality. However, this eating disorder is not more common in higher socioeconomic groups. Some experts have suggested that conflicts within a family may also contribute to anorexia. It is thoughts that anorexia is a way for a child to draw attention away from marital problems, for example, and bring the family back together. Other psychologists have suggested that anorexia may be an attempt by young women to gain control and separate from their mothers. The causes, however, are still not well understood. The purpose of treatment is first to restore normal body weight and eating habits, and then attempt to resolve psychological issues. Hospitalization may be indicated in some cases (usually when body weight falls below 30% of expected weight). Supportive care by health care providers, structured behavioral therapy, psychotherapy, and anti-depressant drug therapy are some of the methods that are used for treatment. Severe and life-threatening malnutrition may require intravenous feeding.

Anxiety
Anxiety is an emotion that can signal just the right response to a situation. It can spur you on, for example, to add the finishing touches that transform an essay, painting, or important work document from good to excellent. However, if you have an anxiety disorder, exaggerated anxiety can stop you cold and disrupt your life. Like many other illnesses, anxiety disorders often have an underlying biological cause and frequently run in families. Anxiety disorders range from feelings of uneasiness to immobilizing bouts of terror. Symptoms range from chronic, exaggerated worry, tension, and irritability and appear to have no cause or are more intense than the situation warrants. Physical signs, such as restlessness, trouble falling or staying asleep, headaches, trembling, twitching, muscle tension, or sweating, often accompany these psychological symptoms. Anxiety is among the most common, most treatable mental disorders. Effective treatments include cognitive behavioral therapy, relaxation techniques, and biofeedback to control muscle tension. Medication, most commonly anti-anxiety drugs, such as benzodiazepine and its derivatives, also may be required in some cases. Some commonly prescribed anti-anxiety medications are diazepam, alprazolam, and lorazepam. The non-benzodiazepine anti-anxiety medication buspirone can be helpful for some individuals.

Anxiety Disorders
Anxiety disorders range from feelings of uneasiness to immobilizing bouts of terror. Most people experience anxiety at some point in their lives and some nervousness in anticipation of a real situation. However if a person cannot shake unwarranted worries, or if the feelings are jarring to the point of avoiding everyday activities, he or she most likely has an anxiety disorder.

Any willing provider
A requirement that a health plan contract for the delivery of health care services with any provider in the area who would like to provide such services to the plan's enrollees.

Appropriate services
Designed to meet the specific needs of each individual child and family. For example, one family may need day treatment, while another may need home-based services. Appropriate services for one child and family may not be appropriate for another. Appropriate services usually are provided in the child's community.

Appropriateness
The extent to which a particular procedure, treatment, test, or service is clearly indicated, not excessive, adequate in quantity, and provided in the setting best suited to a patient's or member's needs. (See also, medically necessary)

Asian
A person having origins in any of the original peoples of the Far East, Southeast Asia, or the Indian subcontinent including, for example, Cambodia, China, India, Japan, Korea, Malaysia, Pakistan, the Philippine Islands, Thailand, and Vietnam.

Assertive Community Treatment
A multi-disciplinary clinical team approach of providing 24-hour; intensive community services in the individual's natural setting that help individuals with serious mental illness live in the community.

Assessment
A professional review of child and family needs that is done when services are first sought from a caregiver. The assessment of the child includes a review of physical and mental health, intelligence, school performance, family situation, and behavior in the community. The assessment identifies the strengths of the child and family. Together, the caregiver and family decide what kind of treatment and supports, if any, are needed.

Attention Deficit Hyperactivity Disorder (ADD-ADHD)
Attention Deficit Hyperactivity Disorder (ADD-ADHD) is a neurobiological condition characterized by developmentally inappropriate level of attention, concentration, activity, distractibility, and impulsivity. The symptoms typically begin by 3 years of age-Attention deficit: does not pay close attention to details; may make careless mistakes at work, school, or other activities; failure to complete tasks; has difficulty maintaining attention in tasks or play activities; does not listen when spoken to directly; has difficulty organizing tasks; is easily distracted; unable to follow more than one instruction at a time. Many different methods of treatment have been used for ADD including psychotropic medications, psychosocial interventions, dietary management, herbal and homeopathic remedies, biofeedback, meditation, and perception stimulation/training. Of these treatment strategies, the most research has been done on stimulant medications and psychosocial interventions. Overall, these studies suggest stimulants to be superior relative to psychosocial interventions. However, there is no long term information comparing the two. The primary medications used to treat attention deficit disorder include: Dexedrine (dextroamphetamine), Ritalin (methylphenidate), Cylert (magnesium pemoline), tranquilizers (such as thioridazine), alpha-adrenergic agonist (clonidine), and others. Psychosocial therapeutic techniques include: contingency management (e.g., point reward systems, time out...), cognitive-behavioral treatment (self-monitoring, verbal self-instruction, problem solving strategies, self-reinforcement), parent counseling, and individual psychotherapy.

Autism
Autism, also called autistic disorder, is a complex developmental disability that appears in early childhood, usually before age 3. Autism prevents children and adolescents from interacting normally with other people and affects almost every aspect of their social and psychological development.

Auto-enrollment
The automatic assignment of a person to a health insurance plan (typically done under Medicaid plans).

Average Length of Stay
This represents the average time a client receives a specified service during a specified time period. This is generally computed by counting all the days that clients received the service during the time period and dividing by the number of clients that received the service during the same period. (Days a person was on furlough or not receiving are not counted.)

B

Behavioral health care firm
Specialized (for-profit) managed care organizations focusing on mental health and substance abuse benefits, which they term "behavioral healthcare." These firms offer employers and public agencies a managed mental health and substance abuse benefit.

Behavioral Therapy
As the name implies, behavioral therapy focuses on behavior-changing unwanted behaviors through rewards, reinforcements, and desensitization. Desensitization, or Exposure Therapy, is a process of confronting something that arouses anxiety, discomfort, or fear and overcoming the unwanted responses. Behavioral therapy often involves the cooperation of others, especially family and close friends, to reinforce a desired behavior.

Beneficiary
A person certified as eligible for health care services. A beneficiary may be a dependent or a subscriber.

Binge Eating
Binge Eating is an eating disorder characterized by eating more than needed to satisfy hunger. It is a feature of bulimia, a disorder that also includes abnormal perception of body image, constant craving for food and binge eating, followed by self- induced vomiting or laxative use.

Biofeedback
Biofeedback is learning to control muscle tension and "involuntary" body functioning, such as heart rate and skin temperature; it can be a path to mastering one's fears. It is used in combination with, or as an alternative to, medication to treat disorders such as anxiety, panic, and phobias.

Biomedical Treatment
Medication alone, or in combination with psychotherapy, has proven to be an effective treatment for a number of emotional, behavioral, and mental disorders. Any treatment involving medicine is a biomedical treatment. The kind of medication a psychiatrist prescribes varies with the disorder and the individual being treated.

Bipolar Disorder
A chronic disease affecting over 2 million Americans at some point in their lives. The American Psychiatric Association's "Diagnostic and Statistical Manual of Mental Disorders" describes two types of bipolar disorder, type I and type II. In type I (formerly known as manic depressive disorder), there has been at least one full manic episode. However, people with this type may also experience episodes of major depression. In type II disorder, periods of "hypomania" involve more attenuate (less severe) manic symptoms that alternate with at least one major depressive episode. When the patients have an acute exacerbation, they may be in a manic state, depressed state, or mixed state. People who suffer from bipolar disorder, however, have pathological mood swings from mania to depression, with a pattern of exacerbation and remission that are sometimes cyclic. The manic phase is characterized by elevated mood, hyperactivity, over-involvement in activities, inflated self-esteem, a tendency to be easily distracted, and little need for sleep. The manic episodes may last from several days to months. In the depressive phase, there is loss of self-esteem, withdrawal, sadness, and a risk of suicide. While in either phase, patients may abuse alcohol or other substances which worsen the symptoms. The disorder appears between the ages of 15 and 25, and it affects men and women equally. The exact cause is unknown, but it is a disturbance of areas of the brain which regulate mood. There is a strong genetic component. The incidence is higher in relatives of people with bipolar disorder. Hospitalization may be required during an acute phase to control the symptoms and to ensure safety of individuals. Medications to alleviate acute symptoms may include: neuroleptics (antipsychotics), antianxiety agents (such as benzodiazepines), and antidepressant agents. Mood stabilizers, such as lithium carbonate, and anticonvulsants (including carbamazepine and valproic acid) are started as maintenance therapy to relieve symptoms and to prevent relapse.

Black or African American
A person having origins in any of the black racial groups of Africa. Terms such as "Haitian" or "Negro" can be used in addition to "Black or African American."

Borderline Personality Disorder
Symptoms of borderline personality disorder, a serious mental illness, include pervasive instability in moods, interpersonal relationships, self-image, and behavior. The instability can affect family and work life, long-term planning, and the individual's sense of self-identity.

Bulimia
An illness characterized by uncontrolled episodes of overeating usually followed by self-induced vomiting or other purging. In bulimia, eating binges may occur as often as several times a day. Induced vomiting known as purging allows the eating to continue without the weight gain; it may continue until

interrupted by sleep, abdominal pain, or the presence of another person. The person is usually aware that their eating pattern is abnormal and may experience fear or guilt associated with the binge-purge episodes. The behavior is usually secretive, although clues to this disorder include over activity, peculiar eating habits, eating rituals, and frequent weighing. Body weight is usually normal or low, although the person may perceive themselves as overweight. The exact cause of bulimia is unknown, but factors thought to contribute to its development are family problems, maladaptive behavior, self-identity conflict, and cultural overemphasis on physical appearance. Bulimia may be associated with depression. The disorder is usually not associated with any underlying physical problem although the behavior may be associated with neurological or endocrine diseases. The disorder occurs most often in females of adolescent or young adult age. The incidence is estimated to be 3% in the general population; but 20% of college women suffers from it. Treatment focuses on breaking the binge-purge cycles of behavior since the person is usually aware that the behavior is abnormal. Outpatient treatment may include behavior modification techniques and individual, group, or family counseling. Antidepressant drugs may be indicated for some whether or not they have coincident depression.

C

Caregiver
A person who has special training to help people with mental health problems. Examples include social workers, teachers, psychologists, psychiatrists, and mentors.

Case manager
An individual who organizes and coordinates services and supports for children with mental health problems and their families. (Alternate terms: service coordinator, advocate, and facilitator.)

Child protective services
Designed to safeguard the child when abuse, neglect, or abandonment is suspected, or when there is no family to take care of the child. Examples of help delivered in the home include financial assistance, vocational training, homemaker services, and daycare. If in-home supports are insufficient, the child may be removed from the home on a temporary or permanent basis. Ideally, the goal is to keep the child with the family whenever possible.

Children and adolescents at risk for mental health problems
Children are at greater risk for developing mental health problems when certain factors occur in their lives or environments. Factors include physical abuse, emotional abuse or neglect, harmful stress, discrimination, poverty, loss of a loved one, frequent relocation, alcohol and other drug use, trauma, and exposure to violence.

Claim
A request by an individual (or his or her provider) to that individual's insurance company to pay for services obtained from a health care professional.

Clinical Psychologist
A clinical psychologist is a professional with a doctoral degree in psychology who specializes in therapy.

Clinical Social Worker
Clinical social workers are health professionals trained in client-centered advocacy that assist clients with information, referral, and direct help in dealing with local, State, or Federal government agencies. As a result, they often serve as case managers to help people "navigate the system." Clinical social workers cannot write prescriptions.

Cognitive/Behavioral Therapy
A combination of cognitive and behavioral therapies, this approach helps people change negative thought patterns, beliefs, and behaviors so they can manage symptoms and enjoy more productive, less stressful lives.

Cognitive Therapy
Cognitive therapy aims to identify and correct distorted thinking patterns that can lead to feelings and behaviors that may be troublesome, self-defeating, or even self-destructive. The goal is to replace such thinking with a more balanced view that, in turn, leads to more fulfilling and productive behavior.

Collateral Services
Services that include contacts with significant others involved in the client's/patient's life for the purpose of discussing the client's/patient's emotional or behavioral problems or the collateral's relationship with the client/patient.

Community Services
Services that are provided in a community setting. Community services refer to all services not provided in an inpatient setting.

Conduct Disorders
Children with conduct disorder repeatedly violate the personal or property rights of others and the basic expectations of society. A diagnosis of conduct disorder is likely when these symptoms continue for 6 months or longer. Conduct disorder is known as a "disruptive behavior disorder" because of its impact on children and their families, neighbors, and schools.

Consolidated Omnibus Budget Reconciliation Act (COBRA)
An act that allows workers and their families to continue their employer-sponsored health insurance for a certain amount of time after terminating employment. COBRA imposes different restrictions on individuals who leave their jobs voluntarily versus involuntarily.

Consumer
Any individual who does or could receive health care or services. Includes other more specialized terms, such as beneficiary, client, customer, eligible member, recipient, or patient.

Consumer Run Services
Mental health treatment or support services that are provided by current or former mental health consumers. Includes social clubs, peer- support groups, and other peer-organized or consumer-run activities.

Continuous quality improvement (CQI)
An approach to health care quality management borrowed from the manufacturing sector. It builds on traditional quality assurance methods by putting in place a management structure that continuously gathers and assesses data that are then used to improve performance and design more efficient systems of care. Also known as total quality management (TQM).

Continuum of care
A term that implies a progression of services that a child moves through, usually one service at a time. More recently, it has come to mean comprehensive services. Also see system of care and wraparound services.

Coordinated services
Child-serving organizations talk with the family and agree upon a plan of care that meets the child's needs. These organizations can include mental health, education, juvenile justice, and child welfare. Case management is necessary to coordinate services. Also see family-centered services and wraparound services.

Couples Counseling and Family Therapy
These two similar approaches to therapy involve discussions and problem-solving sessions facilitated by a therapist-sometimes with the couple or entire family group, sometimes with individuals. Such therapy can help couples and family members improve their understanding of, and the way they respond to, one another. This type of therapy can resolve patterns of behavior that might lead to more severe mental illness. Family therapy can help educate the individuals about the nature of mental disorders and teach them skills to cope better with the effects of having a family member with a mental illness- such as how to deal with feelings of anger or guilt.

Creditable Coverage
Any prior health insurance coverage that a person has received. Creditable coverage is used to decrease exclusion periods for pre- existing conditions when an individual switches insurance plans. Insurers cannot exclude coverage of pre-existing conditions, but may impose an exclusion period (no more than 12 months) before covering such conditions. (See also, Health Insurance Portability and Accountability Act)

Crisis residential treatment services
Short-term, round-the-clock help provided in a nonhospital setting during a crisis. For example, when a child becomes aggressive and uncontrollable, despite in-home supports, a parent can temporarily place

the child in a crisis residential treatment service. The purposes of this care are to avoid inpatient hospitalization, help stabilize the child, and determine the next appropriate step.

Cultural competence

Help that is sensitive and responsive to cultural differences. Caregivers are aware of the impact of culture and possess skills to help provide services that respond appropriately to a person's unique cultural differences, including race and ethnicity, national origin, religion, age, gender, sexual orientation, or physical disability. They also adapt their skills to fit a family's values and customs.

D

Day treatment

Day treatment includes special education, counseling, parent training, vocational training, skill building, crisis intervention, and recreational therapy. It lasts at least 4 hours a day. Day treatment programs work in conjunction with mental health, recreation, and education organizations and may even be provided by them.

Deductible

The amount an individual must pay for health care expenses before insurance (or a self- insured company) begins to pay its contract share. Often insurance plans are based on yearly deductible amounts.

Delusions

Delusions are bizarre thoughts that have no basis in reality.

Dementia

Refers to a group of symptoms involving progressive impairment of all aspects of brain function. Disorders that cause dementia include conditions that impair the vascular (blood vessels) or neurologic (nerve) structures of the brain. A minority of causes of dementia are treatable. These include normal pressure hydrocephalus, brain tumors, and dementia due to metabolic causes and infections. Unfortunately, most of the disorders associated with dementia are progressive, irreversible, degenerative conditions. The two major degenerative causes of dementia are Alzheimer's disease, which is a progressive loss of nerve cells without a known cause or cure and vascular dementia, which is loss of brain function due to a series of small strokes. Dementia may be diagnosed when there is impairment of two or more brain functions, including language, memory, visual-spatial perception, emotional behavior or personality, and cognitive skills (such as calculation, abstract thinking, or judgment). Dementia usually appears first as forgetfulness. Other symptoms may be apparent only on neurologic examination or cognitive testing. Loss of functioning progresses slowly from decreased problem solving and language skills to difficulty with ordinary daily activities to severe memory loss and complete disorientation with withdrawal from social interaction.

Depression

A term that people commonly used to refer to states involving sadness, dejection, lack of self-esteem, and lack of energy. Feelings of depression are synonymous with feeling sad, blue, down in the dumps, unhappy, and miserable. Most feelings of depression are a reaction to an unhappy event. It is natural to have some feelings of sadness after a loss such as the death of a relative, or after a major disappointment at home or at work. Depression is more prevalent in women than men and is especially common among adolescents. Mild depression comes and goes and is characterized by downheartedness, sadness, and dejection. Short-term episodes of depression or other mood changes can occur with hormone changes, including those that accompany pregnancy or premenstrual syndrome (PMS), and those occurring shortly after the birth of a baby (postpartum "blues"). Sleep disruption and lack of sunlight during the winter months are other biological factors that can precipitate depressive symptoms. Distorted thought patterns, characterized by feelings of worthlessness, helplessness, and hopelessness are part of the "cognitive triad of depression," and can be a risk factor for depression. It appears that a tendency toward depression is often genetic, but that stressful life circumstances usually play a major role in bringing on depressive episodes. Problems with depression usually begin in adolescence, and are about twice as common in women as in men. Noticeably disturbed thought processes, poor communication and socialization, and sensory dysfunction indicate moderate depression. People with severe depression are withdrawn, indifferent toward their surroundings, and may show signs of delusional thinking and limited physical activity.

Diagnostic Evaluation

The aims of a general psychiatric evaluation are 1) to establish a psychiatric diagnosis, 2) to collect data sufficient to permit a case formulation, and 3) to develop an initial treatment plan, with particular consideration of any immediate interventions that may be needed to ensure the patient's safety, or, if the evaluation is a reassessment of a patient in long-term treatment, to revise the plan of treatment in accord with new perspectives gained from the evaluation.

Discharge

A discharge is the formal termination of service, generally when treatment has been completed or through administrative authority.

Drop-in Center

A social club offering peer support and flexible schedule of activities: may operate on evenings and/ weekends.

Drug Formulary

The list of prescription drugs for which a particular employer or State Medicaid program will pay. Formularies are either "closed," including only certain drugs or "open," including all drugs. Both types of formularies typically impose a cost scale requiring consumers to pay more for certain brands or types of drugs.

DSM-IV (Diagnostic and Statistical Manual of Mental Disorders, Fourth Edition)

An official manual of mental health problems developed by the American Psychiatric Association. Psychiatrists, psychologists, social workers, and other health and mental health care providers use this reference book to understand and diagnose mental health problems. Insurance companies and health care providers also use the terms and explanations in this book when discussing mental health problems.

Dyslexia

A reading disability resulting from a defect in the ability to process graphic symbols. There are about 2 to 8% of elementary-age children that have some degree of reading disability. Developmental reading disorder (DRD) or dyslexia is not attributable to eye problems but instead is a defect of higher cortical (brain) processing of symbols. Children with DRD may have trouble rhyming and separating the sounds in spoken words. These abilities appear critical in the process of learning to read. Initial reading skills are based on word recognition. More developed reading skills require the linking of words into a coherent sentence (thought). DRD children may be unable to form images from the meanings of the words or to process the words into an idea which is understandable. At this level, reading may fail at its primary function, which is to convey information. Dyslexia or developmental reading disorder may appear in combination with developmental writing disorder and developmental arithmetic disorder. All of these processes involve the manipulation of symbols and the conveyance of information by their manipulation. These conditions may appear singly or in any combination. Other causes of learning disability and, in particular, reading disability, must be ruled out before a diagnosis of DRD can be made. Cultural and educational shortfalls, emotional problems, mental retardation, and diseases of the brain (for example AIDS) can all cause learning disabilities. Remedial instruction has remained the best approach to this type of reading disorder.

E

Education Services link

Locating or providing a full range of educational services from basic literacy through the General Equivalency Diploma and college courses. Includes special education at the pre-primary, primary, secondary, and adult levels.

Electroconvulsive Therapy

Also known as ECT, this highly controversial technique uses low voltage electrical stimulation of the brain to treat some forms of major depression, acute mania, and some forms of schizophrenia. This potentially life- saving technique is considered only when other therapies have failed, when a person is seriously medically ill and/or unable to take medication, or when a person is very likely to commit suicide. Substantial improvements in the equipment, dosing guidelines, and anesthesia have significantly reduced the possibility of side effects.

Emergency
A planned program to provide psychiatric care in emergency situations with staff specifically assigned for this purpose. Includes crisis intervention, which enables the individual, family members and friends to cope with the emergency while maintaining the individual's status as a functioning community member to the greatest extent possible.

Emergency and crisis services
A group of services that is available 24 hours a day, 7 days a week, to help during a mental health emergency. Examples include telephone crisis hotlines, suicide hotlines, crisis counseling, crisis residential treatment services, crisis outreach teams, and crisis respite care.

Emergency Medical Treatment and Labor Act (EMTALA)
EMTALA also referred to as the Federal Anti- patient Dumping Law link an act pertaining to emergency medical situations. EMTALA requires hospitals to provide emergency treatment to individuals, regardless of insurance status and ability to pay (EMTALA, 2002).

Employed
This is a broad category of employment that includes competitive, supported, and sheltered employment.

Employment/Vocational Rehabilitation Services
A broad range of services designed to address skills necessary for participation in job- related activities.

Enrollee
A person eligible for services from a managed care plan.

F

Family-centered services
Help designed to meet the specific needs of each individual child and family. Children and families should not be expected to fit into services that do not meet their needs. Also see appropriate services, coordinated services, wraparound services, and cultural competence.

Family-like arrangements
A broad range of living arrangements that simulate a family situation. This includes foster care and small group homes.

Family support services
Help designed to keep the family together, while coping with mental health problems that affect them. These services may include consumer information workshops, in-home supports, family therapy, parenting training, crisis services, and respite care.

Fee for Service
A type of health care plan under which health care providers are paid for individual medical services rendered.

Foster Care
Provision of a living arrangement in a household other than that of the client's/patient's family.

G

Gatekeeper
Primary care physician or local agency responsible for coordinating and managing the health care needs of members. Generally, in order for specialty services such as mental health and hospital care to be covered, the gatekeeper must first approve the referral.

General Hospital
A hospital that provides mental health services in at least one separate psychiatric unit with specially allocated staff and space for the treatment of persons with mental illness.

General Support
Includes transportation, childcare, homemaker services, day care, and other general services for clients/patients.

Group Therapy
This form of therapy involves groups of usually 4 to 12 people who have similar problems and who meet regularly with a therapist. The therapist uses the emotional interactions of the group's members to help them get relief from distress and possibly modify their behavior.

H

Hallucinations
Hallucinations are experiences of sensations that have no source. Some examples of hallucinations include hearing nonexistent voices, seeing nonexistent things, and experiencing burning or pain sensations with no physical cause.

Health Insurance Portability and Accountability Act (HIPAA)
This 1996 act provides protections for consumers in group health insurance plans. HIPAA prevents health plans from excluding health coverage of pre-existing conditions and discriminating on the basis of health status.

Hispanic or Latino
A person of Cuban, Mexican, Puerto Rican, South or Central American, or other Spanish culture or origin, regardless of race. The term, "Spanish origin," can be used in addition to "Hispanic or Latino."

Home-based services
Help provided in a family's home either for a defined period of time or for as long as it takes to deal with a mental health problem. Examples include parent training, counseling, and working with family members to identify, find, or provide other necessary help. The goal is to prevent the child from being placed outside of the home. (Alternate term: in-home supports.)

Homeless
A person who lives on the street or in a shelter for the homeless.

Horizontal consolidation
When local health plans (or local hospitals) merge. This practice was popular in the late 1990s and was used to expand regional business presence.

Housing Services
Assistance to clients/patients in finding and maintaining appropriate housing arrangements.

I

In Home Family Services
Mental health treatment and support services offered to children and adolescents with mental illness and to their family members in their own homes or apartments.

Indemnity plan
Indemnity insurance plans are an alternative to managed care plans. These plans charge consumers a set amount for coverage and reimburse (fully or partially) consumers for most medical services.

Independent living services
Support for a young person living on his or her own. These services include therapeutic group homes, supervised apartment living, and job placement. Services teach youth how to handle financial, medical, housing, transportation, and other daily living needs, as well as how to get along with others.

Individual Therapy
Therapy tailored for a patient/client that is administered one-on-one.

Individualized services
Services designed to meet the unique needs of each child and family. Services are individualized when the caregivers pay attention to the needs and strengths, ages, and stages of development of the child and individual family members. Also see appropriate services and family-centered services.

Information and Referral Services
Information services are those designed to impart information on the availability of clinical resources and how to access them. Referral services are those that direct, guide, or a client/patient with appropriate services provided outside of your organization.

Inpatient hospitalization

Mental health treatment provided in a hospital setting 24 hours a day. Inpatient hospitalization provides: (1) short-term treatment in cases where a child is in crisis and possibly a danger to his/herself or others, and (2) diagnosis and treatment when the patient cannot be evaluated or treated appropriately in an outpatient setting.

Intake/Screening
Services designed to briefly assess the type and degree of a client's/patient's mental health condition to determine whether services are needed and to link him/her to the most appropriate and available service. Services may include interviews, psychological testing, physical examinations including speech/hearing, and laboratory studies.

Intensive case management
Intensive community services for individuals with severe and persistent mental illness that are designed to improve planning for their service needs. Services include outreach, evaluation, and support.

Intensive Residential Services
Intensively staffed housing arrangements for clients/patients. May include medical, psychosocial, vocational, recreational or other support services.

Interpersonal Psychotherapy
Through one-on-one conversations, this approach focuses on the patient's current life and relationships within the family, social, and work environments. The goal is to identify and resolve problems with insight, as well as build on strengths.

L

Legal Advocacy
Legal services provided to ensure the protection and maintenance of a client's/patient's rights.

Length of Stay
The duration of an episode of care for a covered person. The number of days an individual stays in a hospital or inpatient facility.

Living Independently
A client who lives in a private residence and requires no assistance in activities of daily living.

Local Mental Health Authority
Local organizational entity (usually with some statutory authority) that centrally maintains administrative, clinical, and fiscal authority for a geographically specific and organized system of health care.

M

Medicaid
Medicaid is a health insurance assistance program funded by Federal, State, and local monies. It is run by State guidelines and assists low-income persons by paying for most medical expenses.

Medicaid client
Mental health clients to whom some services were reimbursable through Medicaid.

Medical group practice
A number of physicians working in a systematic association with the joint use of equipment and technical personnel and with centralized administration and financial organization.

Medical review criteria
Screening criteria used by third-party payers and review organizations as the underlying basis for reviewing the quality and appropriateness of care provided to selected cases.

Medically necessary
Health insurers often specify that, in order to be covered, a treatment or drug must be medically necessary for the consumer. Anything that falls outside of the realm of medical necessity is usually not covered. The plan will use prior authorization and utilization management procedures to determine whether or not the term "medically necessary" is applicable.

Medicare
Medicare is a Federal insurance program serving the disabled and persons over the age of 65. Most costs are paid via trust funds that beneficiaries have paid into throughout the courses of their lives; small deductibles and some co-payments are required.

Medication Therapy
Prescription, administration, assessment of drug effectiveness, and monitoring of potential side effects of psycho-tropic medications.

MediGap
MediGap plans are supplements to Medicare insurance. MediGap plans vary from State to State; standardized MediGap plans also may be known as Medicare Select plans.

Member
Used synonymously with the terms enrollee and insured. A member is any individual or dependent who is enrolled in and covered by a managed health care plan.

Mental disorders
Another term used for mental health problems.

Mental Health
Refers to how a person thinks, feels, and acts when faced with life's situations. It is how people look at themselves, their lives, and the other people in their lives; evaluate the challenges and the problems; and explores choices. This includes handling stress, relating to other people, and making decisions.

Mental health
How a person thinks, feels, and acts when faced with life's situations. Mental health is how people look at themselves, their lives, and the other people in their lives; evaluate their challenges and problems; and explore choices. This includes handling stress, relating to other people, and making decisions.

Mental Health Parity (Act)
Mental health parity refers to providing the same insurance coverage for mental health treatment as that offered for medical and surgical treatments. The Mental Health Parity Act was passed in 1996 and established parity in lifetime benefit limits and annual limits.

Mental health problems
Mental health problems are real. They affect one's thoughts, body, feelings, and behavior. Mental health problems are not just a passing phase. They can be severe, seriously interfere with a person's life, and even cause a person to become disabled. Mental health problems include depression, bipolar disorder (manic-depressive illness), attention-deficit/ hyperactivity disorder, anxiety disorders, eating disorders, schizophrenia, and conduct disorder.

Mental illnesses
This term is usually used to refer to severe mental health problems in adults.

MHA Administration
Activities related to the planning, organization, management, funding, and oversight of direct services.

MHA Data collection/reporting
These are activities to obtain, analyze, and report data for planning, management or evaluation purposes.

MHA Other Activities
Other specific non-direct service activities of State MHAs that further the provision of mental health services in the State.

MHA Planning Council Activities
All activities that comply with the mandate of State MHAs to form and operate a planning council to support the development of a strategic plan for mental health services and assess ongoing operations.

MHA Technical Assistance
Provision or sponsorship of training, education, or technical support in the planning, operation or management of public mental health programs in the State.

MI and MR/DD services
Services designed to address the needs of people with both psychiatric illness and mental retardation or developmental disabilities.

Mobile Treatment Team
Provides assertive outreach, crisis intervention, and independent-living assistance with linkage to necessary support services in the client's/patient's own environment. This includes PACT, CTTP, or other continuous treatment team programs.

More Than One Race
A category of racial grouping for a person who reports multiple racial origins.

N

Native Hawaiian or Other Pacific Islander
A person having origins in any of the original peoples of Hawaii, Guam, Samoa, or other Pacific Islands.

Network
The system of participating providers and institutions in a managed care plan.

Network adequacy
Many States have laws defining network adequacy, the number and distribution of health care providers required to operate a health plan. Also known as provider adequacy of a network.

New Generation Medications
Anti-psychotic medications which are new and atypical.

Non-Institutional Services
A facility that provides mental health services, but not on a residential basis, other than an inpatient facility or nursing home.

Non-Medicaid Services
Services other than those funded by Medicaid.

Nurse Practitioner (NP)
A nurse practitioner is a registered nurse who works in an expanded role and manages patients' medical conditions.

Nursing Home
An establishment that provides living quarters and care for the elderly and the chronically ill. This includes assisted living outside a nursing home.

O

Obsessive-Compulsive Disorder (OCD)
One of the anxiety disorders, OCD is a potentially disabling condition that can persist throughout a person's life. The individual who suffers from OCD becomes trapped in a pattern of repetitive thoughts and behaviors that are senseless and distressing but extremely difficult to overcome. OCD occurs in a spectrum from mild to severe, but if severe and left untreated, can destroy a person's capacity to function at work, at school, or even in the home. Obsessions are unwanted ideas or impulses that repeatedly well up in the mind of the person with OCD. Persistent fears that harm may come to self or a loved one, an unreasonable concern with becoming contaminated, or an excessive need to do things correctly or perfectly, are common. Again and again, the individual experiences a disturbing thought, such as, "My hands may be contaminated–I must wash them"; "I may have left the gas on"; or "I am going to injure my child." These thoughts are intrusive, unpleasant, and produce a high degree of anxiety. Sometimes the obsessions are of a violent or a sexual nature, or concern illness. In response to their obsessions, most people with OCD resort to repetitive behaviors called compulsions. The most common of these are washing and checking. Other compulsive behaviors include counting (often while performing another compulsive action such as hand washing), repeating, hoarding, and endlessly rearranging objects in an effort to keep them in precise alignment with each other. Mental problems, such as mentally repeating phrases, list making, or checking are also common. These behaviors generally are intended to ward off harm to the person with OCD or others. Some people with OCD have regimented rituals while others have rituals that are complex and changing. Performing rituals may give the person with OCD some relief from anxiety, but it is only temporary. People with OCD show a range of insight into the senselessness of their obsessions. Often, especially when they are not actually having an obsession, they can recognize that their obsessions and compulsions are unrealistic. At other

times they may be unsure about their fears or even believe strongly in their validity. OCD is sometimes accompanied by depression, eating disorders, substance abuse disorder, a personality disorder, attention deficit disorder, or another of the anxiety disorders. Co-existing disorders can make OCD more difficult both to diagnose and to treat.

Outcomes
The results of a specific health care service or benefit package.

Outcomes research
Studies that measure the effects of care or services.

P

Panic Disorder
Panic Disorder is when people experience white-knuckled, heart-pounding terror that strikes suddenly and without warning. Since they cannot predict when a panic attack will seize them, many people live in persistent worry that another one could overcome them at any moment. Most panic attacks last only a few minutes, but they occasionally go on for ten minutes, and, in rare cases, have been known to last for as long as an hour. They can occur at any time, even during sleep. The good news is that proper treatment helps 70 to 90 percent of people with panic disorder, usually within six to eight weeks. Symptoms include pounding heart, chest pains, lightheadedness or dizziness, nausea, shortness of breath, shaking or trembling, choking, fear of dying, sweating, feelings of unreality, numbness or tingling, hot flashes or chills, and a feeling of going out of control or going crazy. Cognitive behavioral therapy and medications such as high-potency anti-anxiety drugs like alprazolam can be used to treat panic disorders. Several classes of antidepressants (such as paroxetine, one of the newer selective serotonin reuptake inhibitors) and the older tricyclics and monoamine oxidase inhibitors (MAO inhibitors) are considered "gold standards" for treating panic disorder. Sometimes a combination of therapy and medication is the most effective approach to helping people manage their symptoms.

Pastoral Counseling
Pastoral counselors are counselors working within traditional faith communities to incorporate psychotherapy, and/or medication, with prayer and spirituality to effectively help some people with mental disorders. Some people prefer to seek help for mental health problems from their pastor, rabbi, or priest, rather than from therapists who are not affiliated with a religious community.

Pharmacy Benefit Manager (PBM)
PBMs are third party administrators of prescription drug benefits.

Phobias
Irrational fears that lead people to altogether avoid specific things or situations that trigger intense anxiety. Phobias occur in several forms. Specific phobia is an unfounded fear of a particular object or situation-such as being afraid of dogs, yet loving to ride horses, or avoiding highway driving, yet being able to drive on city and country roads. Virtually an unlimited number of objects or situations- such as being afraid of flying, heights, or spiders-can be the target of a specific phobia. Agoraphobia is the fear of being in any situation that might trigger a panic attack and from which escape might be difficult. Many people who have agoraphobia become housebound. Others avoid open spaces, standing in line, or being in a crowd. Many of the physical symptoms that accompany panic attacks – such as sweating, racing heart, and trembling – also occur with phobias. Social phobia is a fear of being extremely embarrassed in front of other people. The most common social phobia is fear of public speaking. Cognitive behavioral therapy has the best track record for helping people overcome most phobic disorders. The goals of this therapy are to desensitize a person to feared situations or to teach a person how to recognize, relax, and cope with anxious thoughts and feelings. Medications, such as anti-anxiety agents or antidepressants, can also help relieve symptoms. Sometimes therapy and medication are combined to treat phobias.

Physician Assistant
A physician assistant is a trained professional who provides health care services under the supervision of a licensed physician.

Plan of care
A treatment plan especially designed for each child and family, based on individual strengths and needs. The caregiver(s) develop(s) the plan with input from the family. The plan establishes goals and details appropriate treatment and services to meet the special needs of the child and family.

Play Therapy
Geared toward young children, play therapy uses a variety of activities-such as painting, puppets, and dioramas-to establish communication with the therapist and resolve problems. Play allows the child to express emotions and problems that would be too difficult to discuss with another person.

Post-Traumatic Stress Disorder (PTSD)
Post-Traumatic Stress Disorder (PTSD) affects people of all ages if they have experienced, witnessed, or participated in a traumatic occurrence-especially if the event was life threatening. PTSD can result from terrifying experiences such as rape, kidnapping, natural disasters, or war or serious accidents such as airplane crashes. The psychological damage such incidents cause can interfere with a person's ability to hold a job or to develop intimate relationships with others. The symptoms of PTSD can range from constantly reliving the event to a general emotional numbing. Persistent anxiety, exaggerated startle reactions, difficulty concentrating, nightmares, and insomnia are common. In addition, people with PTSD typically avoid situations that remind them of the traumatic event, because they provoke intense distress or even panic attacks. A rape victim with PTSD, for example, might avoid all contact with men and refuse to go out alone at night. Many people with PTSD also develop depression and may, at times, abuse alcohol or other drugs as "self-medication" to dull their emotional pain and to forget about the trauma. Psychotherapy can help people who have PTSD regain a sense of control over their lives. Many people who have this disorder need to confront what has happened to them and, by repeating this confrontation, learn to accept the trauma as part of their past. They also may need cognitive behavior therapy to change painful and intrusive patterns of behavior and thought and to learn relaxation techniques. Another focus of psychotherapy is to help people who have PTSD resolve any conflicts that may have occurred as a result of the difference between their personal values and how behaviors and experiences during the traumatic event violated them. Support from family and friends can help speed recovery and healing. Medications, such as antidepressants and anti- anxiety agents to reduce anxiety, can ease the symptoms of depression and sleep problems. Treatment for PTSD often includes both psychotherapy and medication.

Posttraumatic Stress Disorder (PTSD)
Posttraumatic Stress Disorder is an anxiety disorder that develops as a result of witnessing or experiencing a traumatic occurrence, especially life threatening events. PTSD can cause can interfere with a person's ability to hold a job or to develop intimate relationships with others.

Prader-Willi Syndrome
A congenital (present from birth) disease characterized by obesity, decreased muscle tone, decreased mental capacity, and hypogonadism. Prader-Willi is caused by the deletion of a gene on chromosome 15. For unkown reasons, only the copy of this gene on chromosome 15 that is received from the father is active. The maternal copy of this gene is turned off in all people. When there is a deletion of this gene on the copy received from the father, the disease occurs. This is because the patient is left with only the maternal copy — which is inactive in all people. Signs of Prader-Willi may be seen at birth. New infants with the condition are often small and very floppy (hypotonic). Male infants may have undescended testicles. The growing child exhibits slow mental and delayed motor development, increasing obesity, and characteristically small hands and feet. Rapid weight gain may occur during the first few years because the patient develops uncontrollable hunger which leads to morbid obesity. Mental development is slow, and the IQ seldom exceeds 80. However, children with Prader-Willi generally are very happy, smile frequently, and are pleasant to be around. Affected children have an intense craving for food and will do almost anything to get it. This results in uncontrollable weight gain. Morbid obesity (the degree of obesity that seriously affects health) may lead to respiratory failure with hypoxia (low blood oxygen levels), cor pulmonale (right- sided heart failure), and death.

Pre-existing condition
A medical condition that is excluded from coverage by an insurance company because the condition was believed to exist prior to the individual obtaining a policy from the insurance company. Many insurance companies now impose waiting periods for coverage of pre-existing conditions. Insurers will cover the condition after the waiting period (of no more than 12 months) has expired. (See also, HIPAA)

Prior authorization
The approval a provider must obtain from an insurer or other entity before furnishing certain health services, particularly inpatient hospital care, in order for the service to be covered under the plan.

Psychiatric Emergency Walk- in
A planned program to provide psychiatric care in emergency situations with staff specifically assigned for this purpose. Includes crisis intervention, which enables the individual, family members and friends to cope with the emergency while maintaining the individual's status as a functioning community member to the greatest extent possible and is open for a patient to walk-in.

Psychiatrist
A psychiatrist is a professional who completed both medical school and training in psychiatry and is a specialist in diagnosing and treating mental illness.

Psychoanalysis
Psychoanalysis focuses on past conflicts as the underpinnings to current emotional and behavioral problems. In this long-term and intensive therapy, an individual meets with a psychoanalyst three to five times a week, using "free association" to explore unconscious motivations and earlier, unproductive patterns of resolving issues.

Psychodynamic Psychotherapy
Based on the principles of psychoanalysis, this therapy is less intense, tends to occur once or twice a week, and spans a shorter time. It is based on the premise that human behavior is determined by one's past experiences, genetic factors, and current situation. This approach recognizes the significant influence that emotions and unconscious motivation can have on human behavior.

Psychosocial Rehabilitation
Therapeutic activities or interventions provided individually or in groups that may include development and maintenance of daily and community-living skills, self-care, skills training includes grooming, bodily care, feeding, social skills training, and development of basic language skills.

R

Registered Nurse (RN)
A registered nurse is a trained professional with a nursing degree who provides patient care and administers medicine.

Report Card
An accounting of the quality of services, compared among providers over time. The report card grades providers on predetermined, measurable quality and outcome indicators. Generally, consumers use report cards to choose a health plan or provider, while policy makers may use report card results to determine overall program effectiveness, efficiency, and financial stability.

Residential Services
Services provided over a 24-hour period or any portion of the day which a patient resided, on an on-going basis, in a State facility or other facility and received treatment.

Residential treatment centers
Facilities that provide treatment 24 hours a day and can usually serve more than 12 young people at a time. Children with serious emotional disturbances receive constant supervision and care. Treatment may include individual, group, and family therapy; behavior therapy; special education; recreation therapy; and medical services. Residential treatment is usually more long- term than inpatient hospitalization. Centers are also known as therapeutic group homes.

Respite care
A service that provides a break for parents who have a child with a serious emotional disturbance. Trained parents or counselors take care of the child for a brief period of time to give families relief from the strain of caring for the child. This type of care can be provided in the home or in another location. Some parents may need this help every week.

Respite Residential Services
Provision of periodic relief to the usual family members and friends who care for the clients/patients.

Retired
Clients who are of legal age, stopped working and have withdrawn from one's occupation.

Risk
Possibility that revenues of the insurer will not be sufficient to cover expenditures incurred in the delivery of contractual services. A managed care provider is at risk if actual expenses exceed the payment amount.

Risk adjustment
The adjustment of premiums to compensate health plans for the risks associated with individuals who are more likely to require costly treatment. Risk adjustment takes into account the health status and risk profile of patients.

S

Schizophrenia
A serious brain disorder. It is a disease that makes it difficult for a person to tell the difference between real and unreal experiences, to think logically, to have normal emotional responses to others, and to behave normally in social situations. Schizophrenia is a complex and puzzling illness. Even the experts in the field are not exactly sure what causes it. Some doctors think that the brain may not be able to process information correctly. Genetic factors appear to play a role, as people who have family members with schizophrenia may be more likely to get the disease themselves. Some researchers believe that events in a person's environment may trigger schizophrenia. For example, problems during intrauterine development (infection) and birth may increase the risk for developing schizophrenia later in life. Psychological and social factors may also play some role in its development. However, the level of social and familial support appears to influence the course of illness and may be protective against relapse. There are five recognized types of schizophrenia: catatonic, paranoid, disorganized, undifferentiated, and residual. Features of schizophrenia include its typical onset before the age of 45, continuous presence of symptoms for six months or more, and deterioration from a prior level of social and occupational functioning. People with schizophrenia can have a variety of symptoms. Usually the illness develops slowly over months or even years. At first, the symptoms may not be noticed. For example, people may feel tense, may have trouble sleeping, or have trouble concentrating. They become isolated and withdrawn, and they do not make or keep friends. No single characteristic is present in all types of schizophrenia. The risk factors include a family history of schizophrenia. Schizophrenia is thought to affect about 1% of the population worldwide. Schizophrenia appears to occur in equal rates among men and women, but women have a later onset. For this reason, males tend to account for more than half of clients in services with high proportions of young adults. Although the onset of schizophrenia is typically in young adulthood, cases of the disorder with a late onset (over 45 years) are known. Childhood- onset schizophrenia begins after five years of age and, in most cases, after relatively normal development. Childhood schizophrenia is rare and can be difficult to differentiate from other pervasive developmental disorders of childhood, such as autism.

School attendance
Physical presence of a child in a school setting during scheduled class hours. "Regular" school attendance is attendance at least 75% of scheduled hours.

School Based Services
School-based treatment and support interventions designed to identify emotional disturbances and/or assist parents, teachers, and counselors in developing comprehensive strategies for addressing these disturbances. School-based services also include counseling or other school-based programs for emotionally disturbed children, adolescents, and their families within the school, home and community environment.

Seasonal affective disorder (SAD)
Seasonal affective disorder (SAD) is a form of depression that appears related to fluctuations in the exposure to natural light. It usually strikes during autumn and often continues through the winter when natural light is reduced. Researchers have found that people who have SAD can be helped with the symptoms of their illness if they spend blocks of time bathed in light from a special full-spectrum light source, called a "light box."

Section 1115 Waiver
A statutory provision that allows a State to operate its system of care for Medicaid enrollees in a manner different from that proscribed by the Centers for Medicare and Medicaid Services (CMS), in an

attempt to demonstrate the efficacy and cost-effectiveness of an alternative delivery system through research and evaluation.

Section 1915(b) Waiver

A statutory provision that allows a State to partially limit the choice of providers for Medicaid enrollees; for example, under the waiver, a State can limit the number of times per year that enrollees can choose to drop out of an HMO.

Self-help

Self-help generally refers to groups or meetings that: involve people who have similar needs; are facilitated by a consumer, survivor, or other layperson; assist people to deal with a "life-disrupting" event, such as a death, abuse, serious accident, addiction, or diagnosis of a physical, emotional, or mental disability, for oneself or a relative; are operated on an informal, free-of-charge, and nonprofit basis; provide support and education; and are voluntary, anonymous, and confidential. Many people with mental illnesses find that self-help groups are an invaluable resource for recovery and for empowerment.

Serious emotional disturbances

Diagnosable disorders in children and adolescents that severely disrupt their daily functioning in the home, school, or community. Serious emotional disturbances affect one in 10 young people. These disorders include depression, attention-deficit/hyperactivity, anxiety disorders, conduct disorder, and eating disorders. Pursuant to section 1912(c) of the Public Health Service Act "children with a serious emotional disturbance" are persons: (1) from birth up to age 18 and (2) who currently have, or at any time during the last year, had a diagnosable mental, behavioral, or emotional disorder of sufficient duration to meet diagnostic criteria specified within DSM.

Serious Mental Illness

Pursuant to section 1912(c) of the Public Health Service Act, adults with serious mental illness SMI are persons: (1) age 18 and over and (2) who currently have, or at any time during the past year had a diagnosable mental behavioral or emotional disorder of sufficient duration to meet diagnostic criteria specified within DSM-IV or their ICD-9-CM equivalent (and subsequent revisions) with the exception of DSM-IV "V" codes, substance use disorders, and developmental disorders, which are excluded, unless they co-occur with another diagnosable serious mental illness. (3) That has resulted in functional impairment, which substantially interferes with or limits one or more major life activities.

Service

A type of support or clinical intervention designed to address the specific mental health needs of a child and his or her family. A service could be provided only one time or repeated over a course of time, as determined by the child, family, and service provider.

Single-stream funding

The consolidation of multiple sources of funding into a single stream. This is a key approach **used in progressive mental health systems to ensure that "funds follow consumers."**

State Children's Health Insurance Plan (SCHIP)

Under Title XXI of the Balanced Budget Act of 1997, the availability of health insurance for children with no insurance or for children from low-income families was expanded by the creation of SCHIP. SCHIPs operate as part of a State's Medicaid program (Centers for Medicare and Medicaid Services, 2002).

State Coverage

The total unduplicated count of mental health patients/clients served through State programs, exclusive of Medicaid and Other Coverage.

State Hospital

A publicly funded inpatient facility for persons with mental illness.

State Mental Health Authority or Agency

State government agency charged with administering and funding its State's public mental health services.

Stress

Defined as a feeling of tension that can be both emotional and physical. Emotional stress usually occurs when situations are considered difficult or unmanageable. Therefore, different people consider different situations as stressful. Physical stress refers to a physiological reaction of the body to various triggers.

The pain experienced after surgery is an example of physical stress. Physical stress often leads to emotional stress, and emotional stress is frequently experienced as physical discomfort (e.g., stomach cramps). Stress management refers to various efforts used to control and reduce the tension that occurs in these situations. The attitude of an individual can influence whether a situation or emotion is stressful or not. Negative attitude can be a predictor of stress, because this type of person will often report more stress than a person with a more positive attitude. Stress is not a disease and is a normal part of everyone's life. Stress in small quantities is good: it makes us more productive. For example, the fear of a bad grade can make the student study more attentively. However, too much stress is unhealthy and counterproductive. The same student, if he was recently mugged and or is getting over the sudden death of a friend will not be able to study as well. Persistent and unrelenting stress is called anxiety.

Sub capitation
An arrangement whereby a capitated health plan pays its contracted providers on a capitated basis.

Subscriber
Employment group or individual that contracts with an insurer for medical services.

Suicide
A successful or unsuccessful attempt to intentionally kill oneself. Suicidal behaviors indicate that a person wishes to, intends to, or actually attempts to commit suicide. Suicidal behaviors can accompany many emotional disturbances, including depression, schizophrenia, and other psychotic illnesses. In fact, more than 90% of all suicides are related to an emotional or psychiatric illness. Suicidal behaviors occur as a response to a situation that the person views as overwhelming, such as social isolation, death of a loved one, emotional trauma, serious physical illness, growing old, unemployment or financial problems, guilt feelings, drug abuse, and alcohol abuse. In the U.S., suicide accounts for about 1% of all deaths each year. The highest rate is among the elderly, but there has been a steady increase in the rate among young people (particularly adolescents). Suicide is now the third leading cause of death for those 15 to 19 years old (after accidents and homicide). The incidence of reported suicides varies widely from country to country in the world; however, this may be in part related to reporting (especially in cultures where suicide is considered sinful or shameful). Suicide attempts (where the person tries to harm him- or herself but the attempt does not result in death) far outnumber actual suicides. The method of suicide attempt varies from relatively nonviolent methods (such as poisoning, overdose, or inhaling car exhaust) to violent methods (such as shooting or cutting oneself). Males are more likely to choose violent methods, which probably accounts for the fact that suicide attempts by males are more likely to be successful. Many unsuccessful suicide attempts are carried out in a manner or setting that makes rescue possible. They must be viewed as a cry for help.

Supported Employment
Supportive services that include assisting individuals in finding work; assessing individuals' skills, attitudes, behaviors, and interest relevant to work; providing vocational rehabilitation and/or other training; and providing work opportunities. Includes transitional and supported employment services.

Supported Housing
Services to assist individuals in finding and maintaining appropriate housing arrangements.

Supportive Residential Services
Moderately staffed housing arrangements for clients/patients. Includes supervised apartments, satellite facilities, group homes, halfway houses, mental health shelter- care facilities, and other facilities.

System of Care
A system of care is a method of addressing children's mental health needs. It is developed on the premise that the mental health needs of children, adolescents, and their families can be met within their home, school, and community environments. These systems are also developed around the principles of being child-centered, family- driven, strength-based, and culturally competent and involving interagency collaboration.

T

Telephone Hotline
A dedicated telephone line that is advertised and may be operated as a crisis hotline for emergency counseling or as a referral resource for callers with mental health problems.

Therapeutic Foster Care
A service which provides treatment for troubled children within private homes of trained families. The approach combines the normalizing influence of family-based care with specialized treatment interventions, thereby creating a therapeutic environment in the context of a nurturing family home.

Third party payer
A public or private organization that is responsible for the health care expenses of another entity.

U

Unable to Work
This on-line forum was created especially for the nation's jobless and underemployed workers. This resource is available to help the unemployed learn more about the unemployment system, to share their experiences and concerns, and to participate in the national debate over aid to the jobless.

Underwriting
The review of prospective or renewing cases to determine their risk and their potential costs.

Unduplicated Counts
Counting a client/patient and their services uniquely. Unduplicated counts can exist at different levels: a program, a local system of care, or at the State level.

Unemployed
Not currently employed. This could include people looking for work, or people engaged in other activities such as homemakers, students or volunteers.

Unmet Needs
Identified treatment needs of the people that are not being met as well as those receiving treatment that is inappropriate or not optimal.

Utilization
The level of use of a particular service over time.

Utilization risk
The risk that actual service utilization might differ from utilization projections.

V

Vertical disintegration
A practice of selling off health plan subsidiaries or provider activities. Vertical disintegration was a trend in the late 1990s.

Vocational Rehabilitation Services
Services that include job finding/development, assessment and enhancement of work-related skills, attitudes, and behaviors as well as provision of job experience to clients/patients. Includes transitional employment.

W

White
A person having origins in any of the original peoples of Europe, the Middle East, or North Africa.

www.ingramcontent.com/pod-product-compliance
Lightning Source LLC
Chambersburg PA
CBHW081807300426
44116CB00014B/2268